1985

TO GRANDMA
XMAS 85
WITH LOVE

John

PLYMOUTH
As Time Draws On

written and illustrated by
Chris Robinson

Pen&inK
PUBLISHING

British Library Cataloguing in Publication Data

Robinson, Chris
   Plymouth: as time draws on.
   1. Plymouth (Devon)—History
   I. Title
   942.3'58   DA690.P7

ISBN 0-9510747-0-9

Designed by Chris Robinson and Rob Warren
© Chris Robinson 1985

First published 1985

Typeset, printed & bound in Great Britain
by Latimer Trend & Company Ltd
Crescent Avenue
Plymouth Pl1 3AW, Devon

Published by
Pen & Ink Publishing
34 New Street,
Barbican
Plymouth Pl1 2NA

for my family

Introduction

The first ink drawing I produced of Plymouth was of the Hoe Promenade (see page 44) not long after leaving school in 1973 at the request of my mother who wanted to give some friends a leaving present.

Although I had always suspected that I might earn a living with a pen, pencil or paintbrush I little imagined then that in the next ten years or so many hours would be spent working around the city recording it in this form.

In three years at Leeds University, studying psychology and sociology, I did little formal drawing or painting (though a lot of doodling in seminars, a series of caricatures of lecturers and a 10ft by 12ft mural of Charlie Chaplin and the Kid in the Union Coffee Bar!). It was not until Finals were over that I suggested to some designer friends that we might make some money drawing certain pubs in Leeds. They gave up after a couple of outings but before returning to Plymouth that summer I had drawn or made a start on six public houses, two of which were subsequently printed. One was in Sheffield, the other near Saffron Walden.

At the end of the summer of 1976 I went off to Warwick University to do a research degree with no grant but the idea that a little money could be generated by drawing. For income at Warwick, however, I ended up relying more on mobile disco work (something else I had done since schooldays) than on artwork. Despite spending hours designing and drawing concert posters there was little financial reward to be gained from them. I didn't do any drawings off campus and made little out of two ink sketches, one of the Union Building and the other of the Art Centre. However, I did meet my future wife, Clare, and in 1977 she came to Plymouth with me on the grounds that she would rather do something 'creative' than study German literature. By the time I had finished my post-graduate work, Clare had started the fashion course at Plymouth College of Art and Design. On 30th September, 1978, the day after handing in the thesis at Coventry, I took a studio on the Barbican. Before opening the new first-floor studio I spent six weeks full-time drawing the Island House, Mayflower Memorial, Elizabethan House, Merchant's House, Prysten House and St. Andrew's Church. All within easy walking distance of the studio as we had no transport. After that burst of activity the drawings came slower as I then refused to entertain the idea of working from photographs and was reluctant to leave the studio closed since that meant nothing could be sold. In the middle of December, over a period of two weeks, and well protected against the cold and rain, I went down to Union Street and drew the New Palace Theatre which was just about to re-open. The longest and most detailed of all the drawings at that time, it was an instant success.

On a visit to North Yorkshire around this time (Clare's family live in Middlesbrough) I came across a calendar of 12 line drawings of the area and wasted little time in borrowing the concept to produce a calendar for Plymouth. First printed for 1980, the calendar has been popular ever since, and following the Yorkshire example, I wrote a few lines of historical information to go with each of the drawings. These brief descriptions attracted much interest and I found researching them very enjoyable.

Convinced that prints were potentially profitable, the first drawing I printed in Plymouth was of our local, the 'Hyde Park Hotel'. Embarrassment at appearing at all conspicuous on home ground led to me rushing out a small drawing whilst sitting casually on a bench 'behind' the pub. I wasn't there long enough to be seen by many people. However on confronting the landlord with the finished article he said: 'That's all very well but hardly anyone will recognize the "Hyde Park" from that angle. Go around and draw it from the other side and I'll give you a fiver for it.' It was July 1976 and a pound would still buy about five pints of bitter. The next fine day I was there, sitting on the thin strip of concrete that runs down the middle of Mutley Plain. The new drawing was twice the size of the previous effort, it took more than twice the time to execute and I haven't worried about drawing out of doors since! Next came the 'Fortescue' and the 'Golden Hind', but a suggestion that subjects with more general interest might be more commercial led to a drawing of the Barbican from Coxside, the *Kathleen and May*, the Royal Marine Barracks at Stonehouse and Plymouth College.

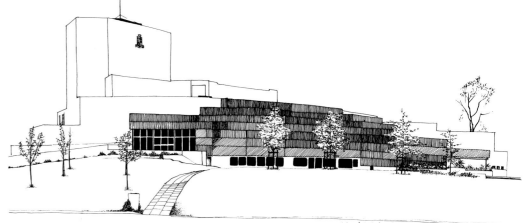

Warwick University Arts Centre Chris Robinson 1977

It wasn't long before I began thinking that, one day, it might be a good idea to put all my drawings into a book with some appropriate historical text. However, like many other schemes with no real pressure or incentive to get the project under way, very little was done about it. Then Horrabridge Parish Council asked me to draw the village bridge. In the course of so doing I was told a little story about Horrabridge's twin town in France for whom the picture had been commissioned. Encouraged to write the story down I took it along with the drawing to the *Evening Herald* offices where it was accepted verbatim and included in the 'Citizen's Diary' page. Not too long after this the Features' Editor of the paper dropped in to the studio and it was then that I first enquired about submitting a series of drawings with accompanying text which later became 'Time Draws On'. Initially the series featured comparisons between my drawings and much earlier engravings or illustrations of the same subject and it ran in that form for forty odd weeks. I had originally hoped that it might run to a dozen or so. After exhausting the supply of comparable old material the series carried on just using my own drawings. Here then was the basis for a book;

the requirement of writing at least one article every week was an excellent discipline and prompted by many enquiries, by the summer of 1984 I had given myself a deadline for its production. This present volume, therefore, represents the first stage in an attempt to produce a comprehensive contemporary record of the City in words and pictures.

Plymouth has played a key role, directly or indirectly, in this nation's history and I believe that the best way to interest people, young and old, in history generally, is to confront them with something with which they are familiar then tell them a part of the story that lies behind it. A post-box may be the inspiration for looking at the history of our postal services; a power station the spark for generating interest in the story of energy supplies. If every picture tells a story it is only because anything man-made tells us something about man, something about ourselves. And learning becomes all the more interesting and meaningful if students can relate to it.

The drawings and articles in this book follow each other in a geographical tour of the city starting with Sutton Harbour the area around which Plymouth is assumed to have evolved. It then moves out from Sutton to Coxside, Cattedown, the Hoe and the City Centre travelling northwards and outwards following the boundary extensions of the city before the other two towns, Stonehouse and Devonport (formerly Plymouth Dock) were incorporated within the city limits in 1914. From Devonport the locations move around from just inside the present city limits taking in the villages now swallowed up by the evergrowing city, St. Budeaux, Tamerton, Crownhill, Eggbuckland via Plymbridge to Plympton, Plymstock, Oreston, Hooe and Turnchapel. Many different subjects are examined along the way with certain themes recurring, notably schools, churches and public houses.

Schools new or old are at one stage compulsory homes for all of us and as one generation succeeds another the school walls forever witness the same age old problems of growing up and learning. Churches, meanwhile, are visited by many of us once or twice a week and most people at least a handful of times on important occasions during their lives. Public houses, on the other hand, are places where people may or may not go, frequently or infrequently, during their lives but I include them regularly in *Time Draws On* precisely because they are buildings in which anyone can socialise if they choose. If you want to explore a different part of the city a public house makes an excellent base. As indigenous to most communities as the local church, the public house and its story can often tell us a good deal about the development of an area and the changes it has seen. Unlike a shop or an amenity, a pub, despite changes in personnel, tends to retain its name and character and therefore over the years it becomes a significant landmark both in time and space. In addition to schools, pubs and churches; cinemas, theatres and historic houses have been included and a variety of other well patronized buildings and locations in the area. I have also featured certain less obvious items which we may all see regularly but seldom notice. A milestone, a boundary stone, a horsetrough, a drinking-fountain and some well-planned trees. They all have their stories and I hope when people read them they will become as fond of these subjects as I have.

When I first left Plymouth I was sure that, of all my friends, I would be one of the last to want to come back home and settle down without having first travelled the world. In the event I was one of the first to return. I have travelled a little and enjoyed it, but I have come to learn the wisdom of the philosophy which teaches you that 'until you know and understand that which is on your own doorstep you will never properly know or understand the rest of the world'.

Plymouth
July 1985

Acknowledgements

Thanks to my mother, Brenda, for her encouragement over the last 30 years, for being my most infuriating critic and for hours and hours of typing. . .to my father, Des, for teaching me the rules of perspective while I was still in short trousers and to both of them for instructing me in the art of self-discipline and amusement. To Clare, my wife, for aiding and abetting and generally putting up with me; to Clare's parents, Laurence and Patricia Greathead, and to James our son for putting life itself into perspective.

To Rob Warren, schoolfriend, designer and watercolourist, and his wife Nita for the day-to-day smooth running of our New Street operations.

From the *Western Evening Herald*, Diana Livingstone and her late husband Malcolm for their interest and introductions and likewise Jill Slight. Thanks to Jim Mitchell, former *Herald* editor who launched the 'Time Draws On' series and Alan Good who had carried it on. To Ken Fenn, Chris Collins, Mike Miller and the late Dennis Simpson who have all seen to it that the weekly deadline is *weakly* met and to Trevor Addis for the promotion of extracurricular *Herald* projects.

To Devon County Council for the Local History Library and Anique Skinner, Polly Lamb and John Smith (my Godfather) who man it. At the same time thanks to Tony Clement, the Barbican bookseller who, over the years, has helped me to stock my own local history library. To Bill Hodges of the Barbican Gallery whose help and advice has been invaluable on more than one occasion and who was the first person ever to sell a picture of mine.

On the print, card, and calendar side, Mike Newton-Perks of Reprocraft for working all hours; Clive Hooper and Dennis Gibbs of Planographic, and Ron, Joe and all the lads at PDS. For the present volume, Vic Brimacombe of PAD and Bill Bugler, Roger Bossom and John Turner at Latimer Trend.

To Mary Browning (my former landlady) and her late husband Dennis for their encouragement of writers, artists and craftspeople by providing very reasonable studio accommodation in New Street for over twenty years now.

Finally, to Angela Lanyon at the Theatre Royal, who, in giving me a date for my first exhibition of original drawings, also provided a necessary deadline for this book.

C.J.R.

Contents

PLYMOUTH
As Time Draws On

The Barbican

'The Barbican generally presents a busy scene for it is really the fish market of the district, and as we pass along we are sure to jostle against fishbuyers, fishermen, fishersellers, besides seamen of various nationalities, and if we mingle in the throng, we shall be almost deafened by the babel of voices which greets our ears.'

So wrote W. H. K. Wright in his 1879 handbook of Plymouth. In the ten years that followed this description the babel doubtless rose to an all time record as the Plymouth fish trade virtually doubled.

In 1890, over 5,000 tons of fish were sent out of Plymouth by rail. Indeed it was not unknown for there to be 300 fishing boats in the harbour with 400–500 handcarts standing by on the quay to handle the catches.

As, by law, the only permitted wholesale fish market was in Sutton Harbour this clearly presented problems and so, in a bid to solve them in 1889 an Act of Parliament was obtained authorizing the building of a new fish market. By 1896 it was opened.

Built in the style of the Great Western Railways buildings the new fish market was constructed on part of the harbour bed. In recent years proper offices and a new ice plant have been built along the quay and today the fish market is serviced by some 60 fishing boats including 8 trawlers and a couple of crabbers.

Still an interesting and exciting place it sadly appears to be better appreciated by the tourist than the local, many of whom seem to have quite lost the art of cooking the fresh fish that's available daily, and cheaply on their doorsteps.

[*WEH* 3.4.82.

Sutton Harbour

Originally almost all the warehouses in the area were built right on the water's edge, for easy loading; today, however, only those at Coxside serve to remind us of how the area once appeared.

Sutton Pool is then much smaller than it ever was in its heyday and it's hard to imagine that a plan was ever mooted, as it was in 1814, to renew an old link between the Pool and the Laira by way of a canal or indeed that until the building of the sixteenth century New Quay (now the Parade) water reached much further west.

For all these changes, however, Sutton Harbour is still the most unspoilt and busiest part of old Plymouth and although a look at the businesses that line this particular area of the 'shallow' pool reveals a lot about the changes in commercial activity over the years it gives no indication of a falling trade.

The buildings off Exchange Street, flanking the seventeenth century 'Three Crowns' pub, fell victim to the Blitz, whilst the pub and Laing's 1820 Customs House today sandwich the Matilda Cafe and Ronnies Night Club. To the left of this fine Customs' building as we look at it, we find a ship owners, a Greek Restaurant and a Marine Sports Shop and then on one of the other Barbican bomb sites, a block of flats.

Opposite the flats stands Tope's sail and tent warehouse, a business established here over 100 years ago.

Across Parade Ope and along the Parade we have a whole string of 'new' Barbican businesses in old buildings with a Pottery Shop, the Barbican Gallery, an Antique Shop and the Wine Lodge, interrupted only by the late eighteenth-century 'Ship Inn', Tamlyn's Ship Agents and a firm producing something inconceivable 100 years ago—sophisticated electronic components for aeroplanes.

[*WEH* 23.10.82

Mayflower Memorial

Of all the tablets and memorials on the Barbican's west Pier, that commemorating the departure of the Mayflower and with it the Pilgrim Fathers must surely be the most widely known and often photographed.

However up until 1891 there had been nothing in the way of a memorial to the Pilgrim Fathers or indeed any obvious indication of their point of departure and so it is that we must thank in large part, the Old Plymouth historian R. N. Worth and his son R. Hansford Worth for securing the same in the Mayorality of J. T. Bond in that year.

It was, however, another 43 years before a combination of local concern, a suggestion from the Old Plymouth Society and a very generous offer from Alderman Sir Frederick Winnicott, saw the erection of the present day memorial unveiled by the Mayor of 1933–4 Mr E. Stanley Leatherby.

Clearly there was no obvious numerical consideration in the timing of these two memorials but together they mark a point in history a little more effectively than the most recent and most defaced of the Barbican tablets, two to their right commemorating in 1970 the 350th anniversary of the *Mayflower* sailing.

Indeed looking again at the strange older memorial one can almost accept that the little Portland Stone, doric-columned gateway affair is, in the words of the late C. W. Bracken: 'Symbolic of the event it commemorates—simple, unostentatious—a gateway giving access to kindly entertainment and courteous use, and enshrining the prospect of the stormy path to an England, a Plymouth beyond the seas'.

What then of the other tablets in the picture? Immediately to the right of the Mayflower Stone we find a memorial commemorating in 1939, the 100th anniversary of the sailing of *The Tory*.

A pioneer ship in the colonization of New Zealand, *The Tory* had on board the founder of the New Zealand Company, Edward Gibbon Wakefield and the following year a group of local merchants founded the Plymouth New Zealand Company which bought 60,000 acres from Wakefield's company.

In a very short space of time the Plymouth Company sent some six ships and 897 emigrants almost all of whom were from Plymouth, Devon and Cornwall—and just as North America had its 'New Plymouth'—so did New Zealand's North Island now have its New Plymouth.

On the other side of the Mayflower Memorial sits an older plaque, ironically commemorating a more recent event.

Laid in 1919 it records the arrival, on 31st May that year, of the American seaplane the NC4. With two pilots and a crew of four, this amazing craft became the first aeroplane to make the Transatlantic Flight.

The NC4 took 23 hours to complete its trip and on arriving in Plymouth the plane's crew were greeted on the Barbican pier by among others Major Waldorf Astor and his wife Nancy and Mayor Joseph Brown who greeted the fliers with the words 'Plymouth is always a point of historic interest to Americans.'

The memorable sailing of the Pilgrim Fathers from this spot, though comparatively unnoticed at the time was an event which has proved to be a point in history of immeasurable interest. Mainly out of that small beginning a mighty people has sprung up, and today, in most dramatic fashion, their descendants have crossed back to us in a way never dreamed of by our forefathers and equalling in scientific development and daring the greatest imaginings of Jules Verne.

[WEH 30.1.83

The Mayflower Steps

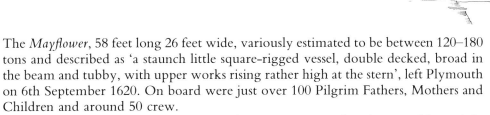

The *Mayflower*, 58 feet long 26 feet wide, variously estimated to be between 120–180 tons and described as 'a staunch little square-rigged vessel, double decked, broad in the beam and tubby, with upper works rising rather high at the stern', left Plymouth on 6th September 1620. On board were just over 100 Pilgrim Fathers, Mothers and Children and around 50 crew.

Their departure ante dated these steps by over 170 years but they would certainly have left from some point on the original Barbican 'Causey' near here. In 1891 a tablet, and in 1934 this strange little memorial were added to the simply carved stone set in cobbles to mark the event, if not the exact location. (The stone bearing the legend 'Mayflower 1620' was moved slightly long ago to prevent excessive wear from traffic.)

However, concern over the precise point often overlooks the fact that it was quite by chance that the Pilgrims left from Plymouth at all. The *Mayflower* only called into the port because its companion ship, the smaller and ill-named *Speedwell* was experiencing difficulties—apparently with both the fabric of the ship and its passengers and crew. In the event the *Speedwell* was sent back to London with those least willing and least fit 'to bear the brunt of this hard adventure' and so the Mayflower was left to complete the voyage alone. Thus we read on 6th September: 'The wind coming east-north-east, a fine small gale, we loosed from Plymouth, having been kindly entertained and courteously used by divers friends there living.'

The pilgrims with their passionate and independent yet unifying religious zeal would certainly have found kindred spirits in Plymouth. They would also have found men with first-hand knowledge of the land for which they were bound.

There had already been several expeditions from Plymouth to the new lands as there had been from other parts of the country. Since 1584 Raleigh, Grenville, Drake and Gilbert amongst others had ventured out, many just to plunder or fish but some with plans to colonize. However, the previous ill-fated attempts had been largely motivated by commercial interests and it was quite probably the Pilgrims determi-

nation, dedication and sense of democracy that enabled their colony, despite being much depleted after the first winter, to survive.

Perhaps too the Pilgrims choice of settlement helped them. They had not aimed for New England—their London Company patents for colonization were for lands over 200 miles to the south, whilst the patents for New England were held by the only other major company in the field, the Plymouth Company. Covering all lands in latitudes 41 to 45 degrees, this included the Indian village of Accomack, described by Captain John Smith after his 1614 visit, as 'an excellent good harbour, good land and no want of anything but industrious people'. In Smith's 1614 map this place is called New Plimouth. It is not clear whether this was Smith's name for the place, someone else's or even the name given it by Prince Charles (later Charles I) who apparently renamed several points on Smith's map before it was engraved.

Either way it is believed that the Pilgrims had a copy of the map and would have known the place by that name and would doubtless have heard in Plymouth, if not before, that Smith believed that in Massachusetts Bay 30–40 men could feed 200 people with as good corn, fish and flesh as the world could show.

So, was their choice of New Plimouth as a home really by accident or was it by design? Or was it done as a superstitious omen on account of the kindness they had received back in mother Plymouth? We will probably never know. But equally this link between the two worlds will always attract latter day 'Pilgrims' to this spot.

[*WEH* 4.5.85

The West Pier

The Barbican today, after the Hoe, is almost certainly the first place the tourist in Plymouth will want to go and it's hard to imagine that only 100 years ago it would probably have been one of the last.

Desperately poor and congested, full of factories, fumes and fish, one writer referred to it in 1880 as an 'historic but odoriferous neighbourhood.'

A naturally shallow pool, Sutton Harbour was at the end of a lot of the city's sewer outlets, and in 1882 contractor John Pethick dredged more than 30,000 tons of sewage from the harbour bed and it was estimated that almost as much again was left.

Proposals that this work be paid for by the Corporation provoked one eminent citizen to proclaim that Sutton Harbour was a natural cesspool and people should accept it as such.

Fortunately, however, attitudes have changed somewhat over the years and this natural pool, while it still niffs a bit at low tide, has now become a prime attraction.

The mouth of this pool was probably formed in the last Ice Age when the water level was 200 feet below its present line. Then streams not strong enough to cut big river paths but substantial enough to create a pool on the edge of Plymouth's limestone coastline, perhaps flowed down from North Hill and settled into the softer slate.

After a time this water cut away and overspilled at the point that became, when the ice finally melted and the tides rose, the harbour mouth.

The present two piers that all but dam the entrance, were constructed in the 1790s upon the remaining rocks which at low tide formed a natural ridge and as speculation has it, perhaps allowed for a completely dry pathway or 'cawsey' from side to side at very low tide.

Indeed, in the days of the Castle Barbican, a fine four-towered fortification which spawned the current civic crest but of which only part of one tower remains, a chain or boom was pulled across this entrance to protect the then tiny city.

The old railway offices and the warehouse to the right of this view have been recently restored and converted inside into flats by the Barbican Association. In 1941 the Blitz claimed the old Mayflower (formerly the Brunswick) Inn and that architectural misfit the Trattoria Capri, now stands in its place. Behind it another recent convert is the Seamen's Bethel, which has been imaginatively transformed into the Serenade Arts Centre.

To the left as we look are the Victorian offices of the Cattewater Commissioners and the pub that takes its name from the man who built the East and West Piers, the Admiral McBride.

Finally, just a little farther up the hill is the Fisherman's Rest, here on the first Friday of each month the Barbican Group meet. An august body led valiantly by Mr. Stanley Goodman, it does the best it can to protect this historic area from bad planning.

[*WEH* 27.11.82]

6

White House Pier

'At five in the morning the cafés are already open and the fishermen have collected freshly baked loaves from the bakery. In the clear morning colours the white and brown furled up sails can be appreciated.

A few policemen anxious to be off their beats approach . . . the street sweepers are industriously brooming and a tramp appears from somewhere glad that the night has gone . . . presently the sails of the trawlers begin to unfurl and nets are hauled down.

Only three or four donkey carts have yet arrived, backed to the edge of the pavement that has to serve as a fish market. Some foreign skippers arrive, bent on an early drink.

At the "Dolphin" it is heard that there has been a catch of some 26,000 mackerel the day before. There is a ringing of bells which is a token that sales are commencing. A crowd of buyers, among them one or two ladies with faded blackened eyes, fiery noses and shrill voices scramble over boxes, dodging between the carts to hear the first sale.

The ladies do not buy and whisper words not usually found in the dictionary—they are scarcely audible against the clatter of up to 90 carts drawn by horses, mules or donkeys.

Throughout the morning the coffee houses and drink shops have plenty of customers . . .' So wrote 'The Idler' in the *Western Figaro* on 9th May, 1884, a time when the Barbican was a slightly busier if not a somewhat rougher place to live and work. These were the days that policemen only ventured out in twos and sometimes threes and there was a police station with cells in The Old Watch House on the West Pier. Demolished in 1933 the role fulfilled by this building was partially replaced by the distinctive little building on the extended quay, built to relieve the congestion described above and to accommodate the much-needed new Fish Market which was completed in 1896. Known as the White House, this neat construction gave its name to the mini pier it stands on and through the 1930s to the 1960s at least, the Barbican Bobby was always based here. Manned by three regular policemen on three shifts, early, late and nights, here the bobby had his water jug and stove for his tea and fresh fish, while among the other items of equipment in the house were great fearsome grappling irons used for retrieving bodies from the harbour.

Well known faces to local folk, Barbican policemen were regular figures who only went missing on high days and holidays when 'strappers' or 'reliefs' would come down from the town. One such strapper in his early days in the force was Stanley Pearce, who during the war years served down there as PC No. 7. Counting them among his happiest days on the beat Mr. Pearce recalls the marvellous family and community spirit that can still just be found on the Barbican and the integral part that policemen played in that environment—a role perhaps best captured by one of the more unusual moments in his career when, on duty one day he was called to help a young woman in New Street and did so by successfully delivering her baby.

[*WEH* 4.6.83

Plymouth's fish quay

'There is no more picturesque or characteristic scene in Plymouth than that which the Barbican presents when the fishing boats, crowding all sail for early arrival, come in.

'In the height of the season the pool hard by is crowded with fishing boats, their brown sails flapping lazily in the puffs of breeze which has brought them in. The quay is filled with hundrds of maunds (baskets) of fish, and lined with scores of carts.

'Hake, mackerel (sic), turbots, whiting, plaice, flounders, pollack, mullet, John Dory, are among the fish most plentifully caught.

'Among the maunds and carts, there is an eager and excited crowd—fishermen and fisherwomen, in costumes from which all distinctive character has not yet departed, fish salesmen and fish buyers; and as auction after auction is held, and the pencil of the auctioneer falls upon his book, maund after maund is loaded into the waiting carts; and off they go, full gallop through the narrow streets of the old town to the railway station.

'In half an hour the once busy scene is deserted: the Barbican is quiet again, and nothing is left behind but that 'ancient and fishlike smell' which is the peculiar prerogative of such localities.'

So wrote R. N. Worth in 1878 for the text that accompanied the review of Plymouth in the Graphic Magazine of March that year.

Talking today with Russell Turner, member of one of the few Barbican fishing families whose ancestors were trading on the quay last century, you get the impression that little has changed.

The catches are much the same except that there's not so much mullet and John Dory landed these days and lemon sole now makes up a fair percentage of the fish caught.

Not so long ago scampi, scallops and queens would have been mostly thrown back, today they are brought home where they have a ready market.

The story goes that in as much as one person could be said to popularize one particular dish, Queen Elizabeth the Queen Mother conferred fame and fortune on scampi sellers when she confessed a liking for the dish back in the 1930s . . . Today, of course, scampi are shipped in great numbers starting out in the now plastic fish baskets and ending up in the now plastic pub baskets.

It is perhaps the mode and means of transportation of fish that has seen the greatest changes; gone are the sail boats, replaced first by steam then diesel, and gone are the horses and carts, replaced by vans, trucks and fleets of insulated container lorries which now carry fish all over the country, as for one reason or another fish have tended not to travel by train since the 1950s. »*Postscript*

[*WEH* 25.9.82.

Plymouth Castle

'At the foot of Lambhay Street is to be seen a small but very substantial building which is all that is left of the Plymouth Castle which was built on the rocky spur at the eastern end of the Hoe, immediately overlooking and commanding the entrance of Sutton Pool, somewhere in the reign of Henry IV.

'When Leland visited Plymouth he found the entrance to Sutton Pool defended by a blockhouse on the south-west and on a rocky hill hard by 'a strong castle quadrate, having at each corner a great round tower'. Risdon also speaks of it.

'From this old 'castle quadrate' the town takes its arms, a saltire between four castles. This interesting relic is now used as a dwelling house,' so wrote W. H. K. Wright at the turn of this century.

By the time C. W. Bracken came to write of it in 1931 this substantial building was no longer used as a dwelling house—it had been known locally as the Round House—and its high roof had disappeared. In the last fifty years it has been allowed to deteriorate further and today wild and weedy growth, the bulk of which I have not drawn, is pushing its way around the stonework and threatening to work loose the whole structure bit by bit. A sad fate indeed for what appears to be the only obvious reminder of a fortification whose outer workings were probably the original waterside defences that gave rise to the name Barbican for this area, as indeed such defences did in other areas, the nearest here being at Plympton St. Maurice.

The exact date of the construction of Plymouth Castle is veiled in the mists of time, different authorities have dated it anywhere between 1220–1420 and Museum Curator James Barber refers to it as medieval.

Whatever, there is little doubt that the original four-towered castle looked down on Sutton Pool in the early fifteenth century and did give rise to the Civic crest first recorded in 1439.

This crest, Plymouth's second of any note, has survived with various modifications to the present day and one would think that this alone would have been sufficient incentive to look after the only surviving tower, the others having long since fallen down or been demolished the most recent disappearing during the last century.

The Castle itself ceased to be of much strategic importance after the building of the Citadel on the Hoe in 1666 and was largely destroyed soon after.

Sir Bernard Gomme, engineer in charge of the citadel project produced a plan in 1665 clearly showing the old four-castelated construction but without a central keep as had been shown in a drawing of 1540.

From the 1660s onward then little civic interest has been shown in the castle quadrate, save for Thomas Darracot who was Mayor in 1704–5 and who evidently 'showed (un)common respect for the remains of the old castle and its outpost as long as he had any influence'.

Today, tourists regularly traipse up Lambhay Hill to view this ancient relic and look at the plaque that reads: 'This, the eastern part of the south port, is the last remnant of the castle 'quadrant' of Plymouth,' and audibly wonder that it is not better kept. Just as locals wonder that the adjacent gardens donated by Lady Astor are not kept open on a regular basis.

Lady Astor apparently bought this land intending to have a bungalow here, however, when her husband died she decided against the idea and gave the plot for gardens to be enjoyed by pensioners and retired fishermen.

Whilst they are seldom open these gardens are at least well maintained unlike the other public gardens here in Lambhay Street which must strike the tourists as being more reminiscent of a city in weeds than in bloom.

[*WEH* 23.7.83]

The Fisherman's Arms

Tucked away towards the bottom of Lambhay Street stands the 'Fisherman's Arms', undoubtedly the most hidden away of the twenty or so pubs around the heart of old Plymouth, the Barbican. And although it cannot claim to be the oldest purpose-built Inn in town, it almost certainly boasts some of the oldest features of any local pub or building. Concealed for many years beneath layers of paint and plaster, these were uncovered soon after the arrival of current licensee John de la Haye back in 1962. Uncovered, treated and varnished now the long and very thick lounge wall, but for its cosmetic work, looks very similar to that of the structure commonly known as the only surviving remnant of Plymouth Castle which stands in line with the Fisherman's frontage some 30 yards down from its door. Other walls around which the pub is built appear to be of similar construction and on either side of the large lounge window are two stone pillars. These are now covered but one sports two hefty iron hinges which would appear to suggest that there was once a substantial doorway here, much bigger than would have been appropriate for an eighteenth century inn.

Whilst there is little doubt that Plymouth Castle was here somewhere, no-one appears to be quite certain just how the last surviving remnant fitted into it or quite where it went, although it is said that the beginning of a town wall did run at least parallel to if not on the actual line of the 'Fisherman's'. and that the wall was there in 1540 and the castle perhaps 100 years or so before that.

Writing in a letter to the *Herald*'s postbag in 1958 in the wake of an earlier article about the Castle local historian G. W. Copeland said: "It is quite possible that the thick and massive stone rubble walls a little further up the street . . . are by their very nature adapted fragments of the medieval castle structure.'

In 1760 long after the Citadel had made the castle redundant, 'the Sutton Pyll Manor was parcelled out' and William Cambers, a victualler, built his court 'behind the remains of Plymouth Castle'. According to the brewery records the 'Fisherman's' was part of it.

In 1814 John Bickell, a carpenter and joiner, took over the lease of the building from Thomas Bridgeman, shoemaker, and in an 1822 Directory we find Bickell listed as 'Victualler, Duke of Wellington, Lammy Hill'. Wellington, the wartime hero, had not long been made a duke in 1822 and although the name 'Fisherman's Arms' was adopted here in 1840, each of the Three Towns had a 'Wellington Inn' 100 years ago.

'The Fisherman's' has since passed through many hands and has been owned by Pope & Allen, brewers; the Harris family: Starkey, Knight and Ford; and Whitbread. John de la Haye, current landlord, first drank here in 1947 when fellow Jerseyman Nobby Lawrence ran the pub. He became a regular, married a Barbican girl, and one day, a few years after Nobby had gone, his successor Taffy Quirk asked John how he'd fancy running a pub and within weeks had handed over to him. In those days the 'Fisherman's' was a little more basic than it is today. Indeed the ladies toilet could only be reached by going outside the pub and a few yards up the street and John kept a brolly behind the bar to issue on rainy days.

Now a popular and comfortable place to drink and eat (the landlord prepares most dishes himself) the 'Fisherman's' remains an historical mystery. A mystery which is only deepened by the 3-foot tunnel under the bar which John believes ran all the way to Tinside. But who can say?

11

[*WEH* 10.10.85

Greyfriars

The buildings currently referred to as 'Greyfriars' and otherwise known as 43 and 44 New Street stand towards the Hoe end of the street at the top of Pin (formerly Pin's) Lane. With their original Georgian brick facade these two former dwelling houses occupy what is believed to have been the north-eastern corner of the sixty acre site that accommodated the late fourteenth-century development of the Franciscan or Grey Friars.

Despite fierce opposition from the parish clergy and outbreaks of apparently anonymous vandalism these medieval monks had by 1391 built their own place of worship upon this land. Land that had, in 1383, been 'alienated' to them by Royal licence. With this as their base these friars, in addition to the earlier settlement of the Carmelite or White Friars on the other side of town—near the present Friary Street—preached and worked around the young town of Sutton. The buildings and activities of the friars doubtless developed over the next 150 years but sadly for them in 1538 everything came to an abrupt end as the Friary became yet another of Henry VIII's dissolution victims.

Thereafter, the Greyfriars' site appears to have been left to crumble rather than be adapted to any secular use and it is likely that the monks stonework was used in the building of what appear to have been two 2-storey late Elizabethan cottages, divided by a wide-paved area, that were built here in New Street.

Not that the street was always called New Street for it was once known as Rag Street and indeed throughout the seventeenth and well into the eighteenth century it was most commonly called Grey Friars Street.

As this thriving seaport developed over the years demand for local accommodation intensified and towards the end of the seventeenth century the two Elizabethan constructions were joined and amended to form the building that we see here today.

Thereafter they were lived in by, at times, a staggering number of people. Around 1850, New Street, which then had no drainage, had some 600 people living in its 43 houses, 26 of which had no privies or W.C.s.

In 1849 17 people in New Street alone died of cholera and typhoid was an ever present hazard. Although conditions improved, well after the second world war there was still terrible over-crowding.

Small wonder then that as the 1960s dawned these buildings were almost derelict with a demolition order hanging over them and their occupants for the most part re-housed. So they were when in 1962 Dennis and Mary Browning bought first 44, then in 1963, 43 New Street.

Much work was done and good sense prevailed and these fine old buildings soon found themselves to be the first in Plymouth to have a demolition order rescinded and a preservation order slapped on in its place soon after. Here, 20 years ago, began the first of the new wave of potteries on the Barbican.

Hospital Radio Plymouth first took to the air from here many years ago and from here five years ago today my pictures were first made available to the general public. Here other open workshops today offer pottery, knitwear, leatherwork, and even hairdressing.

[*WEH* 3.12.83

The Robin Hood

It is thought that there was a Robin Hood Inn here on this site almost 300 years ago and there is definite record of it from 1798 onwards. A succession of landlords saw it through the nineteenth century and two gentlemen Messrs Hughes and Knapman ran it consecutively from the turn of the century to its close around the outbreak of the First World War.

For many years dry and in private hands it reopened, this time as a club in 1967 under the guidance of its owner Mr. E. R. Lonergan. Now run by Roger Thomas, the 'Robin Hood', restored by the Barbican Association, is the nearest thing to a pub in New Street today—a street which in its heyday last century boasted a handful of inns; the East and West Country Inn, the Royal Highlander, the Welchman's Arms and the Anchor and Hope.

Just down the road from the Robin Hood this latter pub had, ironically a landlord in the middle of the last century by the name of John Littlejohns.

In York there is a pub itself called Little John and in Becontree in Essex there is another Robin Hood and whilst Plymouth can claim no direct link with the legend of Robin Hood the influence of this celebrated character has travelled far and wide over 600 or so years. Indeed in recent years films have been made in Italian, Spanish, Japanese—and even Russian telling of his exploits.

For the most part based on the stories that appeared in medieval ballads it would seem that Robin, Little John, Will Scarlett, and Much have been with us since the fourteenth century with Friar Tuck and Maid Marian first appearing late in the fifteenth century.

Whether such a figure ever existed other than in the minds of a public always eager to accept such a hero is less clear. Contenders who have been found in genuine historical documents include a Robertus Hood from the likely area of Wakefield in Edward II's time (1307–27)—he may also be the Robyn Hoode mentioned in Edward's household accounts and who on leaving the court became involved with Thomas, Earl of Lancaster, in his revolt against the King.

There are, however, also several references to a Robin Hood—fugitive, in the pipe rolls of Henry III (1216–72) and should these locate our man then it is possible that this 'Hobbe-hood' could have been active during the reigns of Richard I and John. Such considerations are of little matter though when dealing with the legends themselves which have become among the most well known in popular literature.

These myths and legends are by no means sacred, however, and over the years celluloid Robins including Fairbanks, Flynn and Greene have brought many variations to the role, as has the latest TV version which perhaps more than any of its predecessors has introduced a large slice of magic.

Such is unlikely to detract too much from the character of the man who together with Maid Marion has for centuries presided over May Day celebrations as the Lord and Lady of the May. A traditional time of dancing and fun, May Day had virtually become Robin Hood's day by the sixteenth century.

Robin Hood plays become an integral part of the festivities and characters from the legends featured prominently in the associated Morris Dances. One in particular highlighted when Much the miller's son would play the fool and stun the spectators by banging them on the head with a bladder of peas.

Whether he'll be at it again on Monday somewhere is anyone's guess. One thing, however is certain here in New Street the 'Robin Hood' will be open to entertain revellers until the sun has long gone down.

[*WEH* 5.5.84

Elizabethan Gardens

Visitors to the Barbican are often intrigued to find halfway along New Street a little sign directing them to the 'Elizabethan Gardens'. Entered by an alleyway or snicket between numbers 39 and 40 New Street, these gardens were laid out some 15 years ago. Such recent workings, however, does not mean that these gardens have simply been contrived to look Elizabethan; rather they are designed to appear as they might have done when New Street was developed in the sixteenth century.

Built to house wealthy Elizabethan sea captains and merchants, there are still a handful of properties left in the street which give some idea of how the area would have looked several centuries ago. However it has not always appeared thus. Come the dawn of the eighteenth century the better off members of the community had begun moving out of the inner city areas and, as the original heart of the city, this primarily meant the Barbican. Moving first to North Hill and St. Judes, the gentry then made their way out past Mutley to Mannamead and Hartley then Roborough and beyond. And as the wealthy moved out so the poorer classes moved in. With the population of the growing city increasing and the principal means of transport for most people still their own two legs, so the demand for accommodation in town became intense. Here on the Barbican where fishing and other local industries were approaching their peak almost every available piece of land was covered with a hastily built tenement. Castle Street and New Street boasted populations hard now to conceive and in the area between the large early nineteenth century bonded store and warehouse (Nos. 34–40 New Street where the gardens have now been re-established), almost all the street level back yards had been developed including a good part of the upper level which is the garden area now open to the public. The non-concreted areas immediately to the left and right of the entrance alley, now sporting trees of the sort one might have found in a sixteenth century garden, mark the extent of two such tenements and around the walls of the gardens themselves various tell-tale window shapes and fireplaces indicate others. Partly damaged during the war, the decision to attempt to restore the area to its former glory was taken almost entirely at the instigation of the Old Plymouth Society and the Barbican Association. Through their efforts the City has been spared the loss of a good part of its heritage and again thanks to the efforts of the Barbican Association buildings have been restored and land opened up to the public so that people can perhaps savour for themselves some of that Elizabethan atmosphere. As well as the period garden trees (e.g. Bay, Fig), the herbs, the ornamental hedges and pond, the gardens possess several fine stone pieces, some that were originally here others that have been incorporated into the layout from other sites. The gateway hard by the pond being the most notable example. In 1630 this was the entrance to the Hospital of the Poor's Portion in Catherine Street just next to St. Andrew's Church. Immediately prior to its use as a hostel for the poor, however, in March 1630 'Divers Godly persons of the Counties of Devon, Dorset and Somerset' met here with their spiritual leaders, John Maverick and John Wareham, before setting off to establish Dorchester Church Colony in the New World. Before leaving they carved their motto 'By God's helpe through Christ' above the lintel. Dorchester is today the biggest suburb of Boston, Mass. The Hospital of the Poor's Portion meanwhile saw various uses over the years, eventually being pulled down in 1869 to make way for the present Guildhall. Between then and its incorporation here this doorway spent most of its time in a private garden in Mannamead.

Appropriately enough, in the light of the pioneering spirits of those who once walked through this doorway, the gardens, designed by architect Alan Miller-Williams, were opened in time for the Mayflower celebrations in 1970.

[WEH 29.6.85

New Street

Few streets in Plymouth are older, or even as old, as the Barbican's New Street and certainly no other street has witnessed such dramatic changes of fortune down the years while, at the same time, retaining so much of its original appearance.

Largely developed and built by John Sparke, a much-travelled Elizabethan whom Crispin Gill describes as 'Plymouth's first speculative builder' and 'the first Englishman to mention either potato or tobacco,' the first documentary record of the street appeared exactly 400 years ago.

In 1584 we read that there was trouble with surface water coming down from 'Mr Sparke's new streate'. However it does not appear that the street was then called New Street, indeed up until 1746 it appears to have been known as Rag Street (until recently old Barbican folk referred to the Castle Street approach which runs out of New Street as 'The Rag' or 'Castle Rag'). Furthermore the top, Hoe end, of the street once housed the fourteenth century Greyfriars Monastery and was apparently known as Greyfriars or 'Gray Fryers' Street.

Whatever its name, New Street was built for the successful men of Tudor Plymouth and with Castle Street its houses boasted several prominent owners, the Heles, Sir Thomas Wise, the Pollexfens, Sir James Bagg, the Trelawneys . . . and we are told even in the eighteenth century this was the residential quarter of some of the principal merchants and people of standing in the town.

'It had, however,' wrote W. H. K. Wright in 1899, 'very much deteriorated in the early part of the nineteenth century and has gradually gone lower in the social scale of its inhabitants, as well as in the ricketty character of its buildings.'

Ricketty and unhealthy they might have been, but, when you consider that 100 years ago some 57 people lived in 32, New Street alone and between them 32, 34 and 35 New Street, seen here on either side of the warehouse on the right, housed over 50 children under 16, the houses did well to survive at all.

That they must have done must in part be due to the way in which they were built, 32 and 34 still boast their original pole staircases built around the mast of a ship, and in part due to the men who have been concerned to see their survival.

In 1929 No. 32, now known as the Elizabethan House, was saved from demolition and restored by the Old Plymouth Fund Committee and in the 1950s Nos 34–40 New Street were among those saved and restored by the Barbican Association.

Only a handful of people now live in this part of New Street but the area still thrives today as largely protected from the motor cars it was never designed to admit, many shops and businesses operate here.

No. 32 itself is a showhouse open to the public and with the typically Tudor No. 16 opposite, shows how narrow the street was, a feature which afforded some protection against the wind and rain but allowed little light hence the large window areas.

The warehouse on the left contains among others, potter John Pollex and woodworker Trevor Pate, while former timber merchant Richard Hill is restoring the massive old Palace Vaults warehouse on the right.

Today, 34 New Street, which like 35 still has its original carved Jacobean doorway, now houses my own studios where prints of all the drawings that appear in this Time Draws On series are currently available.

The Island House

No. 9 the Barbican, otherwise known as the Island House is indeed an old construction.

The present building is believed to date from the 1580–1620 period, although an Island House of some description is known to have existed on the site since at least 1495.

Some time around 1610 a fire swept the house and apart from necessary repairs then much renovation and alteration work was carried out in the eighteenth century.

As most Plymothians and certainly most tourists are aware the Island House has had, in recent years, a plaque on its side wall listing the names of some 50 or so male members of that historic party since known as the 'Pilgrim Fathers' who spent their last night on English soil in Plymouth on 5th September 1620.

Having been so 'kindly entertained and courteously used by divers friends there dwelling' the said Pilgrims duly named their first settlement on the other side of the Atlantic, Plymouth.

However, although the Island House was almost certainly here when the Pilgrim Fathers were, there is sadly no evidence to prove that they either did or didn't stay there; but of course as there were so many of them staying here and so few handy Barbican houses remain from that period, the assumption is not unreasonable.

One thing, however, is more certain; in more recent times the changing use of the Island House (currently owned by a member of the Plymouth family, the Baylys, whose ancestors first owned the deeds of the property in 1786) has to some extent reflected the changing fate and fortunes of the whole Barbican area.

George Bryant's ship chandling business was there from 1895 through to the 1920s and indeed between them, Thomas Johnson then Short and Co. had run a ship chandlers there since at least 1850.

In the 1920s for a brief period Robert Turner, the fish merchant, had the place, then in the 1930s a 40-year spell as an antiques business began, until in 1976 the lease was taken up by 'Reynolds Paintings'. »Postscript

[*WEH* 28.8.82.

Elizabethan House

In the text that accompanies an earlier New Street drawing we thus read . . .

'Although called New St., it is one of the oldest streets in the town, and was, in the eighteenth century, the residential quarter of some of the principal merchants and people of standing in the town. It had, however, very much deteriorated in the early part of the nineteenth century and has gradually gone lower in the social scale of its inhabitants, as well as in the ricketty character of its buildings. Two houses . . . with fine overhanging gables and carved corbels and doorposts, are solitary specimens of what Plymouth houses used to be, and even they are doomed.'

And doomed they certainly appeared to be, however in the wake of the slum clearance plans of the 1920s a group calling itself the Old Plymouth Society was formed and in 1926, 32 New St. was rescued and restored and then turned over to the corporation. In 1930 it was opened to the public and has since served as a walkaround Elizabethan show house.

Fascinating as it is architecturally, it somehow lacks that lived in quality—the various pieces of sixteenth and seventeenth century furniture fail either to conjure up the merchants and sea captains for whom John Sparke doubtless constructed this and other houses, or its first recorded owners, Richard Brandon (1631), the Borough Treasurer or William Hele (1633) who was twice Mayor of Plymouth (1630 and 1638).

As for New Street itself, despite having the status of a Grade II listed building, cobbles are still dug up for street workings and then crudely concreted back into place.

[*WEH* 29.5.82.

The Dolphin Inn

Undoubtedly one of the most enduring and unchanging features of the Barbican throughout this century and last is the attractively fronted, yet unpretentious, 'Dolphin Inn'.

Run continuously since the Second World War by one family the Dolphin has preservation orders on both its interior and exterior and as you watch pints being poured straight from the barrel, thanks to nothing more sophisticated than gravity itself it's not hard to picture people and scenes from the past filling a bare floor which has successfully resisted the carpeting craze that seems to have swept public houses throughout the country.

Of the more colourful scenes recalled perhaps the most celebrated one took place on the 17th of March, 1838 when four of the six 'Tolpuddle Martyrs' arrived back in Plymouth after their 7 year deportation sentences had been substantially reduced.

The four—James Loveless, James Brine, Thomas Standfield and his son John received a tumultuous welcome on the Barbican as they landed off the 'John Berry' and were well entertained by Charles Morgan the then landlord with whom they stayed for several days.

It is 150 years since the six Dorset men were found guilty of administering unlawful oaths and it was on the 11th of April, 1834 that they left Plymouth on board the convict ship 'Surrey,' bound for New South Wales, Australia.

In 1956 a plaque was erected on the Barbican to commemorate their early return which had been brought about after many petitions and demonstrations of public support.

The men had been granted full pardons in March 1836 but in those days there was no quick way of telling people on one side of the world what decisions had been made on the other and it was two years before the men were back from Australia (John Hammett was last back in 1839).

Today of course, it is hard to imagine that men were ever treated in this way merely for forming themselves together in order to improve their pay. It had been the industrial revolution with the massive low paid workforce it spawned that prompted workers to form combinations—combinations which were repressed in the Acts of 1799 and 1800 but then given more freedom after these acts were repealed in 1824.

Trade unionism thereafter began to grow fitfully and the judgment against the six Tolpuddle farmworkers (four of them Methodist preachers) was invoked under a statute designed to deal with conspiratorial societies. The unlawful oaths said to have been administered in Tolpuddle were simply variations on the oath of loyalty common among the friendly societies and freemasons on whom early 'unions' were modelled.

Charles Morgan, host to the martyrs was still at the 'Dolphin' 20 years later and indeed the history of the pub is marked with long periods of licensee stability. The McGarrys ran the pub for many years before the war and current licensee Bette Holmes began pulling pints here when she was eleven after her grandparents, Henry and Louisa Nicholls, took the pub over from Edward McGarry during the war.

McGarry then moved to the ill fated Newmarket until it was bombed after which he went to the Britannia at Milehouse. After Louisa, Maudie Nicholls ran the 'Dolphin' for 20-odd years before Bette took charge. Part of an old Barbican family Bette's grandmother also ran a fisherman's restaurant two doors along from the 'Dolphin'. Again a family concern this was open just after the first war and was only sold in the early 1970s.

Meanwhile, as befitting its status as a traditional Barbican institution, the 'Dolphin' still has a pub piano where most now have a juke box and surrounded by an excess of restaurants and takeaways it still only serves refreshments of a liquid kind.

[*WEH* 7.4.84

The Navy

It is perhaps not surprising that the Barbican, which houses a large percentage of Plymouth's oldest pubs, should also have a good proportion of those whose names reflect the city's seaside status.

Here we find the ancient 'Maritime', 'The Ship', the 'Fisherman's', the 'Admiral McBride', the 'Dolphin' and the 200-year-old 'Navy Hotel'.

In 1814 the 'Navy' appeared on a list of Plymouth's principal inns, along with only six others, it was after all one of the town's major hotels and one 'much resorted to by Masters of Merchant ships & C.'

Built on the site of the Tudor home of John Smart, who gave his name at least to the adjacent quayside expansion of 1602, which later became absorbed into the fish market development, the 'Navy' appears to be first documented on a map of 1786 where it is referred to as Ord's public house.

Thought to have been built by Ralph Ord himself on land leased from the Duchy, the 'Navy' enjoyed for most of the nineteenth century, a solid reputation as an hotel of note and three men, Driscoll, Harvie and Luce successively ran the place from just after the turn of the century until the early 1880s.

A fine contemporary photograph of William Luce's 'Navy' hotel shows the main frontage to have changed little in over 100 years and an advertisement of the day informs us that there was a 'Table d'hote daily at 1 p.m. and hearty welcome to all captains visiting the port ... Master marines, passengers and families, it added, will find every accommodation and comfort.'

After enjoying then a considerable period of stability with its licensees, the 'Navy' suddenly found itself in the mid-1880s being passed around like a hot potato. In the next 20 years it changed hands at least nine times and whatever the reasons were for this they doubtless encouraged the Sutton Harbour Company who owned the place, to sell up in 1901. Soon after this the Jacobs family arrived and they stayed for over 25 years.

Bert Ellis and then Alf Miller took the 'Navy' into wartime, a time which, temporarily at least, saw the end of one nearby Southside Street local, the 'Queen's Arms', which was rebuilt in the 1960s and the Dartingtons' 'Royal Oak' at number 10 (at one time or another there have been a dozen or so different drinking houses in Southside Street).

In the succession of landlords at the 'Navy' since the war few have stayed as long or been as popular as Joe O'Leary, who was followed in the late 1970s by Derek Barrett, now at the 'Colebrook' and then by Kevin Nicholson who was here some four years.

For current licensees John and Sue Luckie, the 'Navy' is their first pub but John did have a spell in the trade at the Roxy Nightclub in Union Street, next door to his father's pub, the 'Clipper' (formerly the 'Sydenham'). John's father, however, is by no means his only pub-running relative, his grandfather kept the original 'Unity' in Ebrington Street, his uncle the 'Woodman' in King Street and his great uncle, the 'Galatea', just along the road from it.

And so we find a man with innkeeping in his blood running one of the oldest hotels in Plymouth which, despite its fine harbour views and maze of rooms, is today, like many of its counterparts, run just as a pub and restaurant.

[*WEH* 22.12.84

Barbican Wine Lodge

A little more than ten years ago the local family building firm of F. R. Cross & Son bought No. 7 Quay Road, also known as No. 5 The Quay.

At that time it was a shambling old warehouse that had seen better days and many uses—from an onion sellers through an undertakers to a second hand rope dealers. It was currently then occupied by T. & J. Sanders—metalworkers, coppersmiths and plumbers, who had been in Quay Road since the beginning of the 1930s.

The Quay Road address is itself a comparatively recent one as 100 years ago the water still lapped the warehouse walls, and it wasn't until the building of the Fish Market in the 1890s that a cart path then a road was built along the front of this sixteenth century quay.

Not that the buildings themselves necessarily reflect their Tudor origins as Crispin Gill states in his book on Sutton Harbour (1970)—'the warehouses themselves have been so rebuilt and repaired over the centuries that it would be foolhardy to date them, but one, lower than the others may well contain much original material.'

Certainly if he means the wine lodge building then the Cross family found much to support this notion. The cross beaming from ground floor level ceiling to first level floor, together with the sloping timber floors, the much bowed party wall, the many lintels and the outside coining, all tend to suggest this. There is also the floor of a Tudor courtyard below the present floor level.

Motivated by a love of old buildings, the Cross family, who have restored several such constructions around the city, had no idea to what use the warehouse might be put once its restoration was complete. Cedric (Ziggy) Talbot-Weiss and his stepson Alestair Orr-Ewing, however, had no doubt about what the building should be used for the moment they first saw it.

A successful industrial designer from London, 'Ziggy' had been looking for somewhere to open a wine bar.

In London in the early 1970s there had been a positive outbreak of wine bars—spearheaded by Julia Carpenter's Wolsey Wine Bar chain—in one year she opened 15. Taking the place of the ailing, low profit making coffee bars, whose heyday ended with the arrival of the free'n'easy swinging sixties, wine bars opened up a new market in that as an alternative to pubs they offered women a comfortable and respectable venue for a lunchtime drink and nibble.

Mr. Talbot Weiss made his bid for the building and later applied for his wine bar licence—on the same day, coincidentally as an old schoolfriend of his John Dudley, applied for a similar licence for premises in Southside Street.

John Dudley, perhaps better known today as Cap'n Jasper, the fisherman's friend, had already established Dudley's Wine Bar in Kingsbridge and with the subsequent success of both applications Plymouth soon found itself, in June 1975, with two new wine bar restaurants—the other now being called Oysters.

Both recently changed hands, the busy wine Lodge today with its new proprietor Peter Stadnyk boasts live music—folk and jazz, several nights a week. All this, ironically, coming to Plymouth well over 400 years after Martin Luther was attributed as saying 'Who loves not wine, women and song remains a fool his whole life long!'

[WEH 11.2.84

Kathleen and May

For the greater part of the 1970s the *Kathleen and May* sat in Sutton Pool.

She had been launched at the turn of the century in April 1900 from the little Welsh port of Connah's Quay. Such days in this community were treated as great occasions, the flags would go up around the town and local children had time off school.

A recent Welsh visitor to my studio on the Barbican told me that his mother was one such child and she had gone to school with the two girls, Lizzie and May after whom the boat was originally named.

It was the lot of all children, he added, with careful parents, to go to the launch of a new boat armed with a bucket, so that they might pile up soft soap as soon as the boat had gone down the slipway.

Lizzie (Elizabeth) and May were the daughters of one John Coppack, 'the largest first owner' of the boat. The cost of building the *Lizzie May* is believed to have been £2,700, a figure that makes more sense when compared to the weekly wage of a shipwright in 1900 which was about 25 shillings a week (£1.25).

In 1908 the Coppacks sold the boat for £1,700 to an Irishman who renamed the boat *Kathleen and May* in honour of his own daughter.

The *Kathleen and May* in all her years of service was a light cargo boat, ferrying its loads around the British and Irish coastline. All manner of goods filled her holds from coal to clay, salt to stones and gunpowder to galvanized iron.

In 1931 she was sold again, this time for £700. The new owners were a father and son team, William and Tommy Jewell, who between them ran the triple-rigged schooner for 30 years by which time the Kathleen and May had outlived all but one or two of her hundreds of contemporaries.

That she survived so well is doubtless a tribute to the careful attention paid to her by Tommy Jewell who earned the vessel a lot of admiration and in 1956 the *Kathleen and May* was the subject of a half-hour programme on the old BBC Home Service (Radio 4).

In 1961, 65-year-old Tommy sold his beloved boat for £4,000 to a new owner who had plans of using her for passenger cruising. However the plans didn't materialize and the next ten years saw the *Kathleen and May* in a variety of hands and resting places. That was until almost ten years later when the *Kathleen and May* became the first boat to be acquired by the newly formed Maritime Trust founded by the Duke of Edinburgh.

With further financial assistance from Mr. Y. K. Pao and World Wide Shipping, Hong Kong, the *Kathleen and May* was refitted at Mashfords Yard, Cremyll and opened to the public for the first time in Millbay Docks in 1971.

Moving soon after to Sutton Pool she remained in Plymouth until finances demanded that she be moved to a venue where a greater number of visitors would help to pay her maintenance costs.

And in September 1978 the *Kathleen and May* made another voyage this time to the recently restored Victorian Dock, St. Catherine's in London.

[*WEH* 16.1.83

The Old Custom House

The text written by W. H. K. Wright, accompanying a turn of the century drawing reads thus: 'On the Parade stands a quaint old building, now used as a store, everything but its substantial walls being in a state of decay.

'This was the Custom House of Plymouth in the seventeenth century and the immediate predecessor of the building on the opposite side of the Parade, the later building having been erected in 1820.

'We are however, informed that the corporation paid for work on a Custom House as long ago as 1586 . . . When this old building was erected, what is now known as the Parade, was a creek with private house and warehouse living on both sides of the way, the water flowing almost to the bottom of High Street.

'One authority,' he added. 'suggests that in olden times the Old Custom House, was used as a barracks for artillery and the men used to parade on the open space in front, hence the name.'

Today we can add little to this appraisal either by way of proof or additional information, save that there was at least an 'intermediate' Customs House built on what was then the other side of Exchange Street and is now the 'Three Crowns Beer Garden', and further that the 'New Quay' was built in 1572 and the High Street is no more.

Since this description this quaint old building has nearly disappeared twice. In 1926 it was saved from demolition largely by the action of members of the Old Plymouth Society and during the War it was gutted by enemy bombs.

Now it stands solid once more, quite handsomely restored. At the top of its wooden spiral staircase is the Mayflower fashion workshop whilst downstairs with a lovely touch of irony in the rooms that were once used as stables (Beane's 1903–7. Balkwill's 1907–14) a very different interest is now taken in horses as Mr. Ronald Hooper, registered accountant of the turf conducts his daily business.

22

[WEH 21.8.82.

The Custom House

In an 1821 Guide to Plymouth the following description of the Customs House appeared,

'This establishment was removed from its former mean and inconvenient situation to the newly erected building on the first of January 1820.

'The new Customs House fronts The Parade or coal quay and the warehouse and cellars behind extend into Foyne's Lane (later Woolster Street, now Vauxhall Street). The present edifice was erected by Mr. Ball under the direction of D. Laing, Esq., surveyor.

'The front is built of granite with a colonnade of five arches supported by rusticated piers of the same material. Inside the staircase, likewise of granite, leads to the long-room, a commodious and spacious apartment for the dispatch of general business, adjoining which are the comptroller's and collector's offices.'

But for a few minor alternations in structure and administration little has changed within this, now protected, historical building. The hours of business have been extended form the original 9—3 to 9—4 and the magnificent clock, installed in 1823, has stood up well to the test of time.

Of the other buildings in this block as we look at it however, to the left of the Customs House numbers 8 and 9 have undergone a few character changes with the passing of the years. 100 years ago, No. 8 The Parade housed the offices of John Edmond and Sons, Solicitors and Notaries.

John Edmond himself had been Borough Coroner and the business had been based here for some decades before being replaced by the firm Batchelor and Geake which became simply Arthur Geake, Solicitor, by the turn of the century since when the

building had been used for private habitation until it opened as a Greek restaurant some ten or so years ago.

Next door, in No. 9, the recent history has been somewhat more stable, namely being the premises for a succession of ships' agents and stores merchants passing down through the hands of Triplett's, Pearse & Haswell, then just Haswell and Co., to A. E. Monsen, who, in the mid 1950s, moved their offices to Vauxhall Quay and were then followed by Sanders Stevens and Co. who are still in No. 9 today.

To the other side of the unnumbered Customs House we find No. 10 and 11 The Parade. The latter being the 'Three Crowns' which is almost the oldest inn in the city and certainly has altered little in outward appearance for the greater part of its 380 odd years existence.

Number 10, however, up until relatively recent years, had been the address of two premises, for, level with the front of the Customs House and sticking out in front of about one third of the present No. 10 was a curious little building of uncertain date.

Up until the war this structure had variously housed a wine merchants, tobacconists and sweet shop. Here 100 years ago was Henry Crocker and Co., the wine merchant, whilst in the rest of the building that now houses The Matilda Café, Pilgrim Cabs and in its highest part since 1964, Ronnie's Club, could be found Little John, one of a succession of sailmakers who had in turn shared the building with one R. Ellis and before him, G. Rowe, whose businesses centred curiously enough around the merchandizing of tar and hemp.

[WEH 5.3.83

Barbican Arms

One hundred years ago the 'Porter's Arms', Looe Street, was run by William Perraton, he had been there since the mid 1850s and was to stay there until Charles Gulliver took over in 1895. Perraton's long stay is unlikely to be matched as much because of modern brewery policy as of the licensee's inclination to stop there.

A succession of landlords this century has seen many faces behind the bar here and names such as Billing, Boyes, Quick, Twitty, Williams, Tookey and Darlington have graced the little black and white placard above the front door.

Harold Darlington, however, did more than bring about a change in the name of licensee, for it was he who instigated the name change from the 'Porter's Arms' to the 'Barbican Arms'.

This was reputedly done in the wake of the post Francis Chichester euphoria that swept Plymouth in the late sixties. However, no-one seems to know now where the Arms of the Barbican that decorate the sign outside the pub come from.

The inclusion of a gold, three-masted ship sitting on the waves of the sea all upon a red shield would appear to be a reference to the Arms of Plymouth as recorded by the *Herald's* Visitation of Devonshire in 1575.

'Heraldic Visitations' occurred throughout the country during the sixteenth and seventeenth centuries and were simply visits by officers of the College of Arms who would research and record local coats of arms thereby bestowing some sort of legality upon them.

This particular design, however, was one of two recorded at the College of Arms and a Mayor's seal of 1439 with a saltire and four towers is the one that forms the basis of the Civic coat of arms that we know today. Nevertheless, the ship motif does in some respects predate this and there is one impression of a seal of 1368, of the early Corporation of Sutton which shows a simple single-masted ship upon water.

The pub sign, among its additions to this design, has a crown above sprouting a hand holding an anchor (another feature of the present Civic Arms), it also has a small inset shield, a large fish down either side and the motto 'Audentes fortuna juvat'—Fortune favours the brave.

Whatever its links to Plymouth's heraldic past, the 'Barbican Arms', through its last two licensees at least, had definite links with the past history of Plymouth's public houses.

Harold Darlington himself came from the old 'Princess Royal' in Union Street and Joyce Marston, the current licensee and her husband, Roland (Jim), were in 1971 the last ever landlords of the Ham Street Vaults in Ebrington Street, Indeed for a short time the Marstons ran both the 'Ham Street Vaults' and the then recently renamed 'Barbican Arms'.

While it's still slightly unusual for a pub to change its name these days, a change of name for a restaurant seems to be almost as frequent as a change of management and when the triumvirate of Sarah and Bobby Yardley and Mike Everitt opened Strokers III next door to the pub they chalked up yet another new name for what had been Occasions, Roma in Bocca, before that a café, then earlier this century and at the end of last a 'provision dealer' and Post Office and before that a fish curers' premises . . .

Who said nothing ever changes? After all before 1825 Looe Street wasn't even called Looe Street—it was Pike Street. »*Postscript*

[*WEH* 5.11.83]

The King's Head

'We now enter that portion of the town once called Briton- (Breton)-side, but now included in the general term of Treville Street. This name is a memorial of the destruction of this portion of the town by the Bretons in the early part of the 15th century ... It is a matter of regret that the authorities should have seen fit thus to remove the old landmarks, in the shape of street names ...'

Had the author of the above. W. H. K. Wright, lived another 80 years he would doubtless have applauded the re-renaming of this area as Bretonside in the wake of the building of the bus station in 1958. The Bretonside of today includes part of one of the city's oldest streets, Bilbury Street, first recorded as 'Billabiri' Street in 1342. Running from the northernmost tip of Sutton Harbour (excavation at the rear of the pub revealed some ancient steps under shingle which presumably marked the old sea line) the street curved around to St. Andrews Church, its eastern end just twenty yards or so from the 'King's Head'. According to Crispin Gill, Bilbury is a development of the oldest name we have for the original settlement that became Sutton (Southtown) then Plymouth. Bilbury, he states, 'means Billa's burgh, and a burgh means a defended place'. Originally, Bronze Age men encamped here and had a ridge road running up North Street from here joining with and continuing along the line of Mutley Plain. Billa would have been their chief. Incidentally, Whitfield (1899) spuriously suggests that Bilbury here indicates 'an original locality for bilberries or whortleberries'.

By 1440 the street had become known as 'Byllbury Strete' then sometime later and for no apparent reason it became Lower Broad Street. In 1825 Higher Broad Street was renamed Buckwell Street and Lower Broad Street once again became Bilbury Street, the 'King's Head', occupying numbers 13 and 14. Within 50 years, however, it too had become part of the new Treville Street, where the 'King's Head', without moving, had changed to numbers 45 and 46, as indeed it remained until the last alteration (referred to earlier) which saw the pub with a new postal address—21/23 Bretonside.

Herein lies a great deal of confusion. A situation further aggravated by the very old sign post at the end of Mutley Plain that reads '1 mile to the King's Arms'. Thought by many to refer to the 'King's Head', the wording in fact indicates the 'King's Arms Hotel' in Britonside, this being that part of Britonside that became Treville Street, then Exeter Street, then Bretonside again. By which time the 'King's Arms', which stood between the 'Black Horse' (formerly the 'Friary Hotel' and before that the 'Black Bull') and the 'Regent', had long since ceased to operate (although it continued for some time as a temperance hotel). One can but wonder at the reason for all these name changes, particularly when the present Bilbury Street which runs along the side of the pub (where until recently a house once stood) and around the back of it, bears no relation to its original course!

Whatever, given the antiquity of the original street, it comes as no surprise to learn that the 'King's Head' is believed to be the oldest inn in Plymouth. (Despite appearances—its frontage had to be replaced 10 years ago.) Present deeds date back to the mid 17th century, earlier deeds are believed to have been lost and a beam in the bar bears the date 1629. For centuries a men only establishment, the 'King's Head' had no ladies loo until it was taken over by Fred and Doris Pring in 1964. Previously popularly known as 'Husson's' after the family in whose hands it had been for some 80 years, the 'King's Head' had always been a free house, and one which bottled its own Bass and Guinness. A Courage house for 20 years now, when Garth and Kay Tuxford, arrived in 1981 they became only the third family to run the pub in the last 100 years. In keeping with the area, Garth has introduced certain changes which hark back to earlier days—including a genuine gaslit atmosphere and the long bar still has a solid floor with sawdust on it, not carpet, while an amazing collection of odd artefacts hang from the beams.   »Postscript

[*WEH* 20.7.85

Queen's Arms

There has been a public house on this particular site in Southside Street for centuries, however, it has not always been known as the 'Queens Arms' and the present building has not yet stood for 20 years.

One of the most tasteful, on the outside at least, of the mid 1960s additions to the Barbican, the original 'Queens Arms' was devastated during the air raids of March, 1941 and for some two decades the site lay empty. Designed by Jim Luxton and built to similar overall dimensions to its predecessor the earlier 'Queens' had two doors

angled on to the street, three larger windows at ground level but only one middle one on each level above, facing the street.

Meanwhile, a few yards along Friars Lane and two steps down to the right would take you into the old bottle and jug—snug of the original pub in the area now occupied by the toilets. On the opposite corner of Friars Lane, No. 54 Southside Street (currently the 'Dolls' House') was for many, many years Millman's pawn shop.

In the early 1870s Edwin Millman had taken over Hoppen's pawnbroking business here and when the last war broke out it had passed down in to the hands of Sydney Millman.

A sign of bygone ages a fisherman's wife short of money could leave her husband's best suit here in pawn before eight o'clock on a Monday morning for a few shillings until Friday came around when hopefully she could afford to buy it back.

A sign of a time more long since past, however, is the coat of arms that hangs outside the pub today.

Inscribed with the letters 'E.R.' this piece of heraldry does not relate to the present Queen Elizabeth, in whose reign the pub was built but rather the first Queen Elizabeth, by whose reign Southside Street had undoubtedly been built.

However, whilst there may have been a public house on this site it is unlikely that it was ever called the 'Queens Arms' in those times as the earliest reference to the name appears in the 1860s when another Queen, Victoria, was on the throne. The name by which it was known before then and for the rest of the nineteenth century at least, was the Plymouth Arms.

Ironically there was also around that time another 'Plymouth Arms' in Old Town Street and a 'Plymouth Inn' in Fore Street.

Today, however out of the 220-odd pubs in Plymouth not one bears the name of its town in its title—but there are four other Queens; the 'Queen and Constitution', 'The Queen's Dock', the 'Queen's Hotel' and another 'Queen's Arms'.

What sets this 'Queens' apart from the others, for better or for worse, is undoubtedly the larger than life landlady with the larger than usual hair-do and her impressive collection of china pigs, all of which she has been given.

According to the delightful Flo Kendal, a great-granny and a 'Queen's' regular, Mrs. Winnie Board the landlady here once chanced to remark that if she wasn't running a pub she would like to be running a piggery.

From that moment on she began receiving pigs from her customers. Arriving at the 'Queens' in 1966 with five of them Mrs. Broad had apparently at the last count some 747 of them.

By no means all china and from all parts of the world these piggies are dusted off every two months and look down silently from their shelves upon the customers as they drink their beer and eat their ham sandwiches.

[WEH 30.6.84

Plymouth Gin—Southside Street

When outlining the history of gin a few years go, the late Bill Burke, sales director of Plymouth Gin told his audience that gin was apparently first made around the middle of the sixteenth century in Holland, and probably at the University of Leyden. The Dutch he said had for some time been conducting experiments in distillation in their medical departments, and had produced some strong types of alcohol in the form of colourless spirit.

The practical uses of such spirits, however, soon transcended the various medical ones. The low countries after all during this time were virtually one long battlefield and soldiers (many of them mercenaries often not knowing for whom or why they were fighting) were given copious draughts of these clear spirits to encourage them to take part in the fighting whenever it came their way. Hence the phrase we still use today—Dutch Courage.

One day in the midst of all this someone added oil of juniper (or genievre) to this spirit to make it more palatable. The new addition caught on and so eau de Genievre was born, later it became Genever or Jenever and later still, simply Gin.

The Dutch Bols Distillery was founded in 1575 and the popularity of gin soon took it rapidly around Europe. By 1743 when the population of Britain was well under 7 million one estimate suggests that over 8 million gallons of gin were drunk, a remarkable figure by any standards particularly when the gentry mainly drank Brandy. A lot of British gin stills were illegal in 1743 and although Parliament passed several 'Gin Acts' they were difficult to enforce and mostly ignored.

In 1793 a legal distillery was established in a medieval set of buildings in Southside Street on the Barbican, and since that date to this 'Plymouth Gin' has been produced there. In addition to the Italian Juniper, this particular traditional recipe includes dried Orris plant, also from Italy, Angelica Root from Germany, sun dried orange and lemon peel from Spain, cardomon seed from Ceylon and English coriander seed.

Famed throughout the world Plymouth Gin and until 1975 Blackfriars Gin for years carried a little Black Friar on its label. A simple reference to the Blackfriars' Monastic order which it was believed had previously occupied this site and these buildings. Sadly, however, research by Jennifer Barber suggests that there never was a Blackfriars' establishment in Plymouth and so the exact origins of the buildings are shrouded in mystery.

Old, however, they most certainly are and the Refectory room restored and re-opened in 1961 is said to date from 1425 and it's claimed that the Pilgrim Fathers assembled here before they embarked in 1620.

The Distillery has guided tours from June to September and despite its marvellous museum-like appearance and machinery its stills are still very much alive. Currently around 4 million bottles' worth of spirits leave here each year (about half of which today is vodka which, like gin, now accounts for some 15 per cent of the spirit market—also like gin, vodka is a purified clear barley spirit only it is passed through charcoal rather than being mixed with exotic flavouring).

After it leaves the Barbican, Plymouth Gin with its new ship labels embarks on a journey that takes it to more than 50 countries around the world. »Postscript

[WEH 16.4.83

Merchant's House

'St. Andrew Street may certainly be called one of the oldest streets of Old Plymouth. Taking its name from the church which stands at the top, it was, until recently, full of old world interest.

'Within living memory it contained some good specimens of Tudor architecture. Modern improvements and sanitary considerations, have, however, swept away nearly all that is picturesque.'

Sadly since this was written in 1900, commercial interests and the blitz have taken an even heavier toll in St. Andrew Street and, apart from what we now call the Merchant's House, the Swan Hotel opposite and the few buildings above the Abbey Hotel on the other side of the Magistrates' Courts, there is very little indeed left of the street.

The Merchant's House itself was restored by Plymouth City Council (1972–77). Believed to be a sixteenth century building it is thought to have been much altered and embellished in the early seventeenth century by its first recorded owner James Parker.

Parker, Mayor of Plymouth 1608–9, was a celebrated Elizabethan sea captain and merchant and doubtless funded his work on the house with his privateering spoils procured from the Spaniards in the Caribbean.

Once sandwiched between a men's lodging house and the Mechanics Inn, the Merchant's House has been a taxi office, shop and shoe repairers in recent years.

It housed at least three Lord Mayors in the eighteenth century and today it is open to the public and features displays of Plymouth history up to 1670.

[*WEH* 27.2.82.

28

St. Andrew's Church

Wright's 1879 Plymouth Handbook tells us that ... 'The church itself has been dubbed the "Old Church" and "Old Town Church," and is more frequently known by the former title than by its legitimate one of St. Andrew.'

Twenty years later Wright again made reference to the 'Old Church' in his book *The Streets of Old Plymouth* ... 'The Church of St. Andrew was old,' he said, 'even in the days of Elizabeth; old when the news of Drake's return from overseas was being brought into the Church, all the congregation rushed pell mell to the Hoe, leaving the preacher severely alone; old, when Charles II attended service and touched a number of persons suffering from the King's Evil; and old, when the Pilgrim Fathers reverently passed its sacred portals to their lodging in the Hospital adjoining.

Today as we look upon this old church with its fine fifteenth century tower (the

building of which in 1461 was accredited to Thomas Yogge, the same man who was later responsible for the building of the Prysten House), it is hard to imagine the devastation it suffered during the 1941 Blitz.

But that vision will forever stay in the memory of those who saw it and indeed it was not until 1949 that repair work properly commenced. A service was held to formally inaugurate the work on 15th January and on 22nd October of the same year the then Princess Elizabeth laid a foundation stone to commemorate the beginning of the restoration.

Finally on 30th November, St. Andrew's Day, 1957 the church was officially re-consecrated and re-opened.

[*WEH* 10.4.82.

Magistrates' Court

Opened in 1979 by Prince Charles, on the site of Mumfords Abbey Garage, the Magistrates' Court in St. Andrew's Street is one of the finest pieces of postwar architecture in Plymouth.

With its large basement car park hiding most of the brightly-coloured metal motors that transport people to and from the building, this modern construction blends remarkably well on all fronts with the few ancient city centre blitz survivors that surround it—St. Andrew's Church, the Prysten House, the Merchant's House and the early nineteenth-century 'Swan Hotel' and terrace that leads up from the 'Abbey Hotel'.

Separated from these other buildings, either by existing cobbles or cobbles recently collected and implanted from other old Plymouth streets, the Magistrates' Court manages to evoke a sense of historical dignity that the long, low, somewhat characterless early 1960s Law Court building opposite the Council House seems to lack. Nevertheless it was there, next to the Guildhall, that for some years the magistrates operated.

Much moved around over the years, the magistrates have earlier held courts at Greenbank and in the officers' mess of the old Plumer Barracks at Crownhill.

Part of what is now used by the Treasury in what is left of the 1874 Guildhall complex was used by the magistrates and prior to that they were in the Guildhall of 1800 and the Jacobean one it superseded on the same site, at what was the junction of Whimple Street, Market Street (or High Street) and Looe Street, not very far from where they are today.

So, although Justices of the Peace—those persons entrusted with the conservation of the peace and offences against it—have been with us since the 1361 Justices of the Peace Act, this five-year-old building is the first purpose built 'home' they have had in Plymouth. Furthermore, the level of consultation in making it purpose-built was greater than is usual as the Clerk to the Magistrates himself, Cliff Moiser, was largely responsible for the internal design and layout.

Elaborate 'people flow' charts were produced to ensure that these six adult and one juvenile courts, which together hear around 15,000 cases a year, function as efficiently, practically and as pleasantly as can be expected under what, for most people who appear here, frequently are far from pleasant circumstances. The results can be judged by all as members of the public are generally free to watch any of the courts sitting whenever they want.

The critics, however, gave their opinion some time ago. In the summer of 1980 the Royal Institute of British Architects awarded the project a commendation making it one of only three developments in a national list of awards from an entry of over 353 that year to have been designed by the architects' department of a local authority.

Tony Irish was the project architect and to his, Cliff Moiser's and the rest of the team's credit, the building was completed well inside its budget.

The RIBA jury said the court was a 'welcome change from its forbidding predecessor' while Cliff Moiser who also helped in the design of the recent Dudley courthouse where he was prior to 1971, described the court project as a 'lot of fun'.

[*WEH* 24.11.84]

The Prysten House

The Prysten House, at the top of Finewell Street, known for a good many years as 'the Abbey,' has been for centuries the subject of much historical conjecture.

About 100 years ago, J. Brooking Rowe wrote, in his 'Ecclesiastical History of Old Plymouth' that although he thought that the Prysten House was 'in some way connected with St. Andrew's . . . there is not the slightest clue and any opinion is the purest speculation.'

Nowadays however it is believed that the Prysten House was built to house Chantry Priest and Preaching Canons, in the fifteenth century by the Plympton Priors.

Arriving early in Plymouth the Priors not surprisingly built their house around the best well in the area, the Fine Well from which the street takes its name, and which can be seen in the house today.

Speculation also suggests that there are underground passages from the Prysten House to St. Andrew's (for the priests' convenience) and the Hoe (for the priests' smuggling activities).

Whatever its origins however, the Prysten House was for some 400 years 'converted into base uses', such as a domestic dwelling, a wine merchant's in the seventeenth century, a warehouse, a bacon curing provisions factory and a wholesale grocery store. During the blitz it was used as a training establishment by the ambulance service.

In the 1950s major restoration work was carried out on the house and in 1976 the oldest house in Plymouth today was opened to the public for the first time on a regular basis. »*Postscript*

[*WEH* 6.2.82.

Plymouth's Guildhall

Built between 1870 and 1874, at a cost of almost £50,000 as part of a grand Guildhall, Law Courts and Municipal buildings complex, the Guildhall was for the most part completely destroyed during the 1941 Blitz.

Only the shell was left and it was some ten years before plans were finally approved for its rebuilding rather than its demolition.

Eight more years and almost £500,000 later Lord Montgomery arrived in Plymouth to officate at the re-opening.

The re-designed building had changed little outwardly since the Prince of Wales (later Edward VII) had officiated at its first opening on 13th August 1874.

The ornate towers had disappeared and the entrance had been restructured but inside the building everything had completed changed, even the seating in the main auditorium now faced the other way.

The other municipal building was altogether less fortunate as its shell had been swiftly demolished to make way for Royal Parade.

For those of us who have grown up in post-war Plymouth the Guildhall perhaps does not look so lonely on its own, without the memory of its sister building.

However, lonely it must certainly seem to an older generation, particularly as the building of the Civic Centre, the arrival of the Airdomes and now the building of the Theatre Royal have done so much to take the bustle and glamour away from Plymouth's fourth and perhaps last Guildhall. »*Postscript*

[*WEH* 17.4.82.

Derry's Clock

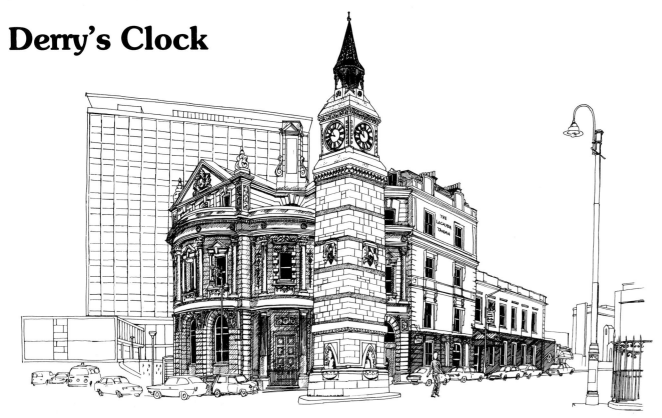

In 1962 one local paper stated quite categorically that: 'Derry's Clock will be re-sited between 1964 and 1966 during which time a complete new scheme is planned for the roundabout.'

But time passed and the unmoved clock ticked on. In the last two or three years, of course, there has been a lot more talk of shifting the Old Tower—one of the few 'The clock, or as it is called Derry's Clock, stands at the centre point from which George Street, Station Road, Lockyer Street and Union Street radiate.

'The Tower was erected by the Corporation—the Clock itself was a present to the city by one of its ex-Mayors in 1862, whose name, will henceforth, in all probability, be immortalised with it.

'It is adorned with what is courteously called four fountains, but these fountains are standing jokes—that is standing, because they never run.' So wrote 'GVK' in May, 1874, in Doidges Guide to Plymouth.

Twelve years earlier in May, 1862, a look at the council minutes shows us that for the first six months of that year the intention was to site the clock at Cornwall Street Gate. It was not to be, however, and for 120 years Derry's Clock has stood resolutely, through foreign wars and civil controversy.

In 1930 its removal was mooted (and not for the first time either). Then it was felt that the clock tower being in the middle of the road slowed traffic and made drivers more careful; it was also a halfway haven for those on foot.

surviving mid-Victorian landmarks in central Plymouth—often sketched and frequently photographed.

One wonders at the sense of trying to redraw a part of the history of a city that has already had so much wiped out.

Derry's Clock is the key point of that once bustling junction and tram terminus. Originally to the right of the Tower was the Royal Hotel, adjoining the old Theatre Royal. In 1874 this first class hotel claimed to be the only place in Plymouth with 'Superior Stabling' and 'replete with Modern Carriages, Wagonettes, Drags, etc.'

Meanwhile, Harvey's Family Hotel opposite boasted that it was patronized by Royalty and replete with every comfort. Today Harvey's Hotel is the Lockyer Tavern and built right on to the front of it, later last century, is the Old Bank Building, once Lloyds and earlier the Wiltshire and Dorset Bank. This extremely distinctive building is constructed of rusticated ashlar—a squared building stone.

My own drawing of Derry's Clock was completed on the same day that the 'diggers' moved in to start work on the New Theatre Royal. The railings and lamp post of the old 'Ladies' and 'Gentlemen' on the right were first to go and the new multi-storey car park, which now looms large in this scene, was the last to be completed.

And now, today, Derry's Clock sends scurrying a whole new generation of Plymouth Theatre Royal patrons. »Postscript

[WEH 13.11.82

The Theatre Royal

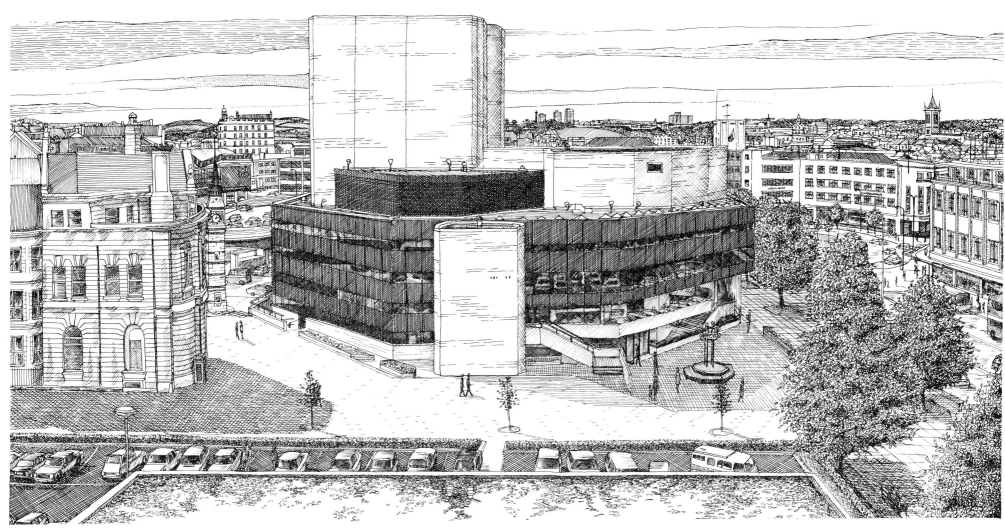

Two Theatre Royals, one built before Bedford Street became the busy thoroughfare familiar to many older Plymothians and one built some 40 years after the street had been virtually flattened by the blitz of 20–21st March 1941.

The first Theatre Royal was built between 1811–13 on the then outskirts of Plymouth from the plans of the newly appointed town architect John Foulston and the entrance at least was constructed according to the proportions of the Temple of Ilissus in Athens.

Internally destroyed by fire in June 1878 and magnificently restored later that year by C. J. Phipps, Foulston's 1,200-seater theatre was destroyed not by the blitz but by Plymouth Council in 1937 and in its place appeared the Royal Cinema, now the ABC.

Ironically the cinema survived the bombs which sadly finished off Foulstons' adjoining Royal Hotel and Assembly Rooms. »*Postscript*

[*WEH* 1.5.82.

Drake Cinema

On the 6th of June, 1958, there was a charity premiere of Rodgers and Hammerstein's *South Pacific* here at the Drake to commemorate the opening of this the first of 20th Century Fox's proposed chain of new cinemas to be opened in Europe.

However, when the curtain first went up it was the Royal Marines' Orchestra of the Commander-in-Chief (Plymouth) that the spotlight fell upon and they were followed by the then Lord Mayor of Plymouth, George Wingett, who performed the official opening ceremony. There then followed the first film to be shown at the Drake—the *Plymouth Story*—the British Movietone News' 'tribute to the people of Plymouth and the building of the city of tomorrow.' Appropriate and undoubtedly ironic that this film should ever be shown in the only purpose-built post-war cinema in the City. A cinema which took Drake as its name and his flagship as its emblem, as indeed did the Plan for Plymouth itself back in 1945 with the small impressed *Golden Hind* illustration on its front cover. Still in Union Street today the Drake now stands a little behind the original south line of the street and the discovery of some bicycles underground in the excavation work on the site points to Currys Ltd., cycle dealers, occupying at least part of this site in pre-blitz Union Street. Local rivals, the Halford Cycle Company, were just across the road at that time, next door to the small Carlton Cinema. Formerly known as the Gaiety it seated around 400 and was briefly known as the Embassy before it was pulled down. Meanwhile back on the south side of the street opposite the old 'Atheneum Inn' on the corner of Queen Street, were to be found Perkin Brothers Outfitters on one side of Curry's and the Hampshire Furnishing Company on the other end. It was towards the back of these premises that the present Drake Cinema was constructed by 20th Century Fox. In the event Fox

didn't add to this chain at all and in 1961 they handed the Drake over to the Rank Organisation.

Peter Bland was the first manager here and after the showing of the *Plymouth Story* it was his job to introduce two live film stars, Richard Todd and Jackie Collins, who was then described as a 'shapely twenty-year-old' . . . and sister of Joan Collins, 'the only British actress who has risen to fame as a Hollywood glamour star under contract to 20th Century Fox'. Todd and Jackie Collins had just completed work on the thriller *Intent to Kill* which was due to be shown later in 1958. Meanwhile Pat Boone and Shirley Jones headed the first full programme here in *April Love*. Projectionist Pat Ahearn, still at the Drake today, was there when the cinema opened, and Pat still rates *South Pacific* as the best film ever to be shown here, although, like his long serving colleague Ron Wilson who was also here in 1958, since the screens were split into three 10 years ago he has only had a chance to see bits of films.

Charles Tappy was the Drake's second manager and he in turn was succeeded by the affable Scot Alex Grieg, one of Rank's most successful managers, who earlier this year moved up in the Organisation and left Plymouth. Today Alan Rosser sits in the hot seat.

In the last twenty-seven years thousands of films have been shown here: however none of them, 'Bond' and *Ghostbusters* included, have yet matched up to the success of *South Pacific*. Shown in several bursts, the film was on screen here for a total of eleven months and was doubtless seen by many thousands of Plymothians, some of them several times over on one enchanted evening or another.

[*WEH* 20.4.85

The ABC Cinema

The marvellous ABC Cinema-shaped retirement cake made for assistant manager Eileen Donovan last week was more or less made on site; for Footlights Restaurant, from whence it came, is part of the Royal Cinema complex and was originally home of Fullers Restaurant.

In later years these premises were occupied by the Coal Utilisation Board and there after for some five or six years it stood empty until Footlights with its genial host Colin Eddy took over in grand style last year.

Built in 1938 the Royal Cinema stands in place of Foulston's original Theatre Royal, built 1811–13 which sadly was pulled down in 1937. In 1954 the lack of a civic theatre and falling cinema attendances, prompted by the arrival of the little TV screen, led to the introduction of fairly regular live theatre at the cinema which was duly rechristened the Theatre Royal Cinema—a move that was marked by the personal appearance of Peter Brough and Archie Andrews.

Four years later, however, in keeping with Associated British Cinema's national policy the Royal was renamed the ABC. Live theatre and one night stands nevertheless continued and over the years such diverse popular figures as Max Bygraves, Billy Cotton, Lonnie Donegan, Ruby Murray, Lita Roza, Tom Jones, the Beatles, the Rolling Stones and most recently the Bay City Rollers, whose May 1975 appearance saw about 100 young girls, aged between 10–15, treated for hysteria, shock and minor injuries. Two years later, however, this particular era ended when on 5th May, 1977 the ABC revealed its split screen and bingo format. A change that came complete with a new manager as Clive Jones became only the third manager at the Royal since 1938. His predecessor Bill Clarke was there nine years and before that Tom Purdie had held the reins for 30 years.

Significant though these changes might have been they certainly have not been as dramatic, in a different sense, as the changes outside. One of the few major buildings in the city centre to have survived the Blitz and the plan for Plymouth, the ABC with the delightful Miss Donovan inside it have witnessed the complete rebuilding of the area. In the view we see here change has been comparatively slow. The original doric columned Athenaeum, also designed by Foulston, was a Blitz victim and many irreplaceable documents and artefacts were lost forever.

Home of the Plymouth Institute since 1818 it was not until 1961 that the new Athenaeum was opened. Primarily a theatre rather than the library, museum or lecture theatre that it had been of old, it was initially hoped that Westward Television would use the building regularly to stage productions. Westward first flickered into action weeks after the Athenaeum opened and its first programmes were beamed out on Saturday 29th April, 1961. Viewing that day included 'The Adventures of Robin Hood' with Richard Greene, Bob Monkhouse hosting 'Candid Camera' and 'The Avengers' with Patrick MacNee as John Steed but with no Emma Peel. Twenty-two years ago, Westward's second sporting Saturday featured live coverage of the Tottenham Hotspur versus Leicester City Cup final.

Since January 1981, of course, TSW have occupied this ITV outpost which perhaps ironically overlooks the car park which stands on the pre-war site of Athenaeum Lane wherein could be found the old studios of the BBC.

[WEH 7.5.83

The Evening Herald offices

Plymouth's first ever newspaper appeared in 1721, under the name *The Plymouth Weekly Journal or General Post*. It cost three halfpence and was printed in Southside Street on the Barbican.

Each week it purported to contain "an impartial account of the most material occurrences—foreign and domestick". Produced at a time when wheeled coach travel to the Westcountry was unheard of, it lasted only two years.

Remember that even in the early nineteenth century when improved roads meant that news travelled faster it still took the Devonport Quicksilver $21\frac{1}{4}$ hours to travel down from London.

Whilst many other newspapers appeared around the country in the 18th century, notably *The Times* in 1785, in Plymouth apart from one or two other short-lived periodicals, no paper of note appeared until the advent of the Napoleonic Wars.

In the wake of these a second weekly journal appeared, this time going under the title of the *Plymouth and Dock Weekly Journal*. First off the presses in August 1819 at a staggering cost of 7d (thanks largely to the Government's repressive newspaper tax) the paper, by the time it was acquired in 1841 by Isaac Latimer, an eminent journalist and friend of Charles Dickens, had simply become known as the *Plymouth Journal*.

Latimer ran this paper successfully for many years and when in 1860, five years after the Government's repeal of the crippling newspaper tax, William Saunders and Edward Spender started up the well received *Western Morning News*, Latimer began thinking about starting his own daily penny paper. Six months later the *Daily Western Mercury* soon to become the *Western Daily Mercury* appeared and by 1863 Latimer had totally merged the *Plymouth Journal* into it.

Thereafter the two papers, by no means exclusively but as main rivals carried on side-by-side for many years. Having absorbed the *Plymouth Mail* in 1862, 10 years after its first edition and the *Devonport Telegraph* in 1866, itself established in 1808, the

Western Morning News enjoyed a slightly wider circulation.

The *Mercury*, however, was busy moving in other directions and by the 1890s it had begun to produce the first non-wartime local evening paper; printed on green sheets it was a Saturday special—the *Football Mercury*, the success of which tempted Thomas Owen, when he took over the paper to plan a new evening paper altogether.

It was organised down to the last detail in the greatest of secrecy and the people of Plymouth, in particular the staff of the *Western Morning News* knew nothing about it until the morning of the day it first appeared on the streets, the 22nd of April, 1895.

Initially it was thought that the new paper should be called the *Echo* and a title block was made for it. However it was felt that rather than merely echo anything the paper should originate and boldly proclaim itself and so instead it was called The *Evening Herald*.

The advantage gained by the Herald's surprise start left it unchallenged by the other papers save for a few months and then a year during the Boer War—bad news is always good news for the media. The *Mercury* itself, however, fared less well and when in 1921 Leicester Harmsworth bought both papers and merged the two it was as the *Western Morning News* and the *Western Evening Herald* that they continued.

The merger meant a move for the *News* away from its Bedford Street premises opposite the old Theatre Royal, now ABC cinema, to the Mercury offices in Frankfort Lane at the back of which in Frankfort Street was built in 1936–38 the splendid building we see here.

Lone City Centre survivor of the Plymouth blitz the front of Leicester Harmsworth House (as it was named by his son Sir Harold Harmsworth almost a year after his death when the building was opened on 1st December 1938) marks the line of the old Frankfort Street now bent round and renamed New George Street, with an extension to the building in the same Georgian style added after the war.

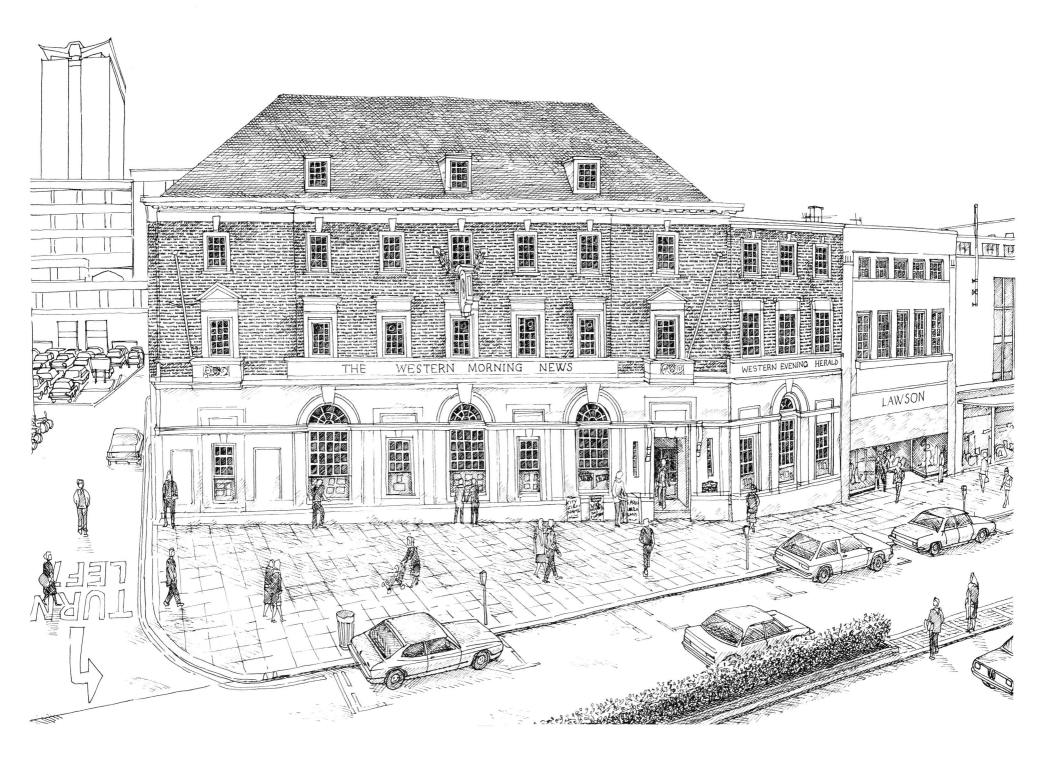

The Hoe Theatre

In 1962, the year that Liverpool gave us the Beatles, Plymouth City Council gave us the Hoe Summer Theatre, a modest prefabricated affair which replaced 'that pole'— that pole being the support for the large tent which for a few years previously had been the venue for the Hoe Summer Show.

On the opening night of a 15-week summer run in the new theatre Hedley Claxton, who devised the 'Gaytime' Show that was enjoying its fourth season on the Hoe, said that he was thrilled with the new alterations and delighted that Plymouth now had a little theatre which was a credit to the city and the people who ran it.

On the same night the star of the show, Gordon Peters, currently at the Palace Panto, was presented with a miniature pole, courtesy of the corporation, as a memento of the tent that he and many others had appeared in.

Twenty years later listening to some of the complaints levelled against this wonderful little theatre one might almost have been forgiven for thinking that the tent was still there, such was the outcry about the cold, the draughts and the raindrops.

However, despite any minor adversities, for 20 years the Hoe Summer Theatre,

which after all wasn't designed as a winter venue, provided Plymothians with many excellent productions.

Indeed it's only seven years since Harvey Crane wrote of the Hoe Theatre Panto, an earlier John Redgrave production of *Cinderella*, that it was the the 'best panto seen for a long time and by far the best and most outstanding amongst the other South West shows.'

In recent years Plymouth Theatre Company came into its own staging several excellent productions on the Hoe's cramped little platform.

One of the best indeed was showing when I did the drawing of the Theatre.

Piaf was a brilliant if not controversial production and I only hope that if someone chooses to adapt that play for the screen, in the same way as *Equus* and *Whose Life is it Anyway*, two other marvellous plays performed in recent years by the Theatre Company on the Hoe, that they choose Plymouth's Piaf, Stella Goodier, for the title role.

Today of course the Theatre has gone and grass grows again on this part of the Hoe and it's almost a year since the Theatre last opened its doors to the public.

[*WEH* 23.1.83]

Register Office

Plymouth's new Register Office was opened in April of last year by Mr. Roger Thatcher, Registrar General, who declared it to be the finest building he had seen, 'for some of the most important events in people's lives'. He added, 'It is important that the building where these human occasions take place should be a good one but this one is outstanding!'

Undoubtedly this new building is a pleasant, light and well situated construction. Virtually on the Hoe, at the top of Lockyer Street and just off Armada Way it is fitting that at last this institution, that most Plymothians will have contact with at least once or twice in their lives, has been set apart and accorded some respect.

Since the Registration of Births, Deaths and Marriages became obligatory almost 150 years ago the Plymouth offices have enjoyed a variety of homes.

Earlier split into sub districts: either North, South East and South, or St. Andrew and Charles; or Plymouth, Devonport and Stonehouse; district registrars have in the past been based all over the city. However, even the Superintendent Registrar himself has enjoyed a number of residencies, most of them now long since disappeared. William Pridham in the 1850s and 1860s was based around the corner in Athenaeum Street; John Matthews, who held the position more than 30 years until 1906, was at 6 Frankfort Street, while his successor Ernest Frank Anthony, who spent 30 years in the post himself, operated from 4 Princess Square.

In 1938 Walter Naylor the new Superintendent Registrar was based at 40 Whimple Street; during the course of the war his offices moved to 13 Thorn Park, then in 1951 he and his staff moved back into town to a hut known as 7 Belle Vue Place, North Road.

In 1962 another move saw the Register Office appear in place of the re-housed Lord Mayor's Parlour in Portland Villas.

Today at last it has these marvellous purpose built premises and Plymouth's current Chief Superintendent Registrar himself, Dan Galliford was consulted in the design.

Here it is then that just over half the people in Plymouth who marry, are joined in wedlock, wedlock being a word made up of two old English words wed, a pledge and lac, action thus meaning the marriage vow and the state of being married rather than the unopenable lock of marriage as is often supposed.

Here it is too that this wedlock is commemorated by the placing of a ring on the fourth finger of the left hand. Why that finger?

Amongst popular theories is that of Macrobius who says that the thumb is too busy to be set apart, the forefinger and little finger are only half protected and the middle finger is too opprobrious (disgraceful) for the purpose of honour and so the only finger left is the pronubus.

On the other hand, Henry Swinbourne worked the Ancients in his *Treaties of Spousals* in 1680 and wrote: 'The finger on which the ring is to be worn is the fourth finger; because by received opinion of the learned—in the ripping up and anatomizing mens bodies, there is a vein of blood, called vena amoris which passeth from that finger to the heart.'

[*WEH* 19.11.83

The Hoe from West Hoe

The Exeter artist George Townsend drew a view from West Hoe in 1853 and in it can clearly be seen the Citadel, the houses of the Esplanade and the drive around the front of the Hoe, formed in 1817.

On the skyline, above the Corporation Seat, which was later restructured to form the colonaded belvedere, we can see the once famous Camera Obscura.

Sadly this has long since gone and today's skyline is dominated by Smeaton's Tower, the longstanding Eddystone lighthouse which was moved to the Hoe in 1884.

A year earlier Drake's statue had been unveiled and later in that same decade there appeared the Armada monument and in front of the Old Saluting Battery, the building of the Marine Biological Association and Aquarium.

Prominent also is the World War Memorial—a reminder of the lost lives, and perhaps too of the lost architecture of Plymouth. One of the war's many local victims was the marvellous Plymouth Pier which might otherwise have dominated this particular view today.

Whatever else however may have changed from this scene, from alongside the Royal Western Yacht Club which resides in the premises of the old West Hoe Baths, one aspect has changed little from the description offered us in a guide book of 1879 . . . "There are few more pleasant methods of spending a spare hour than by taking a saunter on the Hoe on a fine summer afternoon . . . the liveliness of the scene caused by the assemblage of hundreds of persons of both sexes and from amongst the most fashionable classes of society; the gay dresses of the ladies, who here delight to display all the adornments which nature and fashion combined, have bestowed upon them."

[WEH 6.3.82

Hoe Promenade

Plymouth Hoe—'its height being equal to that of any ground in the immediate neighbourhood commands an extensive view and overlooks a vast range of populous communities, including Plymouth, Devonport, Stonehouse and Stoke, which alone are reported to contain one hundred thousand souls.'

So wrote one guide last century. Looking north and westward today these communities, having long since merged are now far more populous. Looking eastwards Plympton and Plymstock have grown greatly from the little villages they were then.

From the south, however, the view and the Hoe itself have not greatly changed and but for the gravel and the grammar the same guide may equally well apply the following description to the Hoe today. 'It is' he wrote, 'an open eminence, devoid of trees or shrubs but overlaid with velvet green sward, in the centre of which is a wide gravelled path, used as a promenade by the inhabitants of Plymouth who have free access to all parts of this delightful spot.'

This fact is perhaps something that we all take very much for granted these days, as we survey the place where Drake played bowls while the Armada threatened and where 'The boys and girls of Plymouth were dancing' (Clemence Dane) while the Germans mustered for further air attacks during the Blitz.

A main feature of the spirit of the city these wartime summer dances on the Hoe were often led by Lady Astor and her husband, Plymouth's Lord Mayor from 1939–44.

The dances were also graced with the occasional presence of such dignitaries as the Duke of Kent, who had some 20 years earlier, as Prince George, unveiled the Plymouth Naval War Memorial, in front of which the dancing always took place.

One of three identical memorials (the others being on the Great Lines at Chatham and on Southsea Common at Portsmouth) to those naval officers and men who fell in the 1914–18 war and who were buried or lost at sea, it was like the others, greatly added to in 1952–54 when wide terraces were constructed to form semi-circular remembrance gardens to commemorate the 46,000 sea service personnel who fell in the 1939–45 war and who had no grave but the sea.   So it was that 30 years after Prince George unveiled this monument, his niece, Princess Margaret unveiled its extension on 20th May, 1954. With over 7,000 names from the First World War and 15,000 from the Second World War the Plymouth memorial is unique, because, at the wish of the countries concerned, it includes the names of some 2,000 members of the Naval forces of Australia, South Africa, Canada and other Commonwealth territories.

Also prominent on the promenade and reflecting a somewhat global flavour are the 18 flags erected in 1970 for the Mayflower celebrations 350 years on.

An attractive addition to the skyline, this feature has recently been 'immortalised' in Colin Gregg's marvellous Plymouth-based award winning film, 'Remembrance' made for Channel 4.

The particular conditions of the opening shots of the flags with the wind and the rain causing the ropes to whip against the poles are not untypical of Plymouth but will hopefully be spared throughout the seasons and especially for each June when Plymouth's marathon runners come up Elliot Street through the bollarded gateway to the Hoe and turn the last bend of the route for the final stretch along the promenade. »*Postscript*

[*WEH* 23.4.83

The Grand Hotel

Built in 1879 by John Pethick, who was also the first owner of the Hotel, the Grand appeared on the Hoe just in time to be included in W. H. K. Wright's *Guide to the City*. At that time, and for several decades to follow, the Grand's proud boast was that it was the only Plymouth Hotel with a sea view and indeed one turn–of–the–century advertisement proclaimed it as occupying 'the Finest Position in Europe'. Even the generally restrained Wright was unusually enthusiastic. 'It is', he wrote, 'a massive structure and by no means belies its name.' Then, after much praise for the fixtures and fittings, he added: '. . . all other necessary accessories of a first-class hotel are provided, and we cannot but hail with satisfaction the opening of such an establishment which will do much towards obtaining for Plymouth the character of a watering place, or, at all events, the centre for a summer holiday for which it is in every way admirably adapted.'

Today, a little over 100 years later, there is the recently built Mayflower Post House nearby, the converted senior naval officers' accommodation at Grande Parade and several other neighbouring hotels which offer sea views. Few, if any however, match the external Victorian splendour of the Grand and it's heartening to know that the new consortium who have taken over the hotel have not only restored the hotel's name on paper but they also intend to do it in atmosphere and appearance inside. A major refitting and refurbishment is taking place under the guidance of the Plymouth Grand Hotel Company formed by directors Bernard Aylward, Carl Berry and Peter Smith, who earlier this year bought the building from the previous owners Berni Inns.

Berni Inns themselves undertook a great deal of 'modernization' back in 1965 when they opened the hotel as just the second of their Mot-Inns (as opposed to Motels) aiming their endeavours at 'the motoring public . . . to give them a service for the hours they are travelling'. Known for the next 20 years as the Berni Grand the emphasis was placed on reasonably priced food rather than accommodation, and indeed in their refurbishments Bernis axed 10 bedrooms.

When they opened under manager Stan Pearson in May 1965 a Grilled Rump Steak could be bought for 11/6d and washed down with a large glass of sherry at 1s 4d (about 7p). One of 80 or 90 Bernis in the 1960s, there are now around 240 nationwide and the selling of the Berni Grand marked the end of an association the Bernis had had with Plymouth since 1935 when Marco Berni (brother of Aldo and Frank who started the company in 1948) started with a café in Courteney Street, which ran north from Derry's Clock before the war.

Before the war right next door to the Grand and extending as far as Leigham Street was the club house of the Royal Western Yacht Club, purpose built in 1882 and now just a flattened bomb site or sight. Not long after its original building members would have been able to witness a spectacle on the Hoe that the historian R. A. J. Walling claimed 'exceeded anything since the days of Drake'. In 1889 some 100,000 people gathered on the Hoe to catch a glimpse of the man who had just addressed a crowd of 10,000 in the Volunteer Drill Hall. Eighty years old, already three times Prime Minister with another term yet to serve, his name was William Ewart Gladstone. In answer to the massive crowd the great man 'a short, spare figure with a noble head, his silver hair shining in the gas light, his cloak wrapped round him against the night air' appeared on the balcony of the Grand Hotel and said a few words. Doubtless only a few would have heard him but the memory would have lingered on and perhaps in the months to come some of that Victorian air may be recaptured at the Grand.

[*WEH* 6.7.85]

The Hoe

'The Hoe proper consists of a series of grassy slopes, surrounded by a spacious promenade, and intersected by numerous paths leading to lower grounds. At the foot of this eminence is a drive, which was formed in the year 1817 by the poor of the town, the cost being defrayed by public subscription.

'Connected with this road are paths leading to the rocks and landing steps at the waters edge ... The promenade at the summit of the Hoe is nearly half-a-mile in length, extending from the Citadel on the east to the West Hoe quarries on the west.'

So wrote W. H. K. Wright over 100 years ago and really apart from a few obvious changes much the same description applies today. A little earlier last century, however, things were different, for not only was there no drive, but there were no quarries either.

In the mid-1800s the West Hoe estate, as it then was, was owned by Thomas Gill and in 1840 he was empowered by an Act of Parliament to erect a pier at Millbay and deepen the bed of the dock.

Gill was a very enterprising man, he started his own alkali and soap factory at Millbay in 1818, he was Mayor of Plymouth in 1836 and from 1841–7 was Liberal MP for the borough. He built houses for his West Hoe workforce and some of his lime kilns survived into this century.

Whatever good he did for himself and local commerce, however, he was also responsible for chipping away the whole of West Hoe as he took his limestone quarrying right up to the very edge of the corporation land on the Hoe.

An unfortunate development and one that perhaps could have been avoided as Plymouth historian C. W. Bracken suggested that 'the town authorities supinely watched the destruction of the magnificent sweep of the Western Hoe, which had curved in a graceful slope to the drill hall site and the Millbay prisons.' (Just down from the Duke of Cornwall Hotel).

This quarrying not only spoilt the sweep and cut down the size of the Hoe it also resulted in most of West Hoe being completely flattened and it was not long before the whole area was full of impressive well ordered terraced accommodation but for the little West Hoe park which sits under the cliff face in the foreground here just beyond the railings.

For the most part the rest of the Hoe has only been altered over the last 100 years or so in such a way as to enhance the locals' appreciation of it. Sadly of course the marvellous Victorian pier and pavilion, which would have celebrated its centenary next year, was a victim of the Blitz, never to be replaced.

Somewhat less expensive to replace, however, would be the Hoe Bandstand. Standing a little away from Smeatons tower, towards us as we look down on it here from the top of the Mayflower Hotel, the Hoe Bandstand was for a good long time the centre for many a happy afternoon.

[*WEH* 10.12.83

Cross on the Hoe

There are many memorials, plaques and tablets on the Hoe but none more simple and perhaps enigmatic than this plain little stone cross, set in the middle of a path that runs along the eastern side of the Naval War Memorial.

Found by standing directly in line with the Naval War Memorial and the Prejoma Clock (on a stick) in the Hoe Gardens, the only marking on this cross is the number 3. A date, a mileage, the holy trinity maybe? No, the three here refers to three Irish marines executed on this spot on the Hoe on the 6th July 1797. Some 10,000 servicemen and thousands more local civilians witnessed the event although few were they, by all accounts, who managed to see any of the proceedings.

Describing the event first hand, however, John Harris (who in 1808 produced what is believed to be the first comprehensive history of the City) said that the march of the doomed men from the Citadel to the Hoe was 'one of the most awful I have ever witnessed'. He added that the men 'were preceded by the Marine Band playing the Dead March in Saul, and each of the culprits had his coffin borne before him by

four men . . . They were allowed their own time for preparation for death'. Then 'the firing party came very near; the culprits knelt each on his shell (coffin) . . . at the end of the first fire two fell' (Caffey and Braning both of the Romish Church) 'but Lee (the ringleader and a Protestant) remained until almost all had fired at him', then adds Harris in graphic detail 'one of them came near and blew his brains out'. The next page of Harris's manuscript is taken up with a plan of the execution drawn up by himself. A fourth marine, John McGennip, a much older man also found guilty of 'Mutiny and Sedition', was given a lighter sentence, he received, at the same time, the first part of 1,000 lashes.

This incident was by no means an isolated event in the late 1790s. Although the British had scored an enormous naval victory over the belligerent French in 1794— the Glorious First of June, there was still a lot of activity in French ports and a major invasion seemed imminent. Meanwhile the grassroots revolutionary fever sweeping France was finding sympathy among the lower decks of Britain's poorly paid and hungry navy. A situation that was seized upon and aggravated by those among them who carried the banner of the United Irishmen (founded in 1791) who had their own additional grievances to add to the situation. Six Irish sailors 'fomenting agitation' had already been 'run up at the yardarm of their frigate'. General naval mutiny however began at Spithead. It swiftly reached Plymouth and Dock but was held off by 'the concession of a shilling a day increase and the promise to refrain from making examples of the ringleaders'. On learning of the violation of this latter agreement revolt spread once more along the south coast and there was much unrest in Plymouth. For days, wrote Whitfield in 1899, 'the harbour was made hideous by the spectacle of jangling corpses (of mutineers) and the ceaseless whish of the 'cat' around the fleet'. Many men were given hundreds of lashes apiece.

The three Irish marines, however, were the first indication that dissent had spread to the land forces. Their conspiracy which entailed joining with locally held French prisoners, was uncovered when a young drummer who had been asleep beneath a furze bush at the crest of Stonehouse Hill, overheard the chief conspirators taking oaths.

Many executions have taken place over the centuries in the City and on the Hoe. Fortunately the last to be recorded came only ten years after all this in 1807. Ironically, like the first recorded execution we have on record (1518) it was of a Spaniard. »Postscript

[*WEH* 13.7.85]

Drake's statue

It was 13th February 1884 and for two or three weeks the weather had been consistently wet and stormy.

On the following day some 3,000 schoolchildren were to be marshalled on to a shelterless Hoe, to witness Lady Elliot Drake unveiling a fine replica of Boehm's striking statue of her famous seafaring ancestor.

Fortunately, 14th February 1884 was a day of glorious sunshine, comparative calm and consequently great rejoicing; indeed according to the commemorative pamphlet published the following day ' . . . the day was observed in the Three Towns (then Plymouth, Devonport and Stonehouse) as a general holiday'.

It was estimated that between 18,000 to 20,000 people turned out, cheering and applauding every stage of the proceedings.

However, while no-one would deny that the statue captured the hearts of the people of an area in whose history Francis Drake had played so great a part, there were those who questioned the sculptor's success in capturing the heart of that hero himself.

Writing in the 'Weekly Mercury' Mr. W. C. Wade stated: 'I will say little of the costume of the statue, although it is so unlike what Drake usually wore, and in which he is usually if not invariably depicted.' It is when he considers the face that he is disappointed in the sculptor's conception of Drake.

'We miss the bullet head, the honest and sturdy, if somewhat hard look of the demon of the sea. Drake was a plain-looking man, and of somewhat under-sized stature.'

Mr. Wade felt that the statue represented 'A rather handsome man, more resembling Sir John Hawkins than his friend Sir Francis Drake.'

Even the commemorative pamphlet stated that 'the likeness is not to be identified with that of any individual portrait extant' adding vaguely that 'it nevertheless has the traditional Drake character stamped upon it.'

In other words although it's not much like the old rogue, it's probably how people would like to remember him.

Today as 'Drake' looks out, the view has changed but little; behind him, however, part of Citadel Road was lost during the Blitz and now we see past the modern Holiday Inn to where the decapitated and restored Guildhall has since the 1960s been overshadowed by the Civic Centre.

[*WEH* 24.7.82.

Drake's Island from The Hoe

'Its really not to be wondered at that we plume ourselves on the Hoe,' said one Plymouth guide over 100 years ago ... 'its promenades are white and clean, its grass for the most part green, and it slopes down to the sea, which comes up to the very feet.'

Nowadays of course a road runs around the front of the Hoe, swimming pools grace its shoreline and the Marine Biological Institute edges out from the Citadel.

It also remains true that, 'Out at sea, far over the blue bosom of The Sound, ship-studded and smiling, may be seen on clear days, just where the sky seems to kiss the sea, the Eddystone, fourteen miles out ...'

The only difference today is that the Eddystone as seen then, now dominates this view, being somewhat less than 14 miles away and a taller tower breaks the skyline in its place.

As to the question of boat trips 100 years ago the writer had a word of warning ... 'If the visitor should desire to go upon the briny wave, and should go down to the restless row of elderly watermen who perch themselves upon the sea wall like a company of crows in blue Guernseys let him beware that the cost of a cruise is implicitly understood before starting or he will find the scale of charges more elastic than agreeable.'

At that time a visit to the Breakwater, for example for one to three people, should have cost two shillings and a trip up around the Hamoaze one shilling and ninepence.

Boatmen were then required by law to state their Christian and surname to any person hiring him if so asked. With the bigger passenger boats we have today the price of a trip upon the briny seems to be one of the few pleasures not to have gone up in price by leaps and bounds.

Out of bounds in a different sense 100 years ago was Drake's Island, then occupied by a group of Royal Artillery, probably then a complement of 50 or 60 men. For the greater part of its inhabited history Drake's Island has had a strictly military use.

However, the building that's believed to be the oldest on the island today is a small round affair that has but one window with access through the roof only. Its likeness to certain medieval Continental structures suggests that this is an 'oubliette,' in other words a cell for lowering prisoners into and leaving them to die.

Although there are no records to confirm this earlier usage the island was certainly used as a State Prison after the Civil War and many notable inmates were detained there at the King's pleasure.

The most celebrated of these, Major-General John Lambert, the man who had seen himself as Cromwell's likely successor, died on the island in 1684 after spending some 15 captive years there. Colonel Robert Lilburn, another Roundhead, was also sent there as was the Presbyterian vicar of St. Andrews and his assistant.

[*WEH* 20.11.82

Tinside

For centuries Plymothians have gone bathing off the Hoe. Clubs such as the 'Seven o'clock Regulars', the 'Shackey Pool Stragglers' and the 'Tinside Champions' have swum and gone.

Ladies and gentlemen have had their own areas for bathing . . . and their own costumes, or lack of them.

In 1886 the Editor of the Western Figaro was clearly relieved to report that 'the wearing of bathing drawers is becoming more and more popular . . .'

Concrete bathing facilities were begun here in 1913.

Built at a cost of little under £3,000 these foreshore improvements did not meet with the approval of all locals and one Press report read: 'Whatever romanticists may think of the taming of Tinside, the Town Council has the blessing of all those who go down to the sea in bathing costumes, and such as are members of the Ratepayers' Association are torn by conflicting emotions.'

The Lord Mayor of the time J. W. S. Godding, hoped, however, that Tinside would not only be patronized by bathers but that somehow room might be found for those who 'love to watch the many twinkling smiles of Father Ocean or to spend a quiet hour in peaceful communion with nature!'

And indeed in accordance with Mayor Godding's wishes there can be few local courting couples who have not whiled away a happy hour at Tinside, particularly since the extensions and developments of the late 1920s and 1930s which culminated in the opening of the New Sea Water Bathing Pool at Tinside on 2nd October 1935, at 7 p.m.

This time it was the turn of Mayor E. W. Rogers to officiate and after declaring open the 180 foot wide semi circular pool he was treated to a combined display by the swimming clubs of the city—a programme that included floating, diving and trick displays by the ladies and a turn of aquatic comedy.

Today at Tinside similar but somewhat more impromptu displays abound throughout the summer, much to the delight of all those who visit this pool with perhaps the best view from any pool in the country.

[*WEH* 7.8.82.

Smeaton's Tower

On this very day, 223 years ago, John Smeaton, a 35-year-old engineer from Leeds, wrote in his diary: 'And so, after innumerable difficulties and dangers we came to a successful conclusion of our venture.'

That venture, which had begun in 1756 was the building of the third Eddystone Lighthouse and the first to be built entirely of stone.

Its predecessors had been constructed in large part of wood on the grounds that this would best withstand the wind and waves. However, the lack of a good solid base saw the first tower (1698–1703) washed into the sea one stormy night, taking its eccentric yet intrepid pioneer architect, Winstanley, with it.

The second Rudyerd's (1706–55) sadly went up in smoke, the fire having been discovered by one of its three keepers, the 94-year-old Henry Hall, who managed to survive the fire but not the seven-ounce lump of molten lead he accidentally swallowed while fighting it.

The 24 candles in Smeaton's lantern house were first lit on 16th October, 1759 and they could be seen five miles away. It wasn't until the following century that candles were replaced, first by oil lamps and then dioptric lights. Smeaton's lighthouse remained on the treacherous Eddystone reef longest of all and might still be there today had not the rock on which it stood been deemed unsafe.

The reef itself is a stretch of very tough rock called 'gneiss' it is perhaps one of the oldest visible rocks in the country, believed to be of the Archaean period it is thought to be 2,000 million years old and part of the earth's original crust.

The decision to renew the tower was announced by James Douglass, engineer-in-chief for Trinity House, in 1877, and it is Douglass's towering replacement (fully automated and unmanned since 1981) that stands today alongside the stump of Smeaton's original.

Smeaton's Lighthouse was in its day a very popular national landmark; in 1860 it was immortalized when it was included in the design of English bronze coinage and although the famous Eddystone light disappeared in 1895 it came back on the penny in 1937 where it remained until decimalization.

Meanwhile local concern for the old tower ensured that the very same steamer, Hercules, that took out all 4,668 tons of granite that made up Douglass's Lighthouse also brought back the hollow upper section of Smeaton's jigsaw-like interlocking granite and Portland stone which was then rebuilt on a simulated hollow stump on the Hoe and the foundation stone for this rebuilding was laid by the then Duke of Edinburgh exactly 100 years ago this month, on 20th October, 1882.

[*WEH* 9.10.82]

Plymouth Hoe from the Citadel

It doesn't matter what time of year it is or what type of weather is prevailing, Plymouth Hoe will never be found quite deserted. In all their many moods the Sound and Hoe together exert an eternal attraction which holds its constantly changing audience however great or small, briefly in its spell.

This is largely due to the way in which the Hoe has been spared from the ravages of modern civilization and left to develop, slowly without any additions or alterations having being well planned and carefully considered.

Even the arrival 100 years ago of John Smeaton's lighthouse from its unsteady home on the Eddystone Reef (a feature which now appears essential to any picture or photograph of the Hoe) has done little to detract from age-old written descriptions of the place, which but for their language one feels could equally well have been written today.

The following, for example, was penned early last century in a guide to the area:

'In a cool evening of a sultry day, the inhabitants of all ranks and conditions may be seen crowding to the Hoe, to inhale the refreshing sea breeze, and there on a plain surface half a mile long, they may escape the lassitude generated by cares and a contracted atmosphere or descending by a gentle declivity to the shore, receive that quiet and solitary satisfaction which is always found in the neighbourhood of the great deep when its waters are still.'

Indeed, even when waters are far from still, such solitary satisifaction can be found, as can "the vast variety of prospect', that our writer goes on to describe. However, his next couple of statements are more open to debate.

'The very 'chef d'oeuvres'' of art and nature are here associated together,' he says . . . 'stupendous proofs of human ingenuity are laid side by side with magnificent objects of nature.'

Attractive and impressive as Grand Parade, Elliot Terrace, the Berni Grand, the colonnaded Belvedere and Charles II's Citadel (from where this view was taken) are, one would hardly call them stupendous proofs of human ingenuity.

The most distinctive of them, the Citadel, while undoubtedly impressive in its construction, must nevertheless be, from the outside at least, one of the most unexciting fortifications of its size in the country.

The views it offers from its walls on the other hand are both breathtaking and illuminating and any Plymothians who have not taken one of the guided summer walks around the walls are missing a rare treat and the chance to relate from on high the number of streets, old warehouses and works that make up the Barbican, Cattedown, Mount Batten and Turnchapel.

Furthermore it is difficult to imagine from outside just how high above sea level this walk and this outlook are and indeed how low Drake's Island appears against the heights of Maker and Mount Edgcumbe.

[*WEH* 15.12.84

George's Statue

Erected by Robert Pitt, 255 years ago, the Statue of George II that today overlooks the parade ground of the Royal Citadel was commissioned by Captain Louis DuFour of the Independent Company of Invalids, who were then quartered in Plymouth.

Originally the statue stood in the middle of what is now the main square, when this now characterless expanse of asphalt was a series of well kept lawns. It was moved in 1903.

George II came to the throne in 1727 and DuFour saw to it that his respectful gesture was well documented by having the following inscription carved into its pedestal: 'This statue of his Most Sacred Majesty King George the Second was erected on the first day of August in the year of our Lord MDCCXXVIII as a memorial of his zeal and loyalty to his Royal Master by Louis DuFour Esq, Military Officer in this Garison under the command of the Honourable Charles Churchill Esq, captain and governor of the town of Plymouth . . .'

On this evidence alone we might be left thinking that the accession of George II was locally well received, however, in his History of Plymouth, C. W. Bracken painted a different picture. 'In the thirteenth year of his reign George I passed away. Minute guns were fired and the church bell tolled.

'Two days afterwards, the new King, George II, was proclaimed to the sound of fife and drum. But while the first George died universally lamented, the accession of the second was celebrated with but one bonfire on the New Quay, 'where was only the rabble, but no appearance of gentlemen nor one spoonful of drink given them'.'

It's hard to imagine, just how Plymothians generally felt about the monarchy all those years ago. After all it was during the reigns of George I and II that the first

Prime Minister, Robert Walpole, fully asserted his position and, as a town that declared for Parliament during the Civil War, Charles II had built the Citadel, in 1666–71, with its guns trained as much upon the town as upon the sea.

What's more there had been disputes during Charles's time and Queen Anne's time (and indeed frequently down the centuries since) over the question of compensation for lands appropriate or rather misappropriated by the Crown, leading to conflicting views over the actual ownership of the land on which the Citadel stands. Does it after all belong to the city?

Whatever, the statue of George II has stood imperiouisly throughout, attired in the classical guise, as was popular at the time, of a Roman Emperor, complete with laurel wreath.

Perhaps in this case, however, the classical pose is not inappropriate, for in 1743 George II led his troops to victory over the French at Dettingen, near Frankfurt, and thereby became the last British king personally to command his men in battle. George emerged unscathed, ironically, however, his statue here in the Citadel sustained damage in battle during the last war almost 200 years later when George VI was on the throne.

A minor victim of enemy air action the statue was removed in 1941 and not replaced until restoration had been completed by HMOW in 1948.

The building behind George II, the former storehouse is one of four remaining original constructions within the Citadel walls, while to its left on the skyline can be seen the fast disappearing pylons at Staddiscombe.

[*WEH* 15.10.83

The Citadel Gate

Writing in the 'Illustrated Handbook to Plymouth, Stonehouse and Devonport' in 1879, W. H. K. Wright says: 'The entrance of the Citadel is very striking.

'After passing the palisadoes the visitor will cross the counter-scarp by a drawbridge, and then pass through a gateway, bearing the Royal Arms and fitted with portcullis and gates, and protected by cannon.

'He will then cross the ditch by a wooden bridge to the inner gate which bears on the entablative the date 1670.'

Sadly, less than ten years later in 1888, there was little or no trace left of these outer works as the ground was levelled, the drawbridge removed and the moat filled in.

In their place appeared a new road and ornamental gardens.

Other changes over the centuries have been minimal except that once a statue of Charles II stood where you now see three cannon balls and according to the account of Miss Celia Fienies in 1695 the armoury and statues were at one time all gilt.

In all other respects the external appearance of the Citadel and its fine Portland stone gateway is much as it was when Wright wrote that the Citadel 'is one of the most complete and best fortifications in the kingdom'.

His after-thought, however, is also worth a mention: 'It is,' he wrote in 1879, 'of course, quite out of date in these days of armour plates and Armstrong guns!'

[*WEH* 17.7.82.

Sutton Pool

Captain John McBride, later Admiral McBride is the man generally credited with securing the Government grants that allowed the building of the two Barbican piers between which since the 1790s the sea has ebbed and flowed.

Prior to this, hard volcanic rocks covered at high tide extended from this, the eastern, Coxside, side . . . whilst on the western stretch of the 'Cut,' as the entrance to the Barbican was then known, were the stonework and rocks upon which the Mayflower's passengers planted their last footsteps before crossing the Atlantic.

Always a natural shallow pool the building of these piers created some problems and by 1806 the accumulation of silt and sewage here was such that at low tide there was no water to be seen in Sutton Pool. To alleviate such problems there has been much dredging over the years . . . there have also been several plans put forward to make a wet dock out of the pool and put gates across the entrance. William Simpson produced a scheme to this effect in 1786, Thomas Tyrwhitt produced an adaptation of it in 1806 and in 1845 I. K. Brunel was commissioned, by men anxious to make Sutton the main railway-served harbour in the area, to produce wet dock plans for the pool.

Thwarted by the Admirality, it was Millbay that became just such a harbour and Brunel again the man responsible for the engineering.

So Sutton then, with its large tidal range has remained a natural harbour of sorts. With higher than average mean low water springs and mean high water neaps it makes an ideal harbour for a good range of working boats. It also makes for a natural focal point for witnessing the occasional 'freak' tides such as we have had this week. Caused by the pull of the moon and to a lesser extent the sun, these extremes are greatest when the sun and moon are in a straight line with the earth and either pull in the same or completely opposite directions to each other.

Tides produced by such alignments are called spring tides, not because they occur at springtime, which coincidentally is around the time one of the two most extreme annual tides occur, but because of the height to which the water rises or springs. This comes, as local weatherman Craig Rich informs me, from the old English 'sprynge,' a head of water that rises naturally from the ground.

The neap tide, meanwhile, occurs when the sun and moon are at right angles to one another through the centre of the earth. Variations between high and low water marks tend to be very slight under such circumstances.

Often if vessels fail to get away after springs they can be stranded or left helpless in sandy or muddy areas during neaps. It is from the old English term for helpless—nep—that we get 'neap' and our 'neap-tides' or nepflods.

With the height of a tide measured in this country as above the mean sea level as established at Newlyn between 1915 and 1921, the greatest spring range forecast in Plymouth was 0.3 metres to 6.1 metres (roughly 19 feet) and the smallest neaps between 2.5 and 4.0 metres in April and 2.6–4.1 metres in November (about five feet).

Although the connection between moon and tide was noticed by the ancients it wasn't until Issac Newton discovered the laws of gravity that a proper explanation appeared.

However, other beliefs cherished by the ancients have yet to be explained and while it is known that through the tides the moon affects some marine animals, the Roman belief that the human mind is also affected by the moon (Latin—luna) has not been fully confirmed. However, those who witnessed the evening swimmers, welly wearers and canoeists on the Barbican this week may well have their own theories on lunacy.

[*WEH* 29.9.84

The First and Last

Known affectionately for many years as the Cradle and Coffin by regulars here at the 'First and Last' in Exeter Street, it is hard now to imagine that when it was built this pub stood outside the main part of Plymouth.

Then, when men travelled either by foot or with horse this was virtually the first building coming into the town and the last going out.

A common name amongst inns similarly situated (the 'First and Last' at Sennen, Cornwall is but a stone's throw from Land's End) there's little doubt now that the 'First and Last' here is far from being the first building one sees coming into the city.

However, for road travellers coming in on the main A38 it is the first inn they encounter and can stop at without either turning on or off the road into the city centre. And so while perhaps not the last chance for ale on the way out, and certainly the width of Exeter Street today is against it, it is still used by many, including all too often visiting football supporters, as their first stop for ale on their way into Plymouth.

Built some time before its next door neighbour of the 1850s, the Church of St. John the Evangelist, Sutton-on-Plym, the 'First and Last' has, over the years, had several addresses. Currently 162 Exeter Street it has earlier been, without moving No. 1 Jubilee Place and No. 34 Jubilee Street. So named after the building in 1809 of the New Eastern Road to commemorate King George's Jubilee, Jubilee Street itself began this new eastern access.

A welcome relief to travellers to and from the city the new road meant that passengers no longer had to 'encounter the dangerous hill and now unfrequented road of Lipson' (1830), a hill described by an earlier commentator (1825) as 'Steep and foilsome.'

Originally three separate buildings in Jubilee Street, the much expanded 'First and Last' began in what today is the lounge bar.

Under the floor of the lounge is an old well and under the rubble of the adjacent bomb site tethering rings have been found suggesting an earlier use perhaps as a coaching inn.

Whatever its uses last century, this century at least saw the lounge bar—then a smoke room—used as a 'surgery' by local councillor Albert Webb who was licensee here from well before the First World War to just before the second.

Today, run by Keith James, a mean table tennis player who at 14 once represented England at the European championships, the 'First and Last' has seen a fair variety of landlords in its long history. Keith himself took over from his father, Reg, in 1978. Reg came here from the Melbourne in 1963 and left to go to the Trelawney before retiring a couple of years ago. Of the various changes and alterations that have taken place here under the James's, one of the more unusual was the introduction of the little aviary just off the public bar. Sporting several delightful finches, the aviary appeared in the mid 1960s around the same time as the 'New' pub sign with its illustration of the hare and tortoise from the famous 'Slow and steady wins the race' fable.

Supposedly written by the slave Aesop in the sixth century BC the story of the complacent and outwitted hare is one well known first and last story.

A much lesser known and somewhat more tenuous one concerns the pub's mid-nineteenth-century landlord whose two initials were strangely enough the first and last letters of the alphabet. Licensee here throughout the 1850s and 1860s his name was Zachariah Atwill.

60

St. John—Sutton-on-Plym

Having reached the corner of Jubilee Street, we proceed past Brunswick Terrace on the right, and the Friary Station on the left to the Church of St. John, Sutton-on-Plym, so called from 'Sutton' the original name of this portion of the locality . . .'

So wrote W. H. K. Wright in his 1879 Handbook of the three towns. The church had been approved by the Commissioners on the 10th May, 1855, and dedicated to St. John the Evangelist on 21st June that year. The parish of Sutton on Plym was carved out of the parish of Charles Church and it was indeed fitting that the new church should be dedicated to this one time Galilean fisherman, brother of James and son of Zebedee. St. John's parish takes in all of Coxside and Cattedown, and the North Quay of Sutton Harbour and, prior to 1954, it had also included Vauxhall Quay.

It was back in 1844 that the Church had first been mooted and the new Ecclesiastical District formed. Apparently the early activities of the church took place in the home of Benjamin Sparrow and in 1849 his children became the first to be baptised in the new Parish. The present building in Exeter Street was designed by Benjamin Ferrey. Ferrey had studied under Pugin, the celebrated Roman Catholic architect of the day, and whilst Ferrey is described as his Anglican equivalent the link is one of many St. John's has with the Catholic Church. Indeed Wright in 1879 apart from stating that 'The Church is considered as one of the handsomest modern ecclesiastical erections in Plymouth' added that 'the service, although not so high as that of some other churches in the neighbourhood, has a ritualistic tendency'. It is possible that these tendencies were first practised by George Greystock Carrigan, Vicar here until 1866, who had been nominated as Minister in 1844. Henry Philpotts, Bishop of Exeter, under whose patronage the church had been consecrated, was a follower of the Oxford Movement and it was he who instituted George Rundle Prynne at St. Peters in 1850. St. John's second Vicar, Charles Coombes, had been assistant to Prynne at St. Peters.

For the last 100 years the patronage of the church has been in the hands of the Wardens, Council and Scholars of Keble College, Oxford, in turn founded by one of the Oxford Movements main protagonists, John Keble.

Sadly the Church's longest serving incumbent, Francis Sanderson, died during the centenary year of 1955 and in the years that followed his death changes in the composition of the parish threatened the existence of the Church. In 1956 the Parish of St. Mary the Virgin and St. Mary Magdalene in Alvington Street, Cattedown, was reabsorbed into Sutton-on-Plym (it had originally been set up in 1911). The advancing industrialization of the area, however, continued to worsen and in 1971 a booklet was produced in St. John's marking the end of its history as the church was added to 'the ever growing list of redundant churches'. Fortunately local pressure forced a reconsideration of this decision and in January 1972 the church was revitalized under first Father Stanley Watson then Prebendary Charles de Cerjat

Then in 1973 Father Brian Lay took up the challenge and is still here today, now in a 'new' Vicarage in nearby Alma Street which has a small carving by the door from one of the fine houses of Brunswick Terrace, now demolished, and in which the Vicarage once stood.

While the population around continues to change, this weekend at least one wedding here harks back to the days of Coxside's glorious past when Shipwrights and Potters dominated the area as today, in St. John's, local girl Rosie Barnfield marries the Barbican Potter from Staffordshire, Paul Acraman.

[WEH 1.6.85]

The Shipwright's Arms

Currently standing on its own a little way down Sutton Road, the 'Shipwright's Arms', Coxside, has witnessed a good many changes over the last two centuries. Changes which at one time even affected the name of the pub itself, as, up to the middle of last century it was known as the Shipwright's and the Potter's Arms.

Thought to have been built in the mid late 1700s (there is a contract dated 1768 between Sir John Molesworth and Thomas Hutchins concerning the sale of the premises) the name Shipwrights and Potters' as we first find it recorded in 1822 was a reflection of the then thriving industries in Coxside.

The celebrated William Cookworthy had set up a pottery nearby, in 1768, in old victualling storehouses and at one time employed over fifty people here. Cookworthy was the first man in England to make true hard paste porcelain. Meanwhile three other Coxside potteries Fills', Algar's and Hellyer's produced a coarse range, while another, founded by William Alsopp, produced blue and white 'Queens Ware' pottery.

All this ceramic activity, however, was tailing off by the second half of the nineteenth century and as the industry became depressed locally the 'Potters' was dropped from the pub name.

Today of course the Barbican potteries are much smaller affairs on the other side of Sutton Pool and only one, Paul Acraman's Three Rivers Pottery, is producing a porcelain line.

By the 1860s then, this pub off Coxside Creek was known simply as the 'Shipwrights Arms'. The pub's mural, painted recently by Doug Stackhouse depicts five stages of the work of a ship-maker or shipwright; work that had been carried out in Sutton Pool since at least the fourteenth century.

Throughout the 1800s three principal shipyards operated here at Coxside: Moore's, Shilston's and Gent's—around the same time Joseph Banks worked from Queen Ann's battery, having moved on from Mutton Cove, Devonport. With possibly the largest concentration of shipbuilders locally, Coxside was by no means the only such area, as indeed the sites of several other Shipwrights Arms confirm; notably in Newport Street, Stonehouse, Lower Street, Plymouth, and until very recently at Turnchapel.

From 1836 to 1899 Plymouth consistently returned the highest number of ship registrations and for some time prior to that was second only to Brixham and Bristol, and although, as Crispin Gill suggests in his book on Sutton Harbour, this does not necessarily indicate that more boats were actually produced here it is certainly a good guide.

With well over 3,000 boats registered here in the 1800s it comes as no surprise when we look at an 1890s street directory and find in the buildings on either side of the pub, W. H. Shilston—shipbuilder, Harris & Penn—timber merchants—Thomas Gregory—sawsman and George Horswell—boat builders.

With the demise of the wooden ship building industry and the use of 'small' wooden ships themselves a lot of associated trades and factories that had grown up around this part of Sutton Harbour fell into decline and today the area has lost a lot of its bustle—a situation further aggravated by the 1969 closure of the old Coxside gasworks.

With the nearby railway tracks and cobble stones of Sutton Road long since asphalted, the 'Shipwrights Arms' is in many ways lucky to be still standing—a 500 lb bomb that landed in the road outside in 1941 did not explode.

Popular with locally stationed 'Yanks' during the war, the pub was kept from the early 1930s until the 1960s by Harry Sussex. Then selling Tivvy, Octagon and Simmond's Ales this spit-'n'-sawdust 'freehouse' has now been comfortably refurbished under Londoner landlord Steve Jewell and his wife Sheila and soon it may offer one of the few waterside drinking areas in this historic seaport.

[WEH 25.2.84

Thistle Park Tavern

Legend has it that as a rule the Danes thought it cowardly to attack an enemy at night, however, there was one proverbial exception.

Attacking their foe north of the English border under the cover of darkness, gradually a now infamous party of Danes crept forwards, barefooted and as quiet as the night itself until one of the men stood on a thistle. He yelped and the Scots, thus alarmed, turned on their adversaries and 'defeated them with terrible slaughter . . .' Ever since then the thistle has been adopted as the heraldic emblem of Scotland.

In 787 Achaius, King of the Scots, is said to have founded the 'Most Ancient' Order of the Thistle (The Scottish Order of Knighthood) and when, in 1567, James VI of Scotland (and later first of England) came to the throne the motto *Nemo me impune lacessit*—nobody touches (or provokes) me with impunity—first appeared on coinage.

Popular donkey fodder and purportedly a cure for 'stitch' the thistle in its many varieties (Scottish, Carline, Globe, Holy, Hedgehog Thistle and others) are more commonly regarded as weeds and troublesome ones at that.

In 1959 the Ministry of Agriculture announced that farmers who did not attempt to prevent the spread of the spear, field or creeping thistle, would be liable to a considerable fine.

Meanwhile, while the thistle is not perhaps the most common weed in the Westcountry, one hundred years ago and more there was, just off Sutton Pool, a large open field known for obvious reasons as Thistle Park.

With its border described in 1856 as the 'Marine Hotel' (now Atlas Signs) and the 'Lord Nelson' (possibly near to or meant to be the 'Breakwater Inn') on the south and Fareham Place and the gas works on the east.

Its north-eastern boundary was marked by the Victoria and the Plymouth Potteries. Operational chiefly in the first half of last century under Messrs Hellyer and Alsopp, rare examples of marked items produced in these potteries are now in the museum.

Today on the site of these potteries we now find more gas board-owned premises, the Chessington tyre and exhaust centre and since 1857 at least the 'Thistle Park Tavern', named after the park but before Thistle Park Cotts and Thistle Park Road in which it now stands.

Today a free house, the sign of the black horse on one of its bar windows tell us not that it ever doubled as a high street bank but rather that it was once a Starkey, Knight and Ford pub. Later becoming a Whitbread house when the local firm was bought out, the Thistle has been a 'free house' before but it is doubtful whether it has ever offered such a range of ales as it does now.

One of the few local hostelries with Murphy's Stout and Bishop's Tipple on draught alongside Hicks, Royal Oak, Wadsworth's 6X and Ushers the pub under licensee Jane MacRitchie (nee Hartop) and her husband, Steve, has a much different bar area than it ever had in the days of Kelly, Bennett, Evans, Jordan, Hobbs, Ernshaw, Crimp et al and in the days when the Coxside Dartmoor Railway used to pass outside its door.

[*WEH* 28.7.84

The Eagle Tavern

These tailors, often finding their resources stretched and pockets empty before pay day would pawn or 'pop' one of their tools to raise some drinking money. Typically they would pawn a type of iron known as a 'weazel' hence the well-known traditional refrain

'Up and down the City Road
In and out of the Eagle
That's the way the money goes
Pop goes the weazel'

Never a common British bird and now extremely rare, Plymouth of course until recently had two 'Eagles', one in Cornwall Street now called 'Silks' and one here in Sutton Road, in a neighbourhood more commonly associated with coal and timber merchants than tailors. Devonport has also had its 'Eagles' in the past with an 'Eagle Inn' in Cumberland Street and an 'Eagle' brewery based in Queen Street, Devonport and Hood Street, Morice Town.

The 'Eagle Tavern' in Sutton Road was built as part of the general development of this part of Coxside in the mid-1850s at the same time as the 'Thistle Park' opposite appeared and significantly a little way away on this side of Exeter Street the Church of St. John Sutton-on-Plym was constructed in 1855. Significantly because not only is it the nearest church to this Tavern but the symbol in Christian art of St. John the Evangelist, to whom the church is dedicated, is the Eagle—hence its use on church lecturns and hence, in all probability, the name of the Tavern. First mentioned by name in 1857 the 'Eagle's' first licensee, George Good, had been recorded as a 'beer retailer' in Sutton Road in 1856 and was to stay here for several years before being succeeded by first George then Albert then Laura Bloye who between them ran the Eagle from the 1860s till the end of the century.

Not long after the end of the First World War this 'Eagle' nearly became extinct as by all accounts the popular local name for the pub became the Screeching Cat. This was evidently due to the endearing tones in which the landlady would address her husband, Irishman Jim Gallagher, after he'd consumed more than his fair share of the ale he liked to drink as well as sell. The 'Eagle' it remained, however, and after the two Maunder men, William and Archie had between them seen the pub through the Second World War and the commissioning of the last HMS *Eagle* Pat and David Bunker arrived in 1960 and immediately began another 24-year regime.

In November 1984 the most recent change saw the arrival of Mike Howett and his wife. After many years in places no Eagles would dare, in her Majesty's submarines, Mike has arrived here in Sutton Road by various trades and a recent spell at the 'Loddiswell Inn', and has been pleasantly surprised to find a friendly local where not only does everybody seem to know everybody else, but in some way or other everybody seems to be related to everybody else.

There are, and have been, a good many 'Eagles' in England plus the odd 'Black Eagle', 'Golden Eagle', 'Grey Eagle', 'Mountain Eagle', 'Spread Eagle' and even 'American Eagle' (Bristol), but perhaps the most famous of the bunch is the 'Eagle Tavern' in City Road, London, at one time much frequented by local tailors.

[*WEH* 2.3.85

Breakwater Inn

In 1788 Mr. Smith, the Master Attendant of Plymouth Dockyard, submitted a proposal to render Plymouth Sound a safe anchorage. Eighteen years later Lord St. Vincent suggested that a Breakwater should be designed for Plymouth Sound.

Messrs. Rennie and Whidbey received instructions in February and by April had submitted a report together with an estimate of £1,171,000—a great deal of money in 1806. It was another five years before John Rennie was instructed to prepare drawings and specifications. By the following year, however, a 25-acre quarry at Pomphlett had been purchased and work had begun.

The first stone was dropped in August 1812 and by the following August labourers were out working on the Breakwater itself. Working against waves, gales and at times the Admiralty, the Breakwater was completed and the lighthouse first lit in 1844. Nearly $3\frac{1}{2}$ million tons of stone had been used and most of it had come from the 'quarries on The Catwater'. Hard and thirsty work and so it's no surprise to find that in 1820 an inn had been built on 'Cat Down' opposite Fareham Place (which stands no more and was doubtless built to house quarry workers).

The 'Breakwater Inn' as it was called even then stands today, still comparatively on its own but no longer surrounded by greenery leading down to the quarries.

In the 1820s Priscilla Bennett would have served the quarryman and in the 1830s and 1840s W. Clark was the licensee. Today the landlord Fred Pelling has no quarrymen to serve but he does have the men of Quarry, as on and off for the last seven years or so one of Plymouth's most accomplished groups, 'Quarry' have appeared here, playing their own unique brand of, what else but 'rock' music.

The 'Breakwater' has been a rock music venue since it was taken over by Ken Stout in the mid 1970s and subsequent landlords have maintained its status; currently the pub provides live music five nights a week.

However, a lesser-known service that the pub has provided for the last couple of years is that of host to the Missions to Seamen, a world-wide organization formed over 100 years ago for sailors of the Merchant Navy. Out of some 90 ports in the world that have their own mission chapel, chaplain and club, Plymouth is one of the only ones not to have a purpose-built club.

The RN is obviously well catered for with the Fleet Club while the earlier seamen's mission on the Barbican dealt primarily with fishermen. Now the merchant seamen's cause is better represented, they have the recently rededicated chapel of St. Nicholas on Drake's Island and the 'Breakwater' displays the Flying Angel pendant of the mission's club.

This means that from here seamen from any part of the world can phone home, change foreign currency and if in any difficulty phone the Plymouth chaplain Donald Peyton-Jones, who works with a number of interpreters. For missions' chaplains the sea is their parish and any ship their church and services, baptisms and weddings are performed happily across denominational barriers.

And so, with the advantage of being within walking distance of the commercial docks, the 'Breakwater Inn' itself now provides a safe haven for seamen of all nationalities, Swedish, Dutch, German, Japanese, Russian or whatever and entertains them with the international language of wine and music under the flag of the Flying Angel.

[*WEH* 26.11.83

Plymouth Power Station

On 12th April, 1849, Mr. J. N. Hearder was invited by the President of the Devonport Mechanics Institute to exhibit the electric light from the top of Devonport Column. Mr. Hearder arranged to have observers at Bovisand and the light was also cast around as far as Trematon Castle.

The thousands of people who collected on the Hoe and in Union Street were disappointed however, as this early searchlight was not shone their way, others were more lucky and witnessed a light 'strong enough for children to make rabbits with their fingers upon a wall more than 500 yards distant from the light itself.'

However, despite the technology that produced this and the excitement that surrounded it, it was to be almost 50 years before the inhabitants of Plymouth had access to a city electricity supply with the building of the Power Station at Prince Rock in 1898.

Instituted under the Plymouth Electric Lighting Order in 1894 this system was designed for lighting and tramway purposes. In the first year of its operation there were only 82 private consumers connected to the mains, with electricity that cost them $4\frac{1}{2}$d a unit. An amount that would be worth far more now in real terms than the $5\frac{1}{4}$ pence a unit that we pay now.

Over the years that followed the station, Plymouth 'A' (as it became known more recently), was added to and amended so that by the late 1920s all the original machinery had been replaced. The following decade saw the station connected to the national grid and within another dozen or so years the whole system had been taken over as the industry was nationalized under the collective banner of the British Electricity Authority.

Around the same time, 1948, preliminary site clearance work was undertaken for Plymouth 'B', the larger and more powerful station that we see today. Constructed in two phases, one ending in 1953 and the other in 1959, Plymouth 'B', initially planned as a coal fired station, went over to oil with the completion of its second half in 1959. For the next 14 years the two stations operated side by side until in 1973 Plymouth 'A', always a coal fired station, closed down and was soon after demolished.

That was just ten years ago, at the time there were some 300 employees at the two stations, with the closure of 'A', that number halved and then more recently with the decision to shut down Plymouth 'B's' generators and put this station in reserve, that number has gone down to a mere 15.

Built on the site of a Civil War fortification and nearby the oldest known residences of man in the Plymouth area, this giant red brick building with its 300 and 350 feet chimneys today stands still, acting for the time being as a substation for the national grid system. Fronted by a large lawn that marks the site of its Victorian predecessor, it is the property of the Central Electricity Generating Board and the electricity which is fed out through the three giant transformers here via the National Grid is sold to the South Western Electricity Board (SWEB) who, in turn, sell it to us to drive all the weird and wonderful electronic contraptions that have found their way into our homes and work places in the 152 years that have passed since Michael Faraday first created electricity by rotating a little loop of wire in a magnetic field.

[*WEH* 13.8.83]

Passage House Inn

The 'Passage House Inn' here at Cattedown stands on one of the oldest inn sites in Plymouth and is thought (like the 'Crabtree Inn' further up the Plym which was demolished in 1974) to date from the fifteenth century.

Today only the thick cellar walls bear witness to this as the visible part of the Passage House dates from the beginning of this century—replacing its predecessor which was pulled down around 1902.

Recorded photographically at least, this delightful ramshackle old building for centuries entertained prospective passengers for the Oreston ferry.

A principal link between Cornwall, the Three Towns and routes to London via Oreston, Plymstock and Elburton, Cattedown Road ran to the ferry here from the old turnpike at the end of Jubilee Street. Today that road is crumbling near its highest point and is barely passable there, even for pedestrians which is something of a pity for one of the oldest thoroughfares in the area.

Indeed, as far as we know man stalked around here before ever settling in Plymouth. The oldest known human remains were found nearby in the Cattedown Caves (discovered almost 100 years ago) and in age are roughly contemporary with the Iron Age findings at Oreston and Mount Batten. Far from reflecting man's early presence in Cattedown, however, this part of Plymouth has in recent centuries tended to reflect the heavy industrial side of life.

Never a very populous place, the flat open spaces left here after extensive quarrying have given way to factories and depots and even before the dawn of the twentieth century there were several chemical works and oil and petroleum stores here.

As the various bridges superseded the ferries so the passing trade of the Passage House fell off and was doubtless responsible for the decline of the inn towards the end of last century. However there has always been sufficient trade to support at least one if not two public houses here and despite being a war restricted area in the early 1940s, the Passage House and the Freemason's Arms, just a few yards up the road, enjoyed fairly prosperous times during the war.

The Freemasons otherwise known as Dirty Dick's, was run then by George 'Chalkie' White. It was pulled down almost 30 years ago.

The Passage House on the other hand was managed during wartime by Flo Nicholls, the first manageress taken on by Plymouth Breweries as menfolk went to work or war. Fortunately for Flo, Harry, her husband, worked across the road for Shell Mex. At this time both pubs had to supply the authorities with lists of all those friends, relatives or businessmen that they might expect to visit them so that they might be admitted through the handful of police gates that staked out this area, an area that included Shapter's Field, first home to many American servicemen at this time (their second home being one or other of the local pubs).

After seeing out some happy times in adversity Flo and Harry Nicholls stayed here until 1954; their son, Harry (Nick) Nicholls who grew up at the 'Passage House', now manages the 'Cherry Tree' at Pennycross.

Following a succession of short-stay landlords the pub has, since 1972, been run by John Ball who is quite happy here in this quiet, isolated inn which affords fine views of Oreston, the Cattewater, the Sound, the depots and the power station.

[*WEH* 24.3.84]

The Grenville

'Here die I Richard Grenville with a joyfull and quiet mind, for that I have ended my life as a true soldier ought to do, that hath fought for his countrey, Queene, religion, and honour, whereby my soule most joyfull departeth out of this bodie, and shall always leave behind it an everlasting fame of a valiant and true soldier, that hath done his dutie as he was bound to do.'

Quoted by a Dutch writer, Van Linschoten, these were apparently the last words of the famous Elizabethan sea captain, Sir Richard Grenville, who breathed his last in 1591 on board a Spanish ship just off the Azores at the end of an epic battle with over 50 Spanish vessels that he had fought alone in Drake's old flagship the *Revenge*.

The first Englishman to talk of colonization, it was he who took out the first party of colonials to Roanoke in 1585 and who later left a further 15 after Drake had brought back the first settlement. It was Sir Richard too who sold Buckland Abbey to Francis Drake in 1588. This Richard, however, was by no means the first noteworthy Grenville nor was he the last. There is record of a succession of Richard Grenvilles from 1129, and in 1347 we find Sir Theobald Grenville, Sheriff of Devon. The grandfather of the aforementioned Sir Richard, also Sir Richard Grenville had, in 1549, been flung in Launceston gaol by a Cornish army of Rebels marching against the King angered by the 'Act of Uniformity' which had made the English prayer book compulsory. Elizabethan Sir Richard's father, Sir Roger Grenville meanwhile is remembered for having been a commander of Henry VIII's ship, the recently refloated *Mary Rose*.

However, the Grenville after whom the pub is named is most likely to be a grandson of Sir Richard—yet another Sir Richard Grenville. This was the man who, having promised his support to Parliament, been given a commission in their Army and learned their plans, then marched to Oxford and joined the King. Outraged at this treachery a gibbet was erected in London with a proclamation setting out his offence and denouncing 'the said Grenville, Traitor, Rogue, Villain and Skellum, incapable of all acquaintance and conversation with men of honesty and honour'.

The nickname Skellum 'an obscure and obsolete word derived from an old German word schelme—a scoundrel' (Bracken) has stuck to this Grenville ever since. Annoyed as Parliament may have been, however, Grenville did them a favour for, according to the historians, his poor local leadership contributed substantially to the failure of the Royalist siege of Plymouth.

Grenville Road, St. Judes, the beginnings of which antedated the hotel by ten years, was built around the same time (the mid 1880s) as neighbouring Cromwell Road and Desborough Road. Two further names which hark back to the days of the Civil War. John Desborough was an army general who married Oliver Cromwell's sister and was later (May 1659) made Governor of Plymouth. A post which two years later, when the Monarchy had been restored, was in the hands of Sir John Grenville, son of Sir Bevil and nephew of 'Skellum'. Indeed, the foundation stone of the Citadel facing the sea inscribed 'Jo Earle of Bathe 1666' refers to John Grenville and the title bestowed upon him by Charles II.

Meanwhile, back in the Grenville itself, we find Jim and Wendy James here after four years of running the 'Woodland Fort' at Honicknowle. They succeeded Ron Sinclair who retired from here after ten years as tenant. Archie Maunder and his wife Eileen were here for a similar period (before that having succeeded Eileen's aunt Beat Dunbar and her husband George). As a family, however, the Williams's had it longest, arriving here in 1905 and keeping it until 1940.

[*WEH* 16.5.85]

St. Jude's Church

'Whoever thought to build a church on such a lonely spot?
We've got St John's and that's enough,' said Mary Caldicott.
And the Jordans at the Round House could not believe it true
Until they saw the hedge pulled down and building stone in view.
Then came a sign announcing that St Jude's Church would be there,
Which made the Friary courting folks near topple with despair.'

So wrote one local man in *The Master Builder*—the ballad of the building of St. Jude's in which in a little over 100 lines the writer recalled the masons and men with whom he had toiled back in 1875–6. That way he conveyed an atmosphere akin to that in which the celebrated Westcountry poet and novelist Thomas Hardy set his mason, coincidentally named Jude (The Obscure) in 1895.

Son of a mason and builder himself. Hardy had been articled in 1856 as an ecclesiastical architect. However, by the time Plymouth architect James Hine had drawn up designs for St. Jude's, Hardy had already embarked on a different course.

When building finished here in 1876 and Bishop Temple came to consecrate the completed church, there was no spire on St. Jude's and indeed it wasn't until 1881 that work on one began.

By now the area around the church was beginning to see change. After the improvement of the approach roads and the selling of the massive Tothill estate, housing development pressed on apace.

The parish of St. Jude's had been carved out of the parish of Charles, along with that of St. Luke's and Emmanuel, to help cater for the rapidly expanding population.

However, when first built although allocated a 4,000 strong parish. St. Jude's was still geographically 'out in the sticks'.

Directly opposite the gates and lodge of Beaumont there was then no Tothill Avenue.

Tothill Road, until recently, had been a narrow lane and the turning that is now Beaumont Road would, 100 years ago, have conducted the visitor to 'some charming country lanes and thence by Love Lane to Woodside and Lipson'.

No wonder Friary courting couples were unhappy then, as within two decades this country area had vanished under the orderly ranks of terraced housing that stretched up to Mount Gould Road across Beaumont Road down to Prince Rock on the other side of the railway.

Throughout this period of great expansion, parishioners were guided spiritually by St. Jude's first vicar, the Rev. Thomas Howard (1876–1902) and blessed by the generosity of Rev. T. A. 'Squire' Bewes, a man of 'large property and great benevolence.'

Squire Bewes lived in Beaumont House and in a series of generous acts helped St. Jude's with land, the building and the furbishing of the church.

Over 100 years have now passed and St. Jude's (which takes its name from the epistle said to be written by Jude 'Servant of Jesus Christ and brother of James,'—that is Judas—the Apostle, not Iscariot) has seen eight vicars.

After Thomas Howard came Joseph Sturdy, William Weeks, Harold McMaking, Kenneth Prior, John Blyth, Peter Pytches and the present incumbent (since 1971), David Lumb, who has not only followed in his father's footsteps by going into the Church but, more specifically, by going into this church as, between 1923–7, his father Alec Lumb was here as curate.

[*WEH* 10.11.84

Greenbank horse trough

THE MERCIFUL MAN
IS MERCIFUL TO HIS BEAST

One of the nice traditional things about Christmas has been the way in which Santa Claus has always relied on his reindeer to get him about when clearly with all the technology his helpers must have to produce the Space Age toys and presents of today he could doubtless be whizzing around the world in a fully automatic sleigh if he wanted to.

So spare a thought as Rudolph and his companions no doubt do every Christmas, for all their four-legged out-of-work horse friends who, less than 100 years ago, used to pull trams, carriages and cabs around the streets of Plymouth.

Mostly classic 2CV vehicles (that's *deux cheveux*, your actual French for two horses or 2 horse-power) Plymouth's first public transport system based around the horse was really quite extensive.

The Plymouth, Stonehouse and Devonport Tramways Co., was founded in 1872 in the wake of the 1870 Parliamentary Tramways Act. Horse buses had been known to run in Plymouth since at least 1832; however, very little evidence of the era of horse travel survives today.

There are only a few equine service stations, or horse troughs, around now and fewer still in their original position. This one at Greenbank was itself moved in January 1983 from the other side of the Lipson Road junction to allow for the provision of new traffic lights.

Despite the fact that horses provided the principal means of transport for centuries it was not really until the early nineteenth century that people began to consider effective means of providing water for them. Up until this time owners had to rely on rivers, streams, ponds and buckets to succour their beasts of burden. In 1824 the Animal Protection Society was formed (it later became the RSPCA) and early troughs, often wooden, began to appear. In 1867 another body, the Metropolitan Drinking Fountain Association (founded partly to encourage temperance among pedestrians in 1859) added 'and Cattle Trough' to its title and in the years that followed nearly 1,000 MDF & CTA troughs were set up all over the country.

About half of these were in the London area, but one bearing the full Metropolitan Drinking Fountain and Cattle Trough Association title still stands on its original site just outside Holsworthy.

The trough here at Greenbank bears the legend 'The Merciful Man is Merciful to his Beast' and above the water level sports the Plymouth City Arms. The mention of water level of course is not to suggest that anything other than rainwater ever sits in the trough today.

Instead, the demise of horse-drawn transport has meant that this has long since been used as a rubbish dump like so many of its counterparts, although some, including the Miles Memorial in Exeter and an extremely ornate Victorian Jubilee trough in Chipping Sodbury, are now used as flower beds. »Postscript

[WEH 29.12.84

Salisbury Road School

Officially opened exactly 80 years ago last week Salisbury Road School has always been somewhat other than ordinary. Originally it was constituted as four separate sections—one for defective and epileptic children, one for deaf children, a section for pupil teacher instruction and finally the main school.

Sadly, however, the special school section was virtually wiped out during the blitz and today only a single floor annexe exists. The school is still unusual in so much as whilst it has a mixed infants and junior school section on the ground and middle floors respectively, the top floor contains a single-sex secondary school.

An all-girl institution it has its male counterpart just down the road on the top floor of the Prince Rock School building. Such educational rarities have numbered days, however, and it will not be long before this particular pair of single-sex secondary schools will be swelling the numbers at the new Lipson Comprehensive.

The departure of the senior girls will leave Salisbury Road School even more like its architectural 'twin' Hyde Park School which has always been a straightforward upstairs/downstairs, junior and infants school. Founded around the same time as Salisbury Road the greatest difference between the schools is not due to any obvious original design feature but rather to an unfortunate wartime incendiary bomb at Hyde Park which necessitated the rebuilding of the roof. Sadly the rebuilding did not follow the old plan which is why Hyde Park now sports a modern flat roof. Originally of course it looked much the same as the one we see at Salisbury Road.

What we cannot really see in this back view of Salisbury Road School, however, is the infants' floor which is hidden behind the long high wall which borders the school. In the last week or so this floor and its large hall have been the centre of a great deal of activity, many former pupils having been in to leave memories and mementoes. Now a fine museum of Salisbury Road School bits and pieces is building up. Thanks for this are due mainly to the energy and enthusiasm of the infants' school sixth headmistress Margaret Bate, her colleagues and her current pupils' parents.

While 80 years may be a long time it somehow seems very short when very active old pupils come in and are filled with memories of the very first years and teachers at the school.

Well remembered were Headmistresses Miss Angier (1903–22) and Miss Oliver (1922–42) who between them cover almost half the school's life to date, whilst one-time pupil Pauline Membrey (1928–32) who returned to the school to teach in 1950 was well known to all but the most recent pupils as she only retired two years ago. Actual structural changes in the school have been slight. Typically, however, most adults returning to their infants school find it much smaller than they remembered it.

However, while the steps and corridors are little changed the same cannot be said of the conditions and it is hard now to imagine the need for attendance medals and the impact of nits, rickets, and diptheria, a severe epidemic of which in 1926 necessitated the incineration of all school books—diptheria immunisation was introduced in 1929.

Used as a hospital during the First World War and oft times as a billet for troops in the Second, the school has been overlooked from this corner of Pentyre Terrace since 1949 by the family butcher's business of A. R. Lavers and Son whose awning protrudes a little into this Salisbury Road sketch.

[*WEH* 30.4.83]

Lipson milestone

The opening of the £34 m Parkway road through the city this week with its great wide carriageways is a far cry from the roads that first bore traffic away from the city.

Indeed the whole development of local roads tells a fascinating story and one in which the greatest excitement has taken place only over the last 200 years or so.

'Early roads' we are told 'were not constructed in the ordinary sense of the word, but used' (Harold Peake 1917).

Although the Romans built fine road systems, their departure was followed by the disintegration of most of these wonderful long ways and throughout the Middle Ages a road was little more than a right of passage and their maintenance primarily meant the removal of any impediments.

In 1555 every parish in England was made responsible for its roads and every inhabitant was called upon for six days' labour each year. Later a 1593 Statute of Elizabeth I mentions the English mile in the length we know it—eight furlongs of 40 perches (rods) of $16\frac{1}{2}$ ft—that is 5,280 ft. (The original mile of the Romans, 1,000 (double) paces, was nearer 4,833 ft).

Elizabethan England also witnessed the introduction of coaches to this country. Coming initially from Holland and Germany, it was some time before they came this far west; not surprisingly either when you consider the state of the roads.

In 1695 Celia Fiennes in her account 'Through England on a Side Saddle', describes her trek into Plymouth thus: 'Here the roads contract and the lanes are exceeding narrow and so covered up you can see little about; an army might be marching undiscovered by anybody, for when you are on those heights that show a vast country about you, you cannot see one road. The ways now become so difficult that one could scarcely pass by each other, even the single horses.'

Indeed only four years earlier an Act had been passed directing that 'no horse causey shall be less in breadth than three foot'. Despite various measures taken and the turnpike acts of the eighteenth century, it was not really until the great coaching boom which began in the 1780s that significant improvements were made.

Prompted largely by the Post Office and their striving to make journeys ever quicker this era almost instantly began with a great jump in speed for coach travel from 'four miles to nine within the hour'.

Meanwhile the Great West Road out of Plymouth towards London had been constructed in 1758. Superseding the old route via Tavistock, it passed along here and down Lipson Hill a stretch, by all accounts, both difficult and unpleasant to negotiate. (Local conservationist Stanley Goodman well remembers the rough red slate rocks scored deeply by the iron cartwheels where the carters jammed them hard up against the rock to assist the braking on the way down.)

Soon after its completion this roadside milestone doubtless appeared. Just at the top of the hill, opposite Queen's Road, as the city is about to come into view, it bears the legend 'I mile from Plym-o'.

This particular stone is possibly the only milestone left standing inside the city. E. N. Masson-Phillips, the local boundary stone expert, believes others that he located some years ago have since been lost.

The Museum does have one that formerly stood near the 'Old Road Inn', Laira, which James Barber hopes they will soon be able to reinstate. This second one shows II(2) Miles from Plym-o, and like the one here was doubtless in place before 1800 for soon after then (1809) the new Embankment Road from Plymouth to Crabtree effectively bypassed this as the main road out of town.

Incidentally in attempting to answer the question 'I mile to exactly what point in Plymouth' I generated much interest but little information for no one seems quite sure.

But after speaking to people at the Reference Library, the City Engineer's Dept, Ordnance Survey and the School of Navigation, it was suggested that it might be the flagpole outside the Guildhall, while the RAC said they used St. Andrew's Cross roundabout, which has in its favour its proximity to both the parish church and the main post office. »Postscript

[WEH 6.4.85.

From Freedom Fields

It is perhaps ironic that the massive Royalist structure the Citadel should once have loomed so large in this view from the area which witnessed the greatest local Royalist setback in the Civil War on Sunday 3rd December 1643. A setback traditionally known as the 'Sabbath Day Fight' and seen as 'The Great Deliverance' from the long siege which was never again to yield to an attack on Plymouth's entrenched Parliamentarians.

Freedom Fields does not, however, take its name from this encounter, rather it dates from a much earlier local victory. In 1403 raiding French Bretons were defeated in fighting around Bretonside and thereafter annual 'freedom' celebrations were held, with 'organised and tolerated' fighting between the Old Town Boys and the Burton (Breton) Boys.

As Plymouth expanded the venue for these fights was moved out to what then became Freedom Fields. (In 1782 these annual fights ended after 'some young gentlemen had their collarbones broken').

In 1830 the eye could still stretch from here across Bretonside, the Sound and out past Staddiscombe and Edgcumbe on either side, thereafter, however, most of the green fields fore and aft have been built upon.

In 1849 at the top of the hill the Borough jail was built to accommodate up to 70 prisoners; just beyond it in 1858 appeared the New Workhouse, moved from Catherine Street and able to accommodate some 600 inmates; while on the other side of the road the new South Devon and East Cornwall Hospital (Greenbank) was completed in 1888, it too having moved up from the Barbican.

So it was that around the turn of the century this area was known as Faith, Hope and Charity as various inmates either prayed for health, escape or food and clothing.

Today it is possible to gain this view of Plymouth either by going to the top of Greenbank or in this case the much newer Freedom Fields Hospital which stands on the site of the old workhouse.

[*WEH* 14.8.82.

The Trafalgar

Widened, lengthened, bombed and shortened, Ebrington Street has had somewhat of a chequered history over the last 150 years. Many shops have come and gone as have several pubs and two cinemas.

Built in the first half of last century the street was named after the much respected Earl Fortescue—Viscount or Lord Ebrington. One of a handful of zealous noble political reformers, including his friend and neighbour Lord John Russell, Ebrington first won a Devon seat for Reform in 1818 and a dinner was given in his honour by local freeholders.

Although he lost this seat in 1820, he later sat for Tavistock and gradually the Reform movement gained momentum.

When Ebrington won a Devon seat again in 1830 he was met on the city's eastern extremity and his carriage was triumphantly carried along this new road to the Royal Hotel where there was a victory dinner.

Plymouth felt very strongly about reform and when the Lords first threw out the Bill, shops were closed and flags were flown at half mast, then some weeks later when the Bill was finally passed, flags were hung out everywhere and ten thousand men took to the streets with bands and banners.

A tablet on the Hoe commemorates a gathering of over 20,000 inhabitants of the three Towns in the Bull Ring and the efforts of Russell, Ebrington, and others in securing the passing of the Reform Bill, which even then only gave the vote to occupants of houses worth £10 rent a year, whether freehold or leasehold.

This still meant that there was an electorate of less than 1 million in a population of 24 million.

In 1841 the 3rd Lord Ebrington was elected MP for Plymouth, a seat which he held until 1852 by which time No. 4 Ebrington Street was better known as the 'Lord Ebrington' public house which stood towards Old Town Street until 1895 when Nos 3 to 29 were rebuilt as part of the road widening scheme that took place after the inauguration of the municipal tram service.

Ebrington Street, of course, then ran, as it did until 1964, as far as Burtons' below the present Drake Circus and the original 'Unity' pub, now in Eastlake Street, was No. 21 Ebrington Street.

Gone altogether now, however, is the 'Norley Inn' and the 'Ham Street Vaults'.

Ham Street originally ran straight on from Ebrington Street and the 'Trafalgar', rebuilt in 1895, was variously known, between 1860 and 1899 as first 12½ then 9½, 10 and finally, 11 Ham Street before becoming 62 Ebrington Street.

With a sign depicting action in the famous sea battle of 1805, news of the historic British victory first reached Plymouth when an actor rushed onto the theatre stage, interrupted the play, silenced the crowd and announced the triumph.

When the cheering had abated somewhat he raised his hand again and gave the news of Nelson's death, reducing, after a moments stunned silence, the jubilant crowd to tears and sadness.

Since its reconstruction the 'Trafalgar' has changed little.

Cyril Phipps was the man behind the bar here for more than 20 years from the early 1930s.

When he first arrived his customers would have included patrons from the Cinedrome opposite.

Opened around 1912 bomb damage sustained during the 1941 Blitz, meant that it never reopened as a cinema; however, part of its distinctive frontage stands today as the entrance to Gould's clothing store . . . better fate than that met by the massive old iron-roofed Palladium which originally opened in 1910 as a Roller Skating Rink.

Meanwhile in the 'Trafalgar' today, we find Roger Bennett. Born just along the way in Beaumont Road, Roger started out as manager of 'The Earl Grey', named ironically after the man, a former resident of Devonport and leading Whig, who introduced the Reform Bill in 1831 (the pub has since changed its name to 'The Brewery Tap').

After an earlier spell here and at the 'Britannia' at Milehouse, Roger came to the 'Trafalgar' early in 1982.

[*WEH* 20.10.84

Sutton High School

At the end of this academic year the doors of this 90-year-old building in Regent Street will no longer admit schoolboys as instead it will become yet another annexe of the College of Further Education.

Meanwhile, the boys of Sutton will see out their schooldays at Keppel Place sharing the building of Stoke Damerel School for Girls, thereby turning full circle, something that began 160 years ago, when in 1821 Stoke Public School was opened.

Later becoming Keppel Place School it ultimately merged in 1926 with Regent Street School and here became Sutton Secondary School. Regent Street School itself started life in nearby Mount Street and when that school moved here in 1897 it was split physically into upper and lower schools with a girls' school sandwiched in the middle floors.

In 1986 Sutton High School (a title it acquired in 1938) and also Stoke Damerel as presently constituted will cease to exist, thereby ending a fine academic tradition in the city.

Sutton High, always a happy school, with the arms of St. Wilfred—patron saint of fishermen—as its badge, 'Ut Serviatur'—that I may serve—as its motto, has twice missed out on moves and developments that might otherwise have shed a different light on its future. Redevelopment had been on the cards since 1949 and a much mooted move in the 1960s to a large site at Pennycross looked all set for realization, as did a plan ten years ago to construct a 24-acre, sixth-form entry Sutton School at Derriford, but alas it was thwarted by last-minute Government economy cuts.

Always, therefore squeezed into these congested Victorian premises just off the cobbled North Street, which runs along the line of what is perhaps the most ancient thoroughfare in the area (a ridge road ran past here from the head of Sutton Pool through to Roborough Down in Iron Age times), Sutton has managed to survive everything but the British politician.

Indeed, during the war, when many pupils were evacuated to St. Austell, the school emerged unscathed, thanks in no small measure to Mr. Lamerton, the school caretaker, who single-handedly threw half a dozen incendiaries off the school roof. A graphic account of the 'School at War' was written by the school's second headmaster Charles Jones, who saw the school through 23 years from 1935–58.

Mr. Jones also later compiled a fuller more detailed history of the school and in fact the school has long been well documented. Brian Moseley, an old boy from the early 1960s, who in 1982 produced an invaluable post war local history book *Vanishing Plymouth*, published an account of the school's history in 1963 which he later revised in 1970.

More recently the Old Suttonians commissioned 6th former Andrew Leigh to compile a history of the school from Mr. Jones's departure to the present day. As befitting a school where many have spent the happiest days of their lives, Sutton has a pretty healthy old boy organization and although soon to lose its influx of new blood, its future looks set for many years to come.

Indeed there are even in its ranks today old boys from Regent Street School itself. The late Jack Train, radio and TV comic was a Regent Street boy, as was the father of the current headmaster of Sutton Dr. James Rowe, who took over here in 1971.

My own father Des Robinson and his two brothers Bob and Derek are all old boys and like many others remember well Mr. Herbert 'Bert' Rogers who joined the school in January, 1928, as its first chemistry master and stayed there until his retirement 41 years latter in 1969.

Today he lives on the Hoe whilst another contemporary of his Mr. C. A. Phillips who retired that same year after 35 years service currently resides in Horrabridge.

Meanwhile, retiring this year is a man whose career considerably overlapped with these two gentlemen: Doug Fraser who with all his workmates and pupils past and present will greatly miss this celebrated institution, which even today may not have seen its greatest moments.

Staff and students here alike are determined to see that Sutton goes out with a bang and who knows both in the sporting and academic stakes they may yet top their present four provisional Oxbridge candidates and sixth-former Martyn Sweett's three England rugby caps.

[WEH 26.5.84

Wellington Bakery

In his 1879 walkabout guide to Plymouth W. H. K. Wright described it thus: 'Eastward of Tavistock Place will be found an extensive network of streets, mostly of recent erection, but possessing no places of interest or objects of curiosity to tempt us out of our course.

'The names of some of these streets serve, however, to perpetuate men and events of national interest. For instance, we find Nelson, Trafalgar, Wellington, Waterloo, Armada and others in close proximity.'

Four of the five above named streets refer, of course to the 1800–15 Napoleonic Wars. Trafalgar in 1805 and Waterloo in 1815 being the scenes of the two major battles with Nelson and Wellington their respective British heroes.

Prime Minister between 1828–34 Sir Arthur Wellesley (Wesley until 1804), the 1st Duke of Wellington, had like Nelson, been made a Freeman of the City of Plymouth and both great commanders had several occasions to visit the town.

Although it was conferred upon him in 1815 the Iron Duke did not receive his freedom until his first post war visit here in 1819, when the crowds cheering him deemed themselves to be celebrating the beginning of a long reign of peace.

Wellington died at Walmer Castle, Kent in 1852, in that same year in Plymouth, John Major, a baker, was working from his premises in Armada Street. By the end of that year a couple of un-numbered buildings appeared in the newly formed Wellington Street.

By 1862 John Major had moved around the corner into the new bakery at the top of Wellington Street. After a dozen or so years there the business was passed from Major to Martin in whose family the bakery remained until the 1940s when it was taken over by Sambell.

Doubtless here was produced 100 years ago a similar range of foodstuffs to other local bakeries who then boasted such delights as 'Good Currant and Seed Cake Daily,' 'Fancy Biscuits and Tea Cakes in great variety' and 'Superior Brown Bread delivered to any part of the three towns.' The latter being a service adopted by Charlie and Jeannie Wrighton when they revitalized the bakery some years ago.

Recalling the services of two of its old hands, 'Ginger' George and Stan, business boomed in this little backstreet bakery with its great traditional ovens, of the sort preserved in the imagery of artist Anton Peck. Ironically, however this bakery, believed to have the last coal fired ovens in Devon, was converted to gas only a short while before a fire of a more tragic and devastating nature swept the premises in 1981. The building was completely destroyed and today the site is barren.

Meanwhile on the other side of the crossroads the 'Wellington Hotel' forlornly waits for a new three storey flat development to take the place of its long standing neighbour.

[WEH 18.6.83

Built soon after the middle of the last century this bakery and hotel opposite were part of a large community housing development that sprang up from the villas of Regent Street.

Full of corner shops and public houses, this area (thankfully reprieved, temporarily at least from recent demolition plans) is today perhaps the best example of a Victorian housing estate in the whole of Plymouth. But impressive as this maze of tidy terrace accommodation may be today 100 years ago it was just another example of urban sprawl.

Drake's Place reservoir

Despite being 'kist with waters' and having an average annual rainfall well in excess of that in Manchester, Plymouth has oft-times yet had cause to 'pine with thirst' and 400 years ago a Plymouth Water Bill was heard in Parliament and passed with Royal Assent on the 29th of March, 1585.

The Bill was titled 'An acte for the presvacon of the haven of Plymouth' and among the men who helped ensure its passage through the committee stage was the then MP for Bossiney in Cornwall, Sir Francis Drake.

As presented to Queen Elizabeth the Bill made much of the fact that it was her Majesty's ships and the ships and vessels of her Highness's subjects trading in to foreign ports and from port to port that often had great difficulty in obtaining fresh waters within a 'myle of the said Towne or thereabowt, a matter verey incomodiouse ... especiallie in the Sommer Tyme when the Daungers bee greateste.'

Going on to describe the proposals for cutting the leat and diverting part of the Ryver Mevve (known also as the Mevye—Meavy today) it was some years before work commenced. Indeed it was not started until 1590, not long after Drake played his famous game of bowls on the Hoe and the Spanish Armada had been defeated.

There has been much controversy down the years over precisely what Francis Drake's contribution was in the construction of this leat but whatever part he played and however much money he might have made personally from the scheme, there appears to be little denying that he was the figure that people associated then as they do now with the project.

Indeed, even the popular legend that Drake rode ahead of the first flow of water on a white horse along the seventeen mile course of the leat may well be founded on fact according to historian Crispin Gill.

Although parts of Drake's leat, long since disused, are still visible today and the course is true to that planned by Robert Lampen, the leat itself is much more sophisticated than the simple ditch some six or seven feet wide and two feet deep that his brother James and his men originally cut in 1590, as centuries later it was replaced with a concrete floor and granite sides.

Back in the 1590s though, Plymouth's ditch was one of the first municipal aquaducts to be built in this country since Roman times and many places still relied for years to come on springs and wells as Plymouth had done.

To distribute their new supply here, however, the corporation built conduits and it's from the 1598 conduit that part of this arrangement in the wall of Drake's Place Reservoir in Tavistock Road has been taken. Previously, however, this same part, the wording 'Made in the Maioraltie of John Trelawnye 1598' had been incorporated in another conduit when the old town conduit was rebuilt in 1671.

The Arms of Drake and the inscription and crests currently above were then placed below this wording. The granite trough underneath this assembly is a sample of what replaced the brick and board street-gutters in 1746.

Meanwhile, the tablet on the left tells us that 'the stone carvings above are parts of the old public conduit removed from the head of Old Town Street in 1834 ... the wall and the carvings being re-erected in 1874.

Drake's Place Reservoir itself was originally constructed in two separate parts (1825 and 1828) as the tablet on the right tells us, whilst further along the reservoir wall we learn that the whole was reconstructed as one reservoir in 1891, just two years before Burrator was begun.

Today Drake's Place Reservoir serves no other useful purpose than as an unusual and attractive leisure area in the centre of town.

Whilst Burrator, despite having been described by another historian, C. W. Bracken, 50 years ago as assuring Plymouth of 'a pure and sufficient water supply for all time' with 'no need as often in the past to fear either summer's drought or winter's frost' presently awaits the completion of Roadford Reservoir to help augment the city's supply.

[WEH 4.8.84

Charles Church

In 1836 in 'Nettleton's Guide to Plymouth, Stonehouse and Devonport' there appeared the following description: 'The tower and spire of Charles Church have an agreeable outline; but otherwise the exterior of the building can only be described as in the debased Gothic style of a degenerated period.'

If that were not enough to put off the prospective visitor it had this to say about the porch on the south side of the church. 'The Saracenic portico on the south side may win a salam from the Mahomedan, but will be deemed most inappropriate by the Christian critic.'

Ironically enough, today the tower and spire now stand as the most complete remains of Charles Church, although sadly the clocks have gone.

Completed in 1658, building began in 1641, the year King Charles I gave his assent to the building of a new church, to be known as 'The Church of Plymouth called Charles Church.'

The tower itself was not completed until 1708, and until 1766 its spire was one of wood covered with lead.

Built on a piece of land, of what was then Green Street donated by William Warren a wine seller, Charles Church, a victim of the 1941 Blitz, at one time seated 1,716 persons.

Today, unfortunately Charles Church is an inaccessible ruin in the middle of one of the busiest roundabouts in Plymouth.

[*WEH* 13.3.82.

Public School

On Thursday 22nd June 1809 a number of prominent local citizens met in the Whimple Street Guildhall to draw up a plan for the 'Establishment of the Publick School . . . for the Education and Improvement of the Morals of Poor Children'.

Initially for boys, it was two years before the girls school was founded. However, it was not until 1812 that a purpose-built school was established here in Coburg Street. Prior to this the boys had received their lessons overlooking the Pig Market and the Shambles in town and the girls in the Leather Loft of the old Guildhall. Free at first, thanks largely to the generosity of various philanthropic subscribers, the school was obliged soon after the terrible cholera epidemic of 1832 to implement fees of one penny per week. This was later raised to tuppence and around 1860 a fee of sixpence per week was charged for members of the upper school.

Largely run throughout the nineteenth century on a monitorial system, the school consequently very much reflected the abilities of its Heads. Under this scheme the Head would instruct senior pupils who in turn imparted this knowledge to small groups of younger pupils. There were other teachers of course but this system had the advantage of being comparatively inexpensive and a good training for the monitors themselves.

After initial periods of instability at the head of both the boys and the girls school the second half of the nineteenth century was marked by long periods of leadership in both. From 1842–85 George Jago was Head of the boys school and was succeeded by his son Charles who had already a long involvement with the school and who remained Head until 1908. Meanwhile Miss Mary Turner took over as Head of the girls school in 1877 having already been with the school since 1856 and she stayed in her post until 1912; whilst in the infants section, opened in 1861, Miss Louisa Sprague was Head from 1872–1906. At one time during this period Public, with just over 2000 pupils, was the second largest school of its kind in the country. The early history of the school has been well documented by former pupil, teacher and Plymouth

historian C. W. Bracken, whose account also covered the transfer of the school from its original managers to the Education Authority in 1909; the demolition of the original buildings, which were deemed unfit soon after this, and then in 1925 and 1927 the foundation and opening of the new school seen here and which now, in turn, is due to be closed later this year.

Once popularly known as the Palace of Coburg Street, although housing both girls and boys, the school has never really been a mixed one and the two sexes have always been kept separate and independent. The infants, incidentally, merged with Oxford Street—now Pilgrim Primary—in 1924. Hitherto in the background of any account of the school the girls do have a strong sense of tradition and, as the school's current Head, Rita Goodman, points out, the school's success in business and clerical training has meant that many of the City's offices are run by 'old girls'. The most notable 'old girl' in recent years is television's Angela Rippon, whilst international footballer Trevor Francis is one of the better known 'old boys'. Later this year Public will become absorbed by the new Lipson Comprehensive; the Polytechnic will take over these premises, but the little oak tree planted this week near St. Andrews and symbolic of the school's motto, motif and aspirations will serve as a living memory of this historic school.

It's interesting to read from the school's earliest surviving document that it was then 'much to be feared that in the present state of Society (the Napoleonic Wars were still blazing) there are many parents whose Poverty is such as to disable them from paying for the Instruction of their children; it is also to be apprehended that there are many children whose Parents, from Indolence and Incapacity of Mind are inattentive to this Duty: and it is beyond all doubt that there are a vast many children born in the midst of vice, and attain the years of Manhood, without having ever had the least Instruction. '

[*WEH* 23.3.85

The Pennycomequick

The name of the area and the public house known as Pennycomequick, has, over the years, been of great interest to many people, strangers and locals alike. It is, believes the present landlord of the 'Pennycomequick' the reason why he receives so many enquiries from would-be overnight guests despite the fact that the pub has never accommodated them.

The area, which apparently sported only one farm at the time of Domesday and was at the time of the Civil War a point of great strategic importance (and doubtless witnessed many dozens of deaths) has had a great number of theories advanced to explain its unusual name.

Favourite, and most likely, is that it comes from the Celtic 'Peny-cwm-Cuig,' meaning 'the head of the creek valley' for it was here that Stonehouse Creek used to rise to, meeting Houndiscombe Brook which used to flow down from the present Tor Lane area.

Historian C. W. Bracken, however, writing some 50 years or so ago, claimed that Pennycomequick was 'probably a nickname for a prosperous farm'. Another, less likely but also popular story, is the one that suggests that last century there was a penny toll charge here at the top of the creek on the road between Plymouth and Stoke or Devonport and because of the great amount of traffic that passed by 'pennies came very quick'.

However, one of the older recorded accounts of this name and certainly the most colourful was published 130 years ago and later hailed by the nineteenth century public librarian W. H. K. Wright as the best version of the origin of the name:

'In days gone by . . . a well known old female had long fixed her abode in a curiously built hut like cot in the locality in question, the rusticity of which together with the obliging demeanour of its tenants had gradually induced the good folk of Plymouth to make holiday bouts to this retired spot for the purpose of merry making. As years rolled on the shrewd old dame became a general favourite with the pleasure seekers; the increasing frequency of these picnics suggesting to her an opportunity which might be turned to good account, namely that of providing her visitors with the cheap requisite—boiling water—for brewing their sober afternoon's beverage, at the low rate of a penny a head.

Still later in the autumn of life . . . she would recount to her pleased auditory how many a time and often she had made the 'penny come quick' by the above recited inexpensive vocation, until at length her saying became a byword in the neighbourhood and universal consent fixed on the triplet as a fitting appellation for the then nameless and retired little nook, but now thickly studded grounds of Pennycomequick.

Whether true or not this charming story at least gives us a tiny insight into the nature of our pleasure-seeking forebears. Meanwhile tonight here and in many other hostelries around the town some of today's pleasure-seekers will be flocking, perhaps no rowdier than their ancestors, but certainly greater in number, so spare a thought for the barmen and barwomen who may well see the 'pennies come quick' but will have to put up with much in the process.

As the anonymous poet wrote of the barman who's passed on . . . 'As Saint Peter sees him coming he will leave the gate ajar, for he knows he's had his hell on Earth, the man behind the bar.'

Traditionally the most drunken night of our calendar, landlord Eric Christie will tonight open the 'Pennycomequick' for well over its 100th New Year, the most recent of which have been hosted since the sixties here by landlords Bert Mooney, Ted Jackson, George Ashley and the former Argyle captain Jack Chisholm.

[WEH 31.12.83

Devonport Prison

Between Wake Street and Holdsworth Street at Pennycomequick stands a rather grand Victorian edifice which once housed the governor and porters of Devonport Borough Prison.

Built in 1849 it was completed only months after Plymouth Prison which was 'erected without the precincts of the towns,' just off the top of Greenbank Hill (it was demolished in 1935).

Built at a cost of about £12,500, from the designs of Messrs Fuller and Gingell, Devonport Prison stood immediately behind this gatehouse—it was approached via a large gateway that ran through the tower where we now see a large balcony window.   A large, three-winged affair, it contained cells for '66 prisoners, male and female, a chapel, surgery, baths, convalescent rooms and the necessary offices and apartments . . .' also in the prison were 'four cells for solitary confinement, arranged for the admission of air, but not of light, and twenty four separate airing grounds to accommodate one prisoner each, rotating from a centre in which an officer is placed.'

The idea of detaining individuals in prison, as a punishment in itself, is a comparatively recent one and well into the nineteenth century misdemeanours were punished by whipping, ducking, stocks, pillory or fines.

Even 'ye infamous castle dungeons' were chiefly places to keep enemies or idle serfs and as a private, usually corrupt, institution it was often used for political gain. Grim, unhealthy jails were also used to assist in exacting fines.

More serious crimes, felonies, were punished by death or deportation. However, with the loss of the American colonies, deportation became less viable and in 1779 an Act was passed authorising the building of State Penitentiaries. The timely discovery of Australia and its subsequent use as a penal colony, from 1787, however, removed thousands from their miserable confinement in old ship hulks, on the Thames and other rivers, and was largely responsible for only one major prison—Millbank being completed in 1821.

When transportation to Australia ended demand for prison accommodation intensified and following another Act in 1835, Pentonville, the 'model prison' was built in 1842. In the next seven years 54 other convict prisons were built on the same plan, including those in Plymouth and Devonport. Even Dartmoor Prison which had been built in 1806 to take captives of the Napoleonic Wars was reopened and extended in 1850 (it had closed in 1816). Indeed most closed prisons in Britain today date from this period.

Deemed to be one of the most cost efficient prisons in England at one time, Devonport's weekly food bill per prisoner was one shilling and eight pence (8p) in 1870. Inmates receiving for the most part nothing other than bread and potatoes or Indian meal pudding in their first week, with soup, suet pudding and cheese (on Sundays only), thrown in for longer stays—and even then authorities were concerned that prisoners ate better than some members of the 'humbler classes'. Some of the work at Devonport Prison was productive too, unlike the treadmill and crank that characterized many institutions.

In 1877, however, another Prison Act brought national centralization; 113 prisons were taken over, 38 were closed—Devonport was one. Desolate for a year or two, and once mooted as a naval prison, it was eventually sold in 1881 for £5,500 to John Martin, probably of Martin and Son, the large Devonport firm of builders and contractors. Within the year the prison was gone and part of Wake Street had been completed whilst Holdsworth Street was underway. The gatehouse itself was left and extended to the right, beyond the original part we see here.

[WEH 4.2.84

Ford Park Cemetery

Originally chosen because it was outside the boundaries of the Three Towns and yet convenient for all three, Ford Park Cemetery was originally approached from Pennycomequick by means of Cemetery Road.

In those days underdeveloped, first Devonport Borough Prison was built and then gradually, after the early demise of the prison, housing began to appear and the name of the road was later changed to Central Park Avenue.

Today, where this road meets Ford Park Road we find the original entrance to the Plymouth, Devonport and Stonehouse Cemetery Company's extensive resting grounds for the departed. Established in the wake of an 1846 Act of Parliament, the cemetery was enlarged by a second Act in the 1870s, and at the same time an addition was made to this lodge at the entrance.

Over the years a great many people have been laid to rest here. The first interment was made in December 1848 and as early as 1879 the cemetery was being described as 'a veritable city of the dead'.

Today there are some 30,000 graves in the cemetery, some holding as many as nine or ten and one or two as many as 15 deceased. All in all this 40 acre site houses a population equivalent to that of the entire city of Plymouth today—that's around 250,000 bodies.

Undoubtedly benefitting from the assistance of Manpower Services labour, Ford Park Cemetery today is looking very presentable and, as Jack Walker, foreman for the last 25 years, notes there is much interesting reading to be done around the many stones. Herein lies a member of the Scott expedition; an engineer from the *Titanic*; Dr. John Butter, founder of the Plymouth Eye Infirmary; two V.C. war heroes and many, many more.

Currently the Plymouth, Devonport and Stonehouse Cemetery Company, one of the oldest such private companies in the area, handles around 150–200 burials a year. Burial is, of course, still our usual mode of disposing of the body of a deceased person.

However, in other parts of the world it is not unknown for other methods to be or to have been, 'normal'. 'Burying' in water; eating 'in order that the virtues of the dead may enter the bodies of the living'; exposing to nature—usually somewhere on high on the grounds that burial defiles the earth, the gift of the societal god, and cremation defiles his symbol, the sacred fire; preservation, often related to the 'ambivalent wish to both keep and to break the bond with the dead' and artificial decomposition.

English law does not prohibit alternatives to burial and indeed cremation was legal before the passing of the 1902 Cremation Act.

Our laws don't even require burial in a particular place and if in non-consecrated ground a service is not required. However, all burials must be effected in a 'decent and orderly manner' so as not to infringe the Burial Laws Amendment Act of 1880.

Meanwhile, back in the erstwhile Cemetery Road, this lodge has for many years now been unlived in. Once caretaker's accommodation and sometimes used for board meetings of the Plymouth, Devonport and Stonehouse Company, its basement had become rat infested and its roof and windows were deteriorating.

Recently sold, this unusual and attractive listed building is currently being rescued by Barry Menear and his wife, Yvonne, who are both keen to see it restored to its former glory. Barry himself has no qualms about living in a cemetery, Yvonne, however, has her reservations.

[*WEH* 23.2.85

Plymouth Station

During the particularly heavy snowfall of February 1841 the Quicksilver Mail Coach became embedded on its way from Laira to Ivybridge. It was quite some time before any traffic could pass and a gang of seventy labourers were called in to free the vehicle. Meanwhile the mail was conveyed to Ivybridge by saddled horses and 'an array of obstructed vehicles' waited for the road to be cleared. It was not long after this, according to the Plymouth historian H. Whitfield writing in 1900, that the prevailing topic of discussion was 'the wonderful new machine for travelling without horses, which had a body of iron like a barrel, a furnace in the rear, and a perpendicular pipe ten feet high to carry off the smoke'. However, he adds: ' At the first South Devon Railway meeting held in Plymouth, the engineer of the Great Western Company was chiefly concerned in dispelling the fears of the nervous. No accidents could occur—Mr. Price pointed out—if passengers kept their seats until the train came to a standstill, and the rails would be so protected that stage coaches could not possibly drive over them'.

Such fears as there were, however, did not stop the money pouring into the scheme and Isambard Kingdom Brunel was the man entrusted with effecting the arrival of the South Devon Railway in Plymouth. Brunel recommended Eldad 'at the end of Five Fields' as the terminus in order that an extension be made into Cornwall 'if this should be thought expedient'. He was overruled partly due to inter-town rivalry, to which Brunel answered 'Although you speak of your Three Towns, we know only one long, straggling, scattered community'. Time and the great engineer himself were to prove his contentions correct, much to the City's later cost. In 1849 a terminus was set up at Millbay and in no time at all the traffic flow had necessitated widening this route. In the process Plymouth lost the Royal Union Baths which were opened to the south of Union Street in 1828. After their demolition the incline to the railway goods shed later stood here—where currently we find a wide empty eyesore. The Baths were one of John Foulstons more impressive imposing buildings built in the classical style. 'With its two swimming baths, six plunge, nine hot, douche and shampooing baths, its coffee and news rooms, the Union Baths gave Plymouth a social and remedial centre comparable to the Pump Room at Bath', C. W. Bracken 1931. However, even this measure was insufficient and by 1877 another station had been set up at the other end of Five Fields here further along North Road to help cope with all the rail traffic now in the area. Jointly administered by the GWR (Great Western Railway) and the LSWR (London & South Western Railway) the two companies nevertheless had separate booking clerks and ticket collectors.

As it became more and more obvious that North Road was most conveniently placed for the expanding City, indeed no longer Plymouth's North Road but as the neighbouring park now suggests more a central road, so plans to develop the station were drawn up. Delayed by the Second World War, these eventually took shape in the late 1950s. In 1958 Friary Station (opened in 1891) closed its passenger services and the rebuilt North Road station was renamed Plymouth Station. Completed in 1962 it was opened by Dr. Beeching, who was also responsible for speeding up the 'tidying up' of Plymouth's intricate railway network.

Today trains run through Plymouth to places all over the country including Manchester, Liverpool, Newcastle, Aberdeen and Glasgow; the latter run—Penzance–Glasgow—being the longest through run available on British Rail today. Most passengers nowadays are, of course, human. Initially the train was a great boon to farmers who previously had been driving their cattle to London, to the detriment of their weight, strength and value. However, no livestock has been carried by rail for many years now. One association that has blossomed though has been the Mail services. Today not only does the mail to London travel so much quicker than it did on the Quicksilver (which took 24hrs and was about the fastest coach in the country)—on the Great Western Travelling Post Office it also gets sorted on the way.

[WEH 9.3.85

The Patna

Where Patna Place meets North Road West, Plymouth we find the 'Patna Inn'.

Why Patna? No one seems to know. The streets around appear to lend no clues and the only other Patna to be found is the one that has given its name to a type of rice and is currently home to over half-a-million Indians.

Situated in the north of India, on the south bank of the Ganges, Patna is the capital of Biha State and is a busy trading centre.

Patna stands on the site of a city founded some two-and-a-half thousand years ago and this city, known as Pataliputra was considered to have been one of the largest cities of the ancient world and many accounts of it survive in old Greek, Roman and Chinese writings.

By the seventh century AD it had fallen into decline and the small settlement that was then left later grew into medieval Patna.

Of the few older buildings that survive in Patna today, one is the temple built by Ranjit Singh of the Punjab on the site of the birthplace of Govind Rai (1675–1708), who adopted the name Singh (lion) and was the last of the ten gurus who established the modern Sikh religious sect.

Govind Singh organized the sect into a militant commonwealth and its members were known by the five 'K's—kesh (uncut hair), kacch (short drawers), kara (iron bangle), kanga (comb) and kirpa (dagger).

Ironically, or perhaps significantly, it was not long after the two Sikh wars of 1845–6 and 1847–8 which the British won but lost thousands of men in the process, that 'The Patna' appeared here in Plymouth.

The 1860s saw major development either side of North Road, Plymouth, in the wake of the arrival of the railways in 1859 and come 1866 Mrs. Georgina Pike was settled here as licensee of 'The Patna', at number 1, Patna Place.

While roads off it were new, North Road itself had been a public thoroughfare for many years previously, when it had been known as Five Fields Lane, forming the southern boundary of the area known as 'Five Fields' and remembered today in the name of a guest house not far from here.

In 1788 Five Fields was written into local history as the scene of the famous Five Fields' murder when an especially abandoned character in the person of John Richards, a labourer, set upon and murdered Philip Smith, a clerk of the Dockyard who had earlier dismissed Richards.

In his evil act Richards was assisted by William Smith and when the two were apprehended and sentenced, Judge Buller determined that the usual course of giving their corpses to the surgeons for dissection should not be followed, but that they should be 'suspended between Heaven and Earth' as they were fit for neither.

Hanged at Heavitree, their bodies were subsequently transferred to Stoke where an old print records a scene that lasted many years as the bodies were allowed to rot on the gibbet. Smith's skeleton took seven years to drop, while Richards's fell bit by bit into the mud.

Meanwhile, back at 'The Patna', the last 100 years have seen at least three licensees spend around 20 years here; the Jacksons from the 1880s, Stephens before and after the last war and following him, Wally Fenwick.

Currently Dave and Barbara Jennings have notched up $7\frac{1}{2}$ years since 1977. New to the licensing trade, Barbara was in nursing before coming here first to help out their predecessors, Ray Cridge and his wife, while Dave worked for more than 25 years in the publishing department of the Western Morning News Co.

[*WEH* 17.11.84]

Oxford Street School

Oxford Street is old and grey.
'How old it is,' people say.
But alas the day is nigh,
When Oxford Street will say 'Goodbye',
In the sadness and in the gloom,
A kind of happiness will begin to bloom.
Because we'll have a brand new school.
With gardens and a swimming pool.

So wrote Helen Demeranville, a pupil at the school, as it prepared to move out of its old home last year. Today all that remains of this grand building is the small caretaker's lodge that stands on what was the corner of King's Gardens and Hastings Terrace.

Meanwhile, in the area in front of the old school site, Oxford Street headmaster John Pugh has a new school with a new name. 'Pilgrim Primary School' is a low three-building affair set in a mini green belt where until recently could be found Cambridge Lane West and Cambridge Street, of which now nothing remains.

The destruction of the old school and its surroundings and the building of the new has been marvellously chronicled in the national prize-winning efforts of 32 school pupils—much encouraged by deputy head Keith Loze—in three volumes, 'Oxford Street School, Past, Present and Future'. Reading this work it's hard to believe that the following account of this area was written barely more than 100 years ago:

'The visitor will now perceive building operations, or buildings recently erected on every hand, and will therefore not be surprised to know that many years, and in some cases months, have not elapsed since this portion of the town was unencumbered with bricks and mortar.

'We are on the site, partly of Barley House and grounds and Pontey's Nursery.

'Passing through one of the many opes we reach King's Gardens, and the site of the Oxford Street Board Schools, now being erected by Messrs Foot and Lethbridge, from the designs of Mr. Sylvanus Trevail, at a cost of about £4,500.'

That was written in 1879, the following year saw the school officially opened by the then Mayor, William Derry, who in his earlier term of office, 1861–3, had seen his famous clock tower—fountain erected.

In 1880 this particular area of Plymouth was expanding rapidly and Oxford Street School was built as a replacement for its inadequate predecessor, Tracey Street School, housed around the corner in a Wesleyan chapel. Today, of course, the new developments off Western Approach have seen the end of what was left of Tracey Street and once again, albeit temporarily, the area is largely 'unencumbered with bricks and mortar' as yet more City Centre blitz survivors fall victim to the planners.

However, while Oxford Street School has gone and is certainly unlikely to be forgotten, it would be wrong to think it will be remembered as shown here for this particular view was known only for a matter of months.

Indeed, for the greater part of its 100-year existence, James Henry Furguson's Mineral Water Works stood opposite the school in King's Gardens.

Furthermore, the street, once cleared, never had time to go to grass and I drew the grand old school as it could have looked but never did. »*Postscript*

St Peter's

Educated at Devonport then Cambridge, Prynne too was a follower of the Oxford movement and when in 1850 the 750-seater chapel had its new chancel consecrated one of the movement leaders, the Rev. Dr. E. B. Pusey was at the ceremony. For his own safety, however, it was necessary to refer to him as Dr. Grey as local authorities felt that there might otherwise have been riots in the city, as indeed there often were during the early years of Prynne's incumbency, riots led or at least encouraged by the then vicar of St. Andrews, John Hatchard.

Hatchard was a typical low church vicar and like many other people (including Isaac Latimer, the radical new editor of the Plymouth and Devonport Weekly Journal) was fiercely opposed to the 'high-church', 'Anglo Catholic' movement that was being advocated within the Church of England primarily by Pusey, Newman (later a cardinal) and John Keble all of Oxford.

The movement began at the university in the 1830s and emphasized spirituality, ritual, the sacraments and tradition in the church and in following it, even by merely wearing a white surplice, Prynne was attacked verbally and physically by Hatchard and his followers.

Forever breaking 'new' ground, in 1849 Prynne worked with Lydia Sellon another Puseyite who founded in Plymouth the first women's religious community to be established in the country since the Reformation (of which St. Dunstan's Abbey School is a reminder today). A wealthy woman Miss Sellon purchased houses and land in the area and together with Prynne and her sisters of the Society of the Holy Trinity erected a temporary hospital and did a great deal of work fighting the cholera epidemic of 1849 which killed over 1,000 people in the three towns.

In order to strengthen her sisters for their difficult, unpleasant and potentially fatal work, Miss Sellon asked Prynne if they could be allowed to receive Holy Communion daily and St. Peter's thus became the first church in England to restore and continue daily Communion.

G. R. Prynne who later wrote the hymn 'Jesu Meek and Gentle' was at St. Peter's 55 years and eventually he won universal admiration.

In 1882 he saw major work done on the church and apart from the addition of the copper clad spire added after his death in 1903, as a memorial to him and his work, that is how the church remained until the war.

Father George Hardy, vicar at St. Peter's from 1919–45 saw the church gutted in April 1941.

With only the walls left standing it was not until 1956 that St. Peter's was rebuilt and reconsecrated by which time John Tickner had succeeded George Hardy's former curate, nephew and son-in-law Charles Howard, as vicar.

The post-war St. Peter's, however, while retaining as many structural features as possible was rebuilt with a flat roof—the money thereby saved being spent on a grand pipe organ.

Sadly today the now leaky roof poses St. Peter's present vicar Sam Philpott and the organ with a difficult, damp and expensive problem.

John Hawker had been curate at Stoke Damerel church almost 30 years when in 1828 William John St. Aubyn was appointed new rector there. Expecting the post himself a disgruntled Hawker resigned and his many supporters built for him a chapel in what were then the 'Five Fields' and now Wyndham Square area.

Called at first Mr. Hawker's chapel it later became the 'Eldad' (favoured of God) chapel. A strict Protestant, Hawker's actions were partly prompted by his feeling towards the so called Catholic Emancipation in the church, a movement favoured by the new Bishop of Exeter, Henry Phillpotts. Consequently the Bishop was unwilling to consecrate Hawker's Chapel and on his death in 1846 Eldad fell into disuse.

In 1843, however, a bill had been passed for the formation of a new parish in Plymouth and at the end of 1847 the purchase of Edlad was arranged by the new vicar of this parish, Edward Godfrey. Godfrey, however, resigned after six months and in 1848 the chapel was licensed for divine service as the Church of St. Peter's and Bishop Phillpotts instituted his own man, George Rundle Prynne, as vicar.

[*WEH* 7.1.84

Plymouth's Oldest Post Box

The octagonal posting box in the Royal Naval Hospital is not only the oldest in Plymouth but it is also one of the three oldest post boxes in use today in the whole of Britain.

Thought to have been cast by one of the early post office contractors around 1853 it is likely to have received its first mail soon after the first ever mainland pillar box had been installed at Botchergate, Carlisle around September 1853.

Sadly no pictorial record of this box now exists but the box at Barnes Cross, Bishops Caundle, Dorset, cast by John M. Butt & Co., of Gloucester circa 1853, is a very similar design, as are the early boxes cast by Andrew Handyside & Co.

Furthermore, like Handyside's earliest boxes, it does not bear the Royal cipher, nor the lettering Post Office, letter box or indeed any maker's name or stamp. This is undoubtedly because it is not an official Post Office Box, but a private box with mail emptied by Naval Hospital Staff (currently three times a day) and passed over to the Post Office at a central point when they call.

There is another virtually identical box but made of very fine wood in the entrance foyer of the hospital's Trafalgar Block.

Letter boxes, hailed by Anthony Wedgwood Benn as the first visible and public sign of the age of modern communication are believed to have evolved from the 'ecclesiastical tamburi' of Florence.

These were closed boxes with a slit, introduced to the sixteenth century to receive anonymous letters of denunciation against persons believed to have broken the law or suspected enemies of the state.

With the gradual development of the postal system, public and private, Charles I made the facilities of his Royal Posts available to the general public in 1635, a variety of letter receptacles appeared.

The first boxes to be sited away from 'Post Offices' (usually shops or inns) are thought to have been erected in France and there were some on the streets of Paris as early as 1653. By 1800 similar boxes were in use in Germany and in Belgium by 1836. In Britain the incentive for such contrivances came in 1840 with the introduction of Uniform Penny Postage master-minded by Rowland Hill.

However, little was done despite public clamouring until in 1851 the clerk to the Western District Post Office Surveyor was sent over to the Channel Islands to study ways of improving the postal system there. The clerk, Anthony Trollope, who did a lot of writing while on his travels and is perhaps better known as a novelist, recommended an experiment with European style letter boxes.

By November 1852 four had been installed, they were hexagonal, about four-foot high, had a horizontal slit and were painted red. By the following year such hollow pillars were spread all over the mainland in all different shapes, sizes and colours.

Standardization began in 1857 and from 1859 all pillar boxes were hexagonal affairs painted with a dingy 'bronze green colour'. The reversion to pillar-box red as it became known did not take place until 1874 and by 1884 all boxes were that colour. However, at first there were problems with fading, indeed the RN Hospital box is in a fairly advanced stage of fading now. In 1887–9 two of London's pillar boxes were painted chocolate brown, just to see if that colour was more durable, but a stronger scarlet red was chosen and has been retained ever since. Although some boxes were painted blue in the 1930s for Air Mail only.

The national adoption of cylindrical 'boxes' came in 1879 and since then there has been very little change in basic pillar box design. An object associated with the bringers of good tidings and the carriers of the same this curious item was not so well liked by G. K. Chesterton 'in all created nature, there is not perhaps anything so completely ugly as a pillar box'.

Others like myself have great affection for them and Tony Benn, a former Post Master General when introducing J. Y. Farrugia's book The Letter Box in 1969 told the world that he had one in his own front garden and would not swap it for any other piece of sculpture in the world.

[WEH 16.7.83

The Townhouse

'Opened 1868' it says above the door on the corner of this much-changed Victorian public house. Opened that is towards the end of the development of Harwell Street back in the 1860s. Nothing more than a beerhouse for the first half of its life to date, the 'Townhouse' is perhaps better known to most Plymothians as the 'Cardiff Arms'. Visible for the last twenty years or so to traffic travelling north along Western Approach the 'Cardiff Arms' was, before the War, anything but a townhouse; rather it was a little corner boozer in the middle of an extensive residential area and directly opposite the cleaning sheds of the Great Western Railway on the line that, until recently, ran down the western side of Harwell Street across the bridges at King Street and Union Street to Millbay Station opposite the Duke of Cornwall. Today it is hard to believe that such a major piece of railway ever existed here, or indeed that Harwell Street used to run all the way down to King Street along with its parallel neighbours Well Street and Tracey Street.

In 1973 Joseph Uren took over the 'Cardiff Arms' from Dusty Miller. A keen boxer and ex naval CPO, Joe had acquired a taste for the licensing trade at the 'Burton Boys'. However, when the Urens moved here his wife, Ethel, didn't drink and was a staunch non-smoker and non-gambler. And yet when Joe died 5 years later Ethel stayed on and was still here in her early seventies almost 30 years later.

A popular Blundels beerhouse during the war, the 'Cardiff Arms' was near two air-raid shelters and was a regular place for a headcount after the many bombing raids. Popular with sailors too, the Cardiff understandably attracted a lot of visiting Welshmen. (Quite why it was ever called the 'Cardiff Arms' no one seems to know.

Cardiff Arms Park just south of Cardiff Castle is the well known home of Welsh rugby football and Glamorgan's County Cricket.) One particular crowd of Welsh patrons during the war were the crew of the ill fated *Charybdis* which was torpedoed just outside Plymouth after the men had spent a very happy night here. Only one or two came back to tell the tale.

Ethel Uren left the 'Cardiff Arms' herself in 1971. Neither her daughter Joan nor her son Joseph followed her into the trade as by this time one had married a chemist, David Toy, now on the Barbican and the other had become a chemist, now on the Ridgeway at Plympton. John, then Queenie, Walker ran the pub for the next 13 years during which time the Buffs (ROAB Club) who had met here for some time, continued to assemble regularly. Then late last year Courage decided to give the 'Cardiff Arms' a facelift. In the process they negotiated with the Council to lease the building next door and now the restyled pub occupies two sites. The bar itself is in the half leased by the Brewery and the main drinking area, which has been very attractively refurbished, is owned by the Brewery. Much enlarged, the erstwhile 'Cardiff Arms' is now a very comfortable pub with timber alcoves and corners and new 'old' fireplaces giving it a domestic feel. With the new developments on the other side of Western Approach there can be no denying that this is no longer a tucked away local but indeed a 'Townhouse'.

Run since May this year by Eric and Viv Alford, having now got a beer garden all they're waiting for is the sun!

[*WEH* 3.8.85

The Duke of Cornwall

The Duke of Cornwall . . . 'is an excellent example of freely-treated Modern Gothic, differing in style from any other building in the town, and exceedingly picturesque.

'The skyline is remarkably effective, thanks to the happy way in which the roof and chimneys have been treated . . .' so wrote R. N. Worth in 1878 in a description that is almost as true today as it was then.

Built in 1865 by 'Honest John' Pethrick of Hall and Pethrick, from the designs of Charles Forster Hayward, the 'Duke' was commissioned by Railway Directors, who were at the same time responsible for the erection of the Albion Hotel which later took over the site of the old Eye Infirmary and, in 1904, became the Albion and Continental. Today the older name is remembered in the Continental's Albion Bar.

These two grand hotels were then both built to service the busy Millbay Railway Station which had been completed in 1849. By all accounts however, the station itself was never particularly grand. W. H. K. Wright in 1879 described it as being neither an 'elegant' nor 'commodious structure' adding, 'For many years the "shabby shed" at Millbay has been a byword, and it was hoped that the Great Western Railway, on coming into the west, would have added to their other improvements, a new station;

but they have determined otherwise.'

Millbay Station nevertheless received passengers up until 1941 when, along with Mutley Station it was closed to such human traffic. It was, however, used as a goods line until 1971 when it was finally closed down and not long after demolished.

Today only its wall and railings remain and the flattened tarmacadamed site now houses those bizarre white, blue striped blisters which, among other things, are called airdomes.

Behind the 'Duke' once stood the Church of St. James-the-Less. A somewhat sorry religious building, St. James-the-Less literally took a long time to get off the ground.

Constituted in 1847 (the year after St. James-the-Great at Devonport which was also designed by J. Piers St. Aubyn) this church was not consecrated until 1861 and was still not fully completed by 1879.

During the Second World War St. James-the-Less fell victim to the same series of bombing raids that devastated Charles Church and its Mother Church, St. Andrews.

After the war, St. James-the-Less was rebuilt, not here but at Ham and this site became the home of St. Andrew's Primary School.

[*WEH* 2.10.82

The Continental

In the first half of the last century there was little in the Millbay area around here save for Barracks, Prisons and a Soap Manufacturers. The building of Union Street in the late 1820s saw the rapid development of what was then the western extremity of Plymouth; development that stepped up a further gear when the increased use of Millbay Docks led the Great Western Railway Company to place their Plymouth terminal here and not in Sutton Harbour.

Logic dictated that where there were great numbers of people arriving and departing by train and boat there would also be a fairly good number of travellers looking for accommodation. Millbay Station was opened on the 4th April 1849 and by 1865 the Duke of Cornwall had been completed with a board of directors made up (with one exception) of various Railway Company Chairmen and Directors. Within another ten years the Albion Hotel had opened on the other side of the road, right next door to the station.

Meanwhile neighbouring on the Albion's eastern side was the Royal Eye Infirmary. This had been here since 1844 when, on moving from Westwell Street, this worthy institution had taken over what had formerly been an isolated Georgian dwelling known as Buckland House. Much adapted and expanded by 1900, the premises had become too small to house the Eye Infirmary and it moved to a new purpose-built home, ironically just along from the railway station that ultimately superseded Millbay, North Road.

No sooner had the Royal Eye Infirmary moved out than George Fowler, who had held the Albion Hotel for nearly twenty years, had expanded into the building and opened it up as Fowler's Hotel. A year or two later however the whole site had been redeveloped and the imposing edifice that we see here had been built on to the

Albion. By 1904 the two were in business under the collective banner of the Albion and Continental Hotels. The Victorian 'Albion' is seen as the lower western wing of the present Continental block and stood originally alone as an impressive square construction. The name Albion survived until the early 1930s. In the hands of Trust Houses Ltd., for some 50 years, the block was eventually sold by them in 1970 when it was bought 'for an undisclosed sum' by the Hastings based firm Hickmet Hotels Ltd. Trust Houses meanwhile opened the Mayflower Post House on the Hoe.

Over the next few years attempts were made to bring evening as well as overnight guests into the Hotel with the staging of a regular 'West End' type revue known as the Tavern in the Town. Featuring singers, dancers and musicians, one former Tavern regular, Douglas Mounce, then billed as a 'comedian-impersonator' can now be heard daily as one of the main attractions on BBC Radio Devon.

In 1977 the Hotel, after spending three years in the hands of the official receivers, was sold again and the new purchasers were the Plymouth Hotel Company, the same firm that had set up (and still hold) the Duke of Cornwall over 100 years earlier. Their tenure, however, was also a comparatively short one as last year the Continental changed hands once more. This time going to a man who, over the last 25 years, has built up an impressive reputation in the city's catering and leisure business world—Steve Hajiyianni—who, together with Andrew his brother, has recently spent over a million pounds restructuring and restyling the inside of this prominent city landmark. And now, appropriately enough, as it is in the hands of a man who came to Albion (the ancient name for England) originally from Greece, the Hotel has been rechristened the New Continental.

[*WEH* 22.6.85

Millbay Docks

Taking its name from the tidemills at its north east corner, Millbay was a natural inlet in a rural setting until 1756 when John Smeaton, in order to set up a base for the workings of the Eddystone lighthouse, cleared a channel and erected a little wooden jetty in the bay's south west corner.

Eighty-four years later, the West Hoe quarryman Thomas Gill obtained an Act of Parliament to build what is now Millbay Pier. Soon after its completion the Millbay authorities scored a victory over Sutton Harbour when the way was cleared for them to be the first to link a dock in the area with the railway.

And so in 1846 the Great Western Dock Co. was formed, eleven years later the Great Western Docks were opened, built from plans drawn up by I. K. Brunel at 'a cost little short of a quarter of a million sterling.'

To cover the opening the Illustrated London News sent down a reporter and artist.

Quoting the article we read that:

'. . . although the occasion was allowed to pass with little of the ceremonial observances with which the completion of the works of such magnitude are sometimes honoured, there can be no doubt that the undertaking is one which is calculated to promote the commercial interests of the metropolis of the west in a greater degree than any other enterprise which has marked the history of Plymouth'.

Sad to say more than 100 years later when Millbay Docks is again the scene of an enterprise that has great potential for promoting the city far and wide there still aren't as many of the ceremonial observances as there might be:

The dock will be busy all next week, however, as yachts, TV crews and the Press converge there in preparation for next Saturday's start of the Round Britain and Ireland Race.

[*WEH* 3.7.82.

The Grand Theatre

On the 26th of December, 1889, the Grand Theatre in Union Street opened with the production of the Christmas pantomime *Cinderella*, or as it was then otherwise called, *The Desperate Demon's Direful Doings and Cupid's Careful Cautious Cooings*.

The theatre, which had been built in 16 weeks on the site of Snawden and Co., a cabinet manufacturing business, then had the biggest stage west of Bristol.

The man responsible for its construction was Henry Reed, son-in-law of J. R. Newcombe, the late manager of the old Theatre Royal. Reed had been somewhat put out when he failed to get the lease of the Royal on Newcombe's death and wasted no time in setting up in competition.

The first night of *Cinderella* was one of great excitement, particularly as the council had only granted a licence to the theatre the day before. Crowds flocked to Union Street, many paying an extra sixpence on top of their ticket prices to gain admission by the 'early doors' and many being turned away.

Small wonder then that the first words spoken to the 1,300-strong audience were . . . 'You little imps, what's all this row and riot . . .? I'll knock your heads off if you do not keep quiet.' Acted in 17 scenes, several with a local flavour—Cremyll Beach, Mount Edgcumbe, Devonport Market—*Cinderella* was a great success and pantomimes remained the prime attraction at the Grand, although plays, operas and performers such as Henry Irving, Charlie Chaplin, Harry Lauder and Randolph Sutton at one time or another, graced its stage.

Opened and closed many times down the years the Grand suffered from competition from other theatres, notably the neighbouring Palace, which opened almost 10 years later.

It made the change to cinema not long before the war, during which its dressing-rooms were largely destroyed and although the rest of the building was substantially intact it never opened again.

However, there were plans as late as the 1950s to 'rebuild' it and in 1951 the City Council agreed to protect the Grand until 2001.

Sadly the driving force behind the scheme most likely to succeed, Mr. E. F. H. Davey, a part owner, was advised by his doctor to avoid too much anxiety and hard work and so the theatre was sold and in 1963 it was pulled down.

All that remains today is the name, preserved in the pub next door. Originally the 'Foresters Arms', this public house had its name changed to the 'Grand Theatre Hotel' back in 1889, when Mr. Reed's wife took over its licence.

Itself subject to changing fortunes over the years the 'Grand Theatre Hotel' took on a new lease of life this summer with the arrival of its new tenants, Kaye and Brian Hobbis.

After several months hard work they managed to strip some 100 years' worth of paint off all the original woodwork around the bar and walls and clean up the original tile panels inside on the walls, on the porch floor and on the pub façade, so that today the refurbished 'Grand Theatre' has perhaps recaptured more successfully than any other local pub much of its original Victorian glory.

[*WEH* 17.12.83]

The New Palace Theatre

Completed in September, 1898, at a cost of £98,000 (£185,000 if you included the purpose built hotel next door) the New Palace Theatre was a magnificent addition to Union Street—the street that then linked the three separate towns of Plymouth, Stonehouse and Devonport; it was also the first theatre in the area to be built to cater specifically for the celebrated Music Hall Acts that were filling houses all over the country.

As it stands today, comparatively little has changed in this marvellous entertainment emporium. Its distinctive handmade Italian tiles still dominate its exterior together with the fine, slightly faded, representations of Sir Oswald Brierley's Spanish Armada pictures. The original wrought iron canopy has been replaced, but I gather that it's still around and could even be restored one day.

In its 84 year history the Palace has seen a great many famous faces grace its stage; before the Great War, Marie Lloyd, Harry Tate, Harry (Any Old Iron) Champion, Florrie Forde and the Ten Loonies all walked the boards and later Lillie Langtry, Max Miller, Robb Wilton and Dick Henderson (snr) played here; so too did such divers names as Louis Armstrong, Gracie Fields, Laurel and Hardy and Anna Pavlova the great ballet dancer.

The history of variety entertainment has however been a chequered one this century; first hit by the cinema then the radio, then winning audiences back by presenting radio stars live—variety ultimately lost audiences in a major way with the advent of television in the 1950s.

Dwindling audiences then saw this magical palace resort to all manner of entertainment in a fight for survival, culminating in an all-time desperate spell when it functioned only as a bingo hall and strip club.

Today of course, its future is still no by means secure, however, the prospect of its closing down for good must surely be unthinkable. Since its extensive redecoration in 1978 the Palace has repeatedly proved itself to be an excellent venue for all kinds of stage production—pantomime, pop, drama and variety.

Plymouth has already lost too much of its pre-war heritage and a place such as this, that has given so much pleasure to so many people deserves a better fate.

Amateur actors are as important to their art as amateur footballers or amateur artists of any kind—and quite often more entertaining. So let's hope that the Carmenians *Annie Get Your Gun* is a better indication of the Palace's future than the not untypical revue that took the boards some 25 years ago—starring the glamorous Julie and 'Funny Face' Alec Pleon and billed as the most talked about show of the year, it was called *Fanny Get Your Fun.* »Postscript

[*WEH* 6.11.82.

The Longroom Inn

Well over 150 years old itself the 'Longroom Inn' takes its name from a building some 50 yards away that a little over 200 years ago was not only the most impressive building in (East) Stonehouse, it was virtually the only one.

Constructed around the middle of the eighteenth century, for 50 years or so this was one of the most fashionable centres of social life in the area and one to which 'all genteel company never failed to resort from both Dock and Plymouth'.

Here 'on all Birth Nights and other Public Seasons', balls, concerts and assemblies would be held as well as 'every Thursday during the summer season.'

To ensure that these affairs never got too out of hand the Longroom had a simple set of rules, one of which, Rule VII desired that on 'Public Days Gentlemen should not wear swords in the room'.

These were the days when Millbay was just a bay and there was a tree-lined walkway which led from the Longroom to 'a Machine to bathe in the open sea.'

In 1780, however, Lord Edgcumbe who owned most of East Stonehouse (his own Edgcumbe Estate being part of West Stonehouse) sold a substantial part of it to the Marines who immediately began work on a new Barracks.

With initial work conducted off Barrack Street, which last century was swallowed up in the new Barracks extension to the edge of Durnford Street, it was not long before wooden hutted barracks had been built around the Longroom which was soon taken over by the Marines. Used variously as a schoolroom, messroom and today as a gymnasium, the Longroom today retains much of its splendour.

Meanwhile, at the foot of Pound Street, we find the 'Longroom Inn', one of the first sights to greet visitors arriving off the Brittany Ferries and if they deign to stop at this long-established inn they're likely to find behind the bar one of the liveliest and certainly the oldest landlords in Plymouth.

At 72 Bill Puddicombe was already more than 65 when the recent retirement regulations were brought in and despite spending a good many years in the Navy he's already logged over 30 years as a publican, with spells at the Crown, Devonport and the ill-fated St. George's Tavern before coming to the Longroom in 1959.

A survivor of the 1942 Dieppe raid which saw thousands of lives lost, Bill was more notably one of the prime movers in the 1931 Invergordon Mutiny.

Then, a revolt, led by his fellow able seaman Len Wincott, ended up bringing the whole navy to a stop.

The Board of Admiralty subsequently revised their decision to drop lower deck wages from four shillings a day to three shillings a day, instead dropping it by only threepence which represented a cut of only 6 per cent instead of 25 per cent, which was more in line with the proposed officers' cut of only three per cent.

Wincott, however, was dismissed from the Navy and although he spent most of his subsequent days in Russia, his ashes were, according to his wishes, scattered in Devonport with among others his old friend Bill Puddicombe present and with the Navy's blessing.

Inside the 'Longroom Inn', however, you're more likely to meet young Marines and good darts players than men of Bill's rare breed.

[*WEH* 21.4.84.

RM Barracks Stonehouse

Work on the Royal Marine Barracks at Stonehouse began in 1781. The first guard, consisting of one sergeant, one corporal and 12 privates, was mounted there on 6th October, 1783 and by 8th December of the same year the Plymouth Division was in occupation.

Prior to this the Marines had been billeted on the Barbican, parading either on the Hoe or on the 'Parade' on the Barbican's New Quay.

The move to Stonehouse made the Marines the first real residents in the Durnford Street area, for with the exception of the Longroom, which was chiefly an assembly room, there were no other buildings in the area in 1783.

Indeed, on the evidence of an early print, in 1755, there appeared to be no housing at all on that strip of land, between Millbay and Stonehouse Pool.

In 1862, the colonnade was built between the two gateways in the barrack railings; it was furnished with a guardroom, an officers' guardroom and guardroom cells on the ground floor, with the orderly room, Paymaster's Office and Divisional Library upstairs.

In well over 100 years, the only major change has really been a very subtle one; originally the building was, according to the architectural fashion of the day, covered in stucco; today, as we see it this has all been removed, revealing the fine original stonework.

Gone too, sadly, are the performances of the Marines Band, 'justly noted' over 140 years ago even, 'as of more than common excellence' and forming 'a source of genuine delight to the inhabitants of the vicinity,' inducing them to 'promenade to enjoy their dulcet notes.'

[*WEH* 20.2.82.

The Vine Hotel

The Rabbis tell us that the fiend buried a lion, a lamb and a hog at the foot of the first vine planted by Noah and that this accounts for men being made ferocious, made mild or made to wallow in the mire, following copious draughts of wine.

Wine, the suitably fermented juice of the grape freshly picked from the vine, has been drunk in the civilized world since the dawn of history. Furthermore, since tracks first became roads, it has been deemed expedient by any wineseller to advertise his business to travellers, and so it was that one of the earliest recognized signs of such an establishment was a display of vine leaves or a bush.

Traditionally associated with Bacchus, the god of wine, it is believed that this sign was first brought to this country by the Romans and was soon after to be found in general usage. It was only as the population and travelling increased that there was any major need to distinguish between similar premises in the same area.

New signs then appeared as landlords put up their own distinctive sign or symbol doubless adding a name as the population became more literate. Today, of course, our society has reached an advanced stage of literacy and consequently many hotels, inns and taverns have, sadly, abandoned the traditional and formerly functional pictorial sign or symbol.

Fortunately not at the 'Vine' here at Admiral's Hard, Stonehouse. Easily recognized by all who travel on the Cremyll Ferry, which leaves from points along the thin stretch of jetty that runs west from here, it is not unknown for the sea to lap at its door. This was particularly so when the main door was sited at the corner of the building.

Last week's high tides again came very close and the cellar of the Vine filled to a depth of around 2ft as crystal clear sea water filtered up through the stone floor.

Known to have been the 'Vine' for at least 140 years, we find James Warren recorded as licensee here in 1844. At that time this was 22 Strand Street, and although little of Strand Street remains today it continued to house a bustling community until comparatively recently.

The 'Vine' became number 5 Admiral's Hard, just over 100 years ago, and thanks to the demands of the ferry boasts the largest adjacent free car park in the city. Not that such a facility concerns the draymen delivering to the Vine, for this is one local pub which currently takes its beer off the back of a horse-drawn cart.

Inside the 'Vine' the main changes over the last 50 years have been in the gradual disappearance of both its Service and non-Service personnel. The demolition of Strand Street flats and the disbanding of the Royal Marine Band have somewhat depleted its local trade although many exiles still drink here, coming from all parts of the city to do so.

Among recent licensees, few have had as many family ties with city pubs as Fred Pring who was here with his wife Doris, in the early 1960s. Coming from the old 'Cambridge', in Cambridge Street, they went to the Barbican's 'King's Head' for almost 20 years after leaving the 'Vine', brought up in the trade by his parents his two sisters, Olive and Amy, also kept Stonehouse pubs for many years.

In the mid 1960s Ron Sinclair arrived at the 'Vine', leaving for the 'Grenville' in 1974 from where he recently retired. He, in turn, was succeeded by Jeffrey and Thelma Sharples, from whom this is the first and, they say, the last pub they will ever run. Although their 11-year stay already makes them the longest-serving licensees here this century, they're not in a hurry to leave.

[WEH 13.4.85.

St. Paul's, Stonehouse

Nettleton's 1836 guide to Stonehouse describes St. Paul's Chapel as 'An edifice in the earliest Pointed Style, first opened for divine service on the 5th July 1831.' It then goes on to describe how finance dictated that the architect could not afford to be too lavish with the internal decoration but nevertheless . . . 'the building taken altogether, and particularly as regards the exterior (in any point of view), holds out a confident challenge to criticism.'

The architect was John Foulston and like so many of his works that survive around the city today this building reflects a certain grandeur evocative of a prosperous early nineteenth century Plymouth, Devonport and Stonehouse. John Foulston not only built in all three towns, he was also the principal architect of the road that connects Plymouth with Stonehouse and Devonport, the appropriately named, Union Street.

The development of Union Street in the 1820s was prompted partly by the increasing importance of Stonehouse. Following the construction of the highly fashionable assembly and leisure complex of the Longroom (1756) came the Royal Naval Hospital (1758–62), Stonehouse Bridge (1769), the Royal Marine Barracks (1781–3) and the Royal William Victualling Yard (completed 1835). Concurrent with these developments was the establishment of some very substantial local housing. The Edgcumbes, who had owned Stonehouse since 1493, started to develop Emma Place and Durnford Street, a street which in turn owed its name to the Edgcumbes' predecessors the Durnford family.

Before the Durnfords, incidentally, Stonehouse or Stanehus as it was known in Domesday was owned by the Bastard family who held it from 1086–1368. In 1086 however Stanehus was the smallest and poorest of all the local manors with only a single farmer. By 1830 the new fortunes of Stonehouse and its much increased population necessitated the building of a new church and St. Paul's was originally established as a chapel-of-ease to St. George's in Chapel Street.

Stonehouse had had two chapels back in the fifteenth century when St. Lawrence's had stood on Devil's Point and an earlier St. George's had occupied a site a little to the east of its two later successors.

The site of St. Lawrence's is now occupied by the Victualling Yard, however it is believed that parts of this chapel and the second St. George's make up the 'purpose built' ruins at Mount Edgcumbe.

The third St. George's itself was left in ruins after the 1941 Blitz in what H. P. Twyford described as 'one of the most freakish incidents of the city's damage.' The old church tower was neatly sliced in two as one half crumbled completely whilst the other remained intact. After this devastation the two parishes merged, becoming in 1954 the Church of St. George with St. Paul.

Today, however, 100 years after the increased local population had merited, in 1883, the creation of a separate parish of St. Paul's, a falling local population has produced new problems for the people of Stonehouse. As residential areas have been superseded by light industrial developments so the peninsula, despite retaining much of its more fashionable nineteenth century accommodation, has witnessed a steady decline in inhabitants. There has been no resident vicar here for some 15 years now and St. Paul's is today conducted rather like a daughter church of St. Andrew's. However, a thriving community project run under the Manpower Services Scheme is now providing an excellent 'lay' base for the church to build upon. The small but comfortable community centre created inside the church entrance six years ago provides a healthy focal point for a great deal of work and activity. So too does the excellent Stonehouse Community Magazine published by the church and delivered free to every house in the area.

[WEH 15.6.85

The Butchers Arms

Built sometime in the first half of the last century it is probable that the 'Butchers Arms' was constructed not long after the completion of the Royal William Victualling Yard outside whose gates the pub still stands.

Designed by John Rennie, who in 1821 had taken over the building of the Breakwater on the death of his father, the Victualling Yard sported five slaughterhouses just inside its main entrance on the right, 'so arranged that no less than 70 or 80 head of cattle can be slaughtered at one time if requisite,' it is from the proximity of these bloody chambers that the 'Butchers Arms' acquired its name.

Up until some 50 years ago there were, behind the pub, paddocks—receiving fields for the animals bound for this place of mass execution, and recent excavations on the site adjacent to the 'Butchers' revealed what was believed to be a tunnel through which the cattle were led, under the yard walls, directly into the slaughterhouse. According to landlord Michael Hunt this tunnel, which no-one dared explore, runs under the ladies' rest room of the pub.

Licensee here since 1982 Michael Hunt's previous pub took its name from an animal that would little interest most butchers as not only is it too fast to catch but there's very little meat on it—'The Greyhound'. That name has now gone of course and the pub, much extended, is now called 'Sippers'.

Meanwhile, a pub that has lost its name and its spirits is the 'Butchers Arms' in Barrack Street in Devonport which at the end of the 1950s found itself on the wrong side of the wall built around the Dockyard extensions of that time.

Older than the pub here at Stonehouse, I do not know whether that particular 'Butchers' ever sported a coat of arms on its sign but this one certainly doesn't.

Butchers as a Guild obtained a Grant of Arms back in 1544, quite what it is I'm not sure but the 'Butchers Arms' at Sheepscombe near Stroud in the Cotswolds has a sign showing two bulls heads on a shield either side of a pair of crossed meat axes with a boar's head above and a motif on either side.

The basic trade of butchers was first recorded in 150 AD and they were first recognized as a Guild in 1179, originally congregating in Eastcheap, London.

The present site near Smithfield dates from 1885, although the hall itself had to be rebuilt after wartime bombing.

In 1885 here at Cremyll Point, as it was then known, Frederick Barradell was landlord of 'The Butchers'. Come the turn of the century Jason Clogg had stepped into his shoes and just around the corner in January 1899 Alf Pearse was born.

Still a regular here at the pub Alf remembers every landlord from his childhood days onwards, from Mr. Pursey who had the pub in 1905 through a long list that includes the names Salter, Hartley, Clarke, Millet, Screech, Shepherd down to the present day Michael Hunt and in all that time the pub has changed little as indeed has the view of the Victualling Yard gate that you see from its front door.

[WEH 14.7.84]

Royal William Victualling Yard Gate

Work began on the Victualling Yard in 1826 during the reign of George IV. It was not completed, however, until 1835 by which time it had already taken its name from George's brother William, who had succeeded him in 1830.

So it's William IV's statue we see above the gate, a statue described in 1842 as being a most exquisite piece of sculpture and a good likeness of our late sailor king . . . the writer then added 'The ox's head and anchors over each side of the entrance deserve particular mention having been carved wholly of granite by a rustic sculptor.'

Indeed all the features of this impressive 62 foot tall entrance had prompted Nettleton's guide book of 1836 to state that, 'as a piece of sterling architecture, taken together, it forms a propyloeum worthy of the noble establishment to which it leads . . .'

The whole establishment being described in 1879 as 'a magnificent pile of buildings, erected at a cost of a million and a half of money, and covering no less than 13 acres of ground, about one half of which has been recovered from the sea, and most of the rest cleared by hewing away the solid rock' . . . convict labour was used in this excavation work. Architects of the yard were Sir John Rennie and Mr Philip Richards.

Apparently then little has changed here; still today 'immediately within the entrance are apartments for the police, by whom every attention is paid to visitors,' (Nettleton 1836 again); and still today we can take time from the clock, made in 1831, on the top of the Melville block tower.

[*WEH* 8.5.82.

Artillery Tower (Firestone Bay)

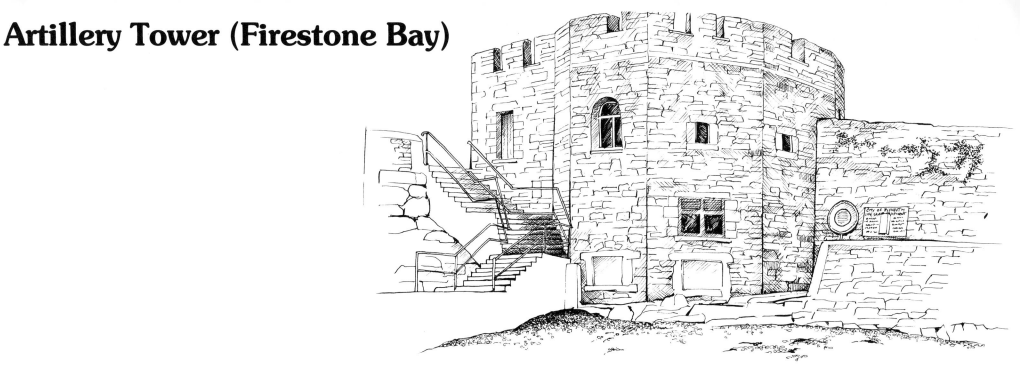

Fronting on to the beach near Devil's Point stands a seven sided fortification of uncertain age believed to have been built as part of Henry VIII's coastal defence system some 450 years ago.

The best surviving example of such constructions locally, others can be seen at Devil's Point itself, Eastern King's above Millbay and Fisher's Nose below the Eastern seaward corner of the Citadel.

Part extended last century it was later converted into a public lavatory by Stonehouse Urban Council.

Since 1981, however, there has been planning permission to convert the tower into a two-storey restaurant to cater for up to 60 people. Plans for the premises have yet to be realized but there is some work in progress.

As architect David Terry said when discussing the restaurant project in the Herald in 1981, 'Old buildings have got to be used and not left to deteriorate,' he added 'as far as we know it's one of the oldest, if not the oldest complete building in Plymouth.'

He was then quoted as saying that it dated from 'the early 1400s,' and thereby added his views to the many conflicting estimates of the building's age.

The Department of the Environment, 'on design considerations,' date it between 1485–1525, although they concede an outside chance of a date in the late 1540s.

A *Herald* feature of 1974 put it 'around 1512' whilst the catalogue of local listed buildings suggests 1537–9 and Sandford's 1828 Guide to Stonehouse says that it was built in the reign of Queen Elizabeth I (1558–1603).

Going back to the DoE official line, however, Mr. B. M. Morley, their inspector of Ancient Monuments said that this was doubtless, 'one of the private enterprise blockhouses of Henry VIII's time such as St. Catherine's Castle at Fowey and the earliest buildings at St. Mawes and Pendennis.'

C. W. Bracken, in his 1931 History of Plymouth lends support to this, referring to 'certain information that Henry VIII licenced Sir Piers Edgcumbe to build turrets and to embattle his manor house in East Stonehouse.'

West Stonehouse was across the Hamoaze.

Looking through the Plymouth Municipal Records we find the following entered under the period 1542–3 that 'the town gave two sets of harness for the war, and Edgcumbe made two new guns of broken ones for £4. Much outlay on defences'.

The absence of further information means that the implications of all this can only be guessed at. One thing, however, would appear to be certain, at various times during the late 1500s Drake, Hawkins, Raleigh *et al* must have all cast their gaze upon what would then have been a free standing castellated tower.

Strengthened 200 years ago (1779) when Lieut. Gen. Sir David Lindsey thought that the French might attempt a landing at Cawsand Bay, the tower has gradually been incorporated into the man-made coastline around Firestone Bay. Used as a coastguard station 100 years ago it is good to know that this important piece of local history is being tidied up and is going to be used again in some way.

Again quoting Mr. Slade of the DoE this is 'the starting point of a series of forts that gives the city a leading position alongside Portsmouth for defence works of national importance as surviving monuments.' »*Postscript*

[*WEH* 23.6.84

Mount Edgcumbe Park

'Lo! the proud Mount whose form in graceful sweep,
Curves like a forest rainbow, o'er the deep,
Which heaves all foamless round its sheltering bay.'

A proud Mount it is indeed, visible from many a point in Plymouth and here seen recently from Devil's Point.

Devil's Point was known until about 1850 as Cremhill or Crimble Point and for many years a ferry service ran from here to Barn Pool opposite, in the Edgcumbe or Cremell Estate.

Among those who appear, at one time or another to have made this trip from East Stonehouse to what was once known as West Stonehouse are the Edgcumbe Deer herd who are believed to be one of the oldest strains in the country.

Happening upon this herd is one of the many delights that have for centuries inspired artists and poets alike to sit and muse: the spectacular views, the wonderful planned English, French and Italian gardens, the orangery and then just off the edge of Barnpool itself, Milton's Temple.

Built by the first Earl of Edgcumbe Milton's Temple stands near the Amphitheatre . . . which is planted with exotic and other trees, forming a prospect such as has been described by the poet, in the following lines, inscribed within the temple:
'Over head up—grew,
Insuperable height of loftiest shade,

Cedar, and fir, and pine, and branching palm,
A sylvan scene, and as the ranks ascend,
Shade after shade, a woody theatre,
Of stateliest view!

An extract from Wrights 1879 guide which provides us with many timeless descriptions of this unspoilt area, few of which surpass the following—'On commanding emminences may be found terraces furnished with seats for the convenience of the weary; romantic zig-zag walks, intricate paths, laurel groves, fern clad dells, and fairy like bowers.'

Wright concluded his look at Edgcumbe by quoting in full Lord Lyttletons 1774 poem which tells of the Gods arguing over the ownership of Edgcumbe, a quarrel that went on . . .
'Till Jove, to finish the debate,
Thus spoke, and what he speaks is fate,
Nor God, nor goddess, great or small,
That dwelling his or hers may call,
I made Mount Edgcumbe for you all.'

And today that's exactly how Mount Edgcumbe stands; free and open to all, all year round.

[*WEH* 30.10.82

The Hamoaze

In 1830 in their extensive review of Devon, Messrs. Britton and Bayley wrote the following text to accompany an earlier drawing from here: 'The magnificent scenery displayed from the height of Mount Edgcumbe, may be partly estimated from the annexed representation of Devonport and the River Tamar, although no pictorial delineation can do justice to the view itself.'

And indeed today this view is every bit as magnificent and as elusive as it must have been 150 years ago.

Britton and Brayley continued: 'Immediately below the eye is that noble estuary the Hamoaze, with the men-of-war and other shipping laid up in ordinary; the Dockyard, with its numerous appendages, next engages attention; beyond lie the town and suburbs of Devonport, with a wide and beautiful expanse of undulating country bounded only by the mountains of Dartmoor' ... Whilst ... 'On the left, the Tamar rolls its silvery waters through a deeply-indented and sinuous upland tract.'

Today the Edgcumbe foreground has but little changed as Devonport, Plymouth and St. Budeaux have grown to meet each other. On the Cornish side Torpoint and Saltash have expanded too, the latter notably after the Tamar had been bridged here first by rail (1859) and then by road (1962).

All this while the cross currented Hamoaze has witnessed a great many changes in the 'men-of-war' that have slipped above and below its silvery silent expanse.

First referred to on paper in 1584 as Ham-oze, in 1643 as Hamwose, and then in 1824 Hamoaze, this name is of uncertain derivation; while commonly believed to have come from Ham—a village or perhaps inside bend of a knee, and the Celtic 'usig', hence 'ooze' 'oaze' or 'wase' meaning end of a tidal river.

The theory has been advanced by the Reverend Worthington Jukes that the name perhaps has a much longer history. In the Hebrew bible the word 'hammoaz' occurs twice—here the 'h' is the definite article 'the,' and the 'moaz' is a fortress.

With appropriate biblical references being made to the Phoenician ports of Tyre and Sidon, Worthington Jukes backs up his theory by suggesting that the Phoenicians, who 3,000 years ago, almost certainly shipped tin out of Cornwall (itself a name with semitic roots) would most likely have erected a fort at the mouth of the river they used for such trading and that, with the passing of the fortress and of time, the adjacent stretch of water would tend to become known locally by the same name.

[*WEH* 11.9.82.

Drake's Island—from Mount Edgcumbe

One of the most curious and attractive follies on our doorstep is undoubtedly that construction known for centuries as the 'Ruins' at Mount Edgcumbe.

Believed to have been built from the remains of two old Stonehouse chapels and a set of barrier gates, the Ruins were apparently erected some time between 1736 and 1755.

Basing our knowledge on contemporary paintings and drawings it would appear that a tall obelisk stood previously on the site.

Whatever else has stood here, however, there can be little doubt that visitors always stop to marvel at the peaceful panorama that breaks up that wonderful coastal trek through Edgcumbe's wooded walkways.

Looking around the Sound today, across to Drake's Island and Plymouth beyond, the view at first glance appears to have changed little; closer inspection shows us, however, just how much Plymouth has grown in a hundred years.

Drake's Island is less changed. Connected to Edgcumbe once upon a time by a ridge, now much eroded by tide and river flow but still partially visible at low tide,

Drake's Island was first referred to in 1135 as St. Michael's Island. It was, along with the chapel that once stood on its summit, later rededicated to St. Nicholas.

Since Tudor times, however, fact and fiction have linked the island with the name of Francis Drake in many different ways, a linking that in 1583, when a petition was sent off asking for Drake to be appointed the island's first governor, appears to have stuck.

From the sixteenth century onwards many types of gun and many hundreds of men have been stationed on the island but it was not until this century that its weaponry was ever used to defend the town.

It was not long, however, after its anti-aircraft guns had seen action in the Second World War that the Ministry of Defence decided to disband coastal artillery and in 1956 Drake's Island ceased effectively to be a military base for the first time in 400 years.

In 1963 it was released by the War Department and today the island is used as an adventure centre for young people and is open to the public.

[*WEH* 31.7.82.

The Italian garden

The Italian garden at Mount Edgcumbe is one of those delightful rare outdoor spots where time really does seem to stand still and it is not hard to imagine that little has changed in almost 200 years.

The fountain in the centre of the garden was a present from Lord Bessborough to Richard, the second Earl of Edgcumbe, at the beginning of the last century.

The females supporting the basin are called Caryatids in the dubious memory of the Carian women who once sided against the Greeks and lost, and were thereafter made slaves by the Greeks. Having instituted this ignominy in life they soon immortalized it in stone by producing building supports in female form, the most famous examples of which are the six on the south porch of the Erechtheum in Athens. This architectural whimsy was later revived in Victorian and Edwardian England.

The statue of Apollo, god of sun, light and prophecy in the middle of the terrace, is a replica of the statue in the Vatican courtyard—Cortile de Belvidere.

Hailed as the ideal of male beauty, this Apollo was originally sculpted in the 5th century and was purchased by Pope Julius II in 1503 after it was discovered in the ruins of Antium. According to art expert Adolf Furtwangler, the lower arm bent forward symbolizes the god's healing power, and his light vigorous gait his looking around to ward off evil.

More generally Apollo is associated with sobriety and rationality in life, aspects opposed by the figure depicted on his left (our right)—Bacchus, the god of wine. Festivals in honour of Bacchus are traditionally distinguished by their licentiousness and debauchery. The ancient philosopher Plato said that he had seen the whole population of Athens drunk at these Bacchanalian revelries.

The third of these statues represents Venus, goddess of love and beauty and sprung from sea foam. This particular Venus is a replica of the work believed to have been done by Cleomenes in the 2nd century BC.

It was dug up in 11 pieces in the 17th century from Hadrian's Villa near Tivoli. All ancient except for the right arm it was moved from the Medici Palace at Rome to the Imperial Gallery at Florence in 1680 by Cosmo III. In the niche underneath these three gods is a bust of the poet Ariosto, whose lines, inscribed below, are so appropriate to Mount Edgcumbe:

"Near to the shore, from whence with soft ascent,
Rises the pleasant hill, there is a place
With many an orange, cedar, myrtle, bay,
And every shrub of grateful scent adorn'd.
The rose, the lily, crocus, serpolet,
Such sweets diffuse from th' odiferous ground,
That from the land each gently breathing gale
Wafts forth the balmy fragrance to the sea"

The scent of oranges, however, is not so great as once it may have been as the orange trees that were once brought out in great numbers each summer, from the 100ft-long Orangery, 'a noble building of Doric order,' are today fewer, not so large and kept inside. With them inside today are a number of other plants and a pleasant café run by Bill Shepherd, who is known, to his wife at least, as William of the Orangery.

Thankfully, however, despite these little changes, this wonderful eighteenth-century building still retains its marvellous spacial quality designed by its principal architect, Lord Camelford of Bocconnoc.

[WEH 2.7.83

Edgcumbe Arms, Cremyll

'There are a few houses of various pretensions making up the village of Cremyll, the principal of which the "Mount Edgcumbe Arms," is an old fashioned well regulated house . . .'

So said Duprez's Guide to Mount Edgcumbe written well over 100 years ago in the middle of last century.

Today the description is just as apt only now the 'Edgumbe Arms' seems that little bit more old fashioned.

Built as the 'Passage Inn' (or 'Passage House') around 1730 when the Cremyll ferry shifted its Western landing-point from Barn Pool, the pub was, for a hundred years or so, along with the rest of Maker, part of Devon. In 1844, however, not long after the completion of the Royal William Victualling Yard, Maker was formally annexed to Cornwall and a borderline curiosity of many centuries standing was logically resolved.

Records of ferry crossings in this area from what was, until comparatively recent times, East Stonehouse to what in years gone by had once been the village of West Stonehouse, go back at least 800 years and as an essential part of the main route into South Cornwall there was doubtless an earlier 'Passage House Inn' at some time at Barn Pool.

When the current Inn became the 'Edgcumbe Arms' is not clear but it would appear to have been sometime in the first half of last century. Certainly it was the 'Passage Inn' when William Stenlake took it over from Robert Bunch at the turn of the century and the 'Edgcumbe Arms' by the time Elizabeth Graves was running it in the 1850s.

One reference (an 1850 directory) calls it the 'Edgcumbe Inn' but nowhere other than in Duprez's text does the name 'Mount Edgcumbe Arms' appear.

Indeed elsewhere in the same booklet there is an advertisement for the 'Edgcumbe Arms Hotel' boasting 'first class wines and spirits . . . with Guinness's Dublin Ale and Bass's Pale Ale available in Draught and Bottle.'

With a boar mounted on a wreath of oak leaves above a crest supported by two greyhounds the 'Mount Edgcumbe Arms' is undoubtedly a more correct title as the seat to which the coat of arms pertain today is not plain Edgumbe but Mount Edgumbe.

The pub run since 1971 by the affable Irishman E. G. 'Pat' Patterson is remarkably the only one that you can sit outside at a table and look out to Drake's Island and the Sound, watching the ferry boats come and go, with all the travellers passing by the toll-house clock bearing that immortal legend 'time and tide wait for no man'.

[*WEH* 10.9.83

Mount Edgcumbe House

Coveted by many, including the Duke of Medina Sidonia, leader of the Spanish Armada and, according to popular legend, Adolf Hitler, Mount Edgcumbe House has over the years had many famous guests.

In 1677 Charles II dined there; some years later the celebrated diarist Samuel Pepys looked in, in 1789 George III, his wife and children dropped by briefly, as did Louis Napoleon and the Empress Eugenie in 1871.

In 1902 Edward VII and Queen Alexandra attended a party there and the following year as Prince and Princess of Wales, George V and Queen Mary stayed as guests of the fourth Earl, William Henry Edgcumbe.

Today's incumbent Edward Piers Edgcumbe is the seventh Earl and succeeded to the seat in 1965 having formerly lived in New Zealand.

Edgcumbe House was built in 1550; in 1539 Sir Piers Edgcumbe had been granted a licence to enclose the grounds of what was then West Stonehouse and eight years later Sir Richard Edgcumbe, his son, engaged the services of Roger Palmer, a mason from North Buckland to undertake the building of the house.

Significant alterations and extensions took place in the seventeenth and again in the eighteenth century only to be almost entirely undone by the incendiary bombs that fell on the night of 22nd April 1941.

The main entrance and outer walls survived and after a recommendation by the Ancient Monuments Department of the Ministry of Works, the War Damage Commission agreed to replace part of the house. This work began in 1958, but the amount of money available meant that the house was restored rather to its original sixteenth century proportions than its rather more grandiose pre-war appearance.

[*WEH* 5.6.82.

The Edgcumbe Hotel

On the edge of Victoria Park, a few yards up from the old Mill Bridge, stands the 'Edgcumbe', a simple early Victorian hotel that helped make up the nucleus of the area around which the present Millbridge has been developed.

Predated by the 'Millbridge Hotel' by a decade at most, the 'Edgcumbe' stands on land bought from the Wise family by the Edgcumbes back in 1525. Then Sir Piers Edgcumbe constructed a tidal sluice across Stonehouse Creek which, at that time, ran past here up as far as Pennycomequick and on it built a bridge and mill operated by the flow of the tide.

As part of the deal Sir Piers had also acquired the rights 'in ferry and road'. However, the subsequent efforts of the Edgcumbe family to enforce these rights almost 300 years later met with major local resistance and it was not until the original grant was produced in court that a compromise solution was arrived at.

Mill Bridge then remained a toll bridge, despite the infilling of the creek to form Victoria Park, until 1924.

Meanwhile, the first recorded licensee at the 'Edgcumbe' was Edward Warden, apparently one of only three Victorian landlords here for, in the late 1880s, Benjamin Leatherby took over and stayed for over 40 years. Succeeded later by his son, Aubrey Leatherby for a long time he owned both this and the Millbridge and was apt to refer to them as top and bottom house.

During this time the 'Edgcumbe' was a free house. Afterwards, however, it was sold to the Octagon Brewery, later becoming first a Simmonds house then the Courage house it is today.

Albert Preddy then took over the licence in 1934 and was followed in 1938 by Les Weaver, an inveterate snuff taker, who became a special constable during the war necessitating the transfer of his licence to his wife, Gladys, in 1941.

In 1946 the Weavers moved to the 'Grenville', later moving on again to the 'Trelawny'. This left the 'Edgcumbe' in the hands of Wilf Phillips who, in turn, was followed by Leslie Frank who was here in 1951, the only year Bertram Mills ever staged his circus in Victoria Park.

A veteran of the Yangtse incident, Les Frank had been a petty officer on the Devonport-based *Amethyst* which, in April 1949, found herself unwittingly caught up in the final stages of the Chinese Civil War.

In the tense and tragic events which followed, many men were lost, the ship sustained much damage and despite naval assistance and negotiation, it wasn't until 31st July, 1949, that the *Amethyst* 'escaped'.

Les Frank, one of the few men to remain on board throughout, was awarded the DSM and in the 1957 film *Escape Of The 'Amethyst'* starring Richard Todd, Frank was portrayed by William Hartnell.

Meanwhile, back in the early 1950s, Frank left the 'Edgcumbe' for the 'Royal Naval Hospital Tavern' and Charlie Casterton began his 24-year stay here. In 1976 he, in turn, was followed by Peter Manley, now running the Salad Bowl in the market, and in November 1983 Mike Smith came here via the 'Breakwater' and 'Old Road Inn'.

Son of a Midlands landlord and an ex-Marine, Mike and his wife, Helen, spent many early courting hours in the 'Edgcumbe' in the early 1960s and are happy to be back in this village within the town.

[*WEH* 16.2.85

The Millbridge

For the greater part of the fifteenth century the Wise family owned the whole of Stoke.

But in 1525 they gave up the rights to the northern bank of Stonehouse Creek so that Sir Piers Edgcumbe, the new owner of Stonehouse, could construct Mill Bridge and 'certain corn mill upon the said work'.

Known also as Stoke Damerel Fleet and Deadlake, this part of Stonehouse Creek, now infilled to form Victoria Park was at various times last century called Mill Creek or Mill Lake.

The Bridge itself was improved almost 180 years ago after a controversial legal battle.

In 1807 the Edgcumbes decided, 'for the first time within the memory of Man', to impose tolls on the bridge and a gate was duly erected.

This caused a huge public outcry and the Mayor and corporation with a large crowd marched to the site to claim public right.

On arriving they dismantled the gate and threw it in the creek.

Whereupon 'the owner of the mill waxed wroth and made use of improper language to the Mayor, who fined him on the spot'.

In the subsequent court wrangle it was established that whilst the owners had been lax in enforcing their right, they were entitled to do so, so a compromise was reached whereby pedestrians went free and horses and vehicles were chargeable.

The potential income from this prompted major repairs to the bridge and led to a much improved road between 'Plymouth, New Passage and Stoke'.

Throughout the nineteenth century then Molesworth Road and the areas off it saw much development and we find record of the 'Edgcumbe Hotel', just up from the 'Bridge', from the 1860s and from the 1850s the 'Millbridge Hotel'.

Both inns have had landlords who have had spells longer than 34 years behind the bar.

Benjamin Leatherby was at the 'Edgcumbe' from 1888 to 1933 and ended his service at the Millbridge whilst Harry Wills (a name familiar to off-licence patrons in Wilton Street) was at the 'Millbridge' from 1870–1907.

Chasing such records, however, is current 'Millbridge' licensee Jack Mitchell who together with his wife Phyl has been here since 1950 and is the longest serving landlord in one pub in Plymouth today.

A cooper by trade Jack Mitchell began his apprenticeship, interrupted by a wartime spell in the Fleet Air Arm, in 1936 with Plymouth Breweries at Stonehouse, just 10 feet from the place of his birth.

Jack worked for only a few years exclusively as a cooper before coming to this 'Popplestone Inn' in 1950.

One of half a dozen Pop's Houses (the 'Crown', the 'Ship', the 'Opporto', 'Jubilee' and 'Picken's Bar' were others) Jack as their first tenant here was able to stock whatever ales he chose and at one time he had 10 draught beers on sale including Plymouth Breweries Bitter and Beer, Bass's Pale LD and No. 6 Mild, Octagon Brewery Beer, Tivvy Beer, Simmonds Heavy, Younger's No. 3 and McEwans.

He also carried a dozen different kegs and a large range of bottled beers.

Some time ago taken over by Watneys, draught Ushers is the beer drinkers tipple today.

Meanwhile, Jack has established over the last 13 years a new reputation for the pub, and it's now considered to be one of the best pub jazz venues in the South West.

Here the Climax Jazz Band appear on Friday nights whilst at other times Hefty Jazz have had residencies here and any Friday night you may find some celebrated jazz musician guesting with the band. As Rod Mason, Keith Smith, Bobby Fox, Ian Wheeler, Pete Allen and many others have done..

Incidentally if you admire the classic paintings on the walls here, they are indeed 'originals' painstakingly recaptured by Jack's brother Stanley, a fine English artist in his own right.

[WEH 6.10.84

Ha' penny Bridge

In 1767 an Act was passed in Parliament (George III VII Cap 73)—'for building a bridge cross Stonehouse Creek from Stonehouse to Plymouth Dock, in the County of Devon'. Up until this time men, women, children and all had been transported from one side to the other in a boat with its 'pilot' moving his craft by pulling on ropes laid across the creek.

The men empowered to build this new bridge were George Lord Edgcumbe and Sir John St. Aubyn and the man they chose to design this construction was the man who some seven years earlier had witnessed the completion of his pioneering lighthouse on the Eddystone Rocks—John Smeaton.

Yorkshire born in 1724 John Smeaton was a careful and innovating engineer and it is to his credit that we can still look today on his lighthouse relocated on the Hoe 100 years ago, only because the Eddystone Rocks on which it stood became unstable, and this bridge, strengthened and widened in the mid 1960s only to accommodate a greater flow of traffic than the man could ever have envisaged.

Completed in 1773 the bridge was opened for the public to cross in 1769. Access was by no means free, however, and from that year and for the next 155 that followed pedestrians were charged a halfpenny for the privilege of crossing.

Initially the toll was charged by men who stood in the open way and it was some years before a gate was erected, a measure which one account describes as 'leading to incidents which at times were sadly lacking in humour'.

The whole situation seemed guaranteed to bring out the worst in people and two nineteenth century guides echoed similar sentiments. 'At the Stonehouse end,' wrote Llewellyn Jewitt, 'is a toll gate, which is a disgrace to the authorities to allow to remain. 'It impedes the traffic, is an unnecessary and unjust tax upon pedestrians and carts and carriages; and is of no use to anyone except the lords of the manors who realize something like £2,000 annually from its receipts.'

Samuel Rowe, writing in 1825, some 99 years before the toll was lifted, said: 'Still it is a matter of surprise that the noble proprietor does not, with his characteristic liberality, relieve the public from this tax, as the greater freedom of communication between the towns would doubtless induce many artisans and others whose daily vocations call them to Devonport, to fix their residence at Stonehouse and thus enhance the value of his lordship's property in that town.'

His lordship did at the time indeed own most of Stonehouse and the most popular expression of frustration was in song:
"Lordy Edgcumbe, earl divine,
All the bakey fish are thine.
All the fishes off Penlee,
Lordy Edgcumbe belong to thee.
Lordy Edgcumbe, we are told
That you've bags and bags of gold
So lift the toll, for this is true
What's much for us is nought for you.
Lordy Edgcumbe, good and great,
Open wide the Halfpenny Gate,
For your credit and renown
Pull the bloody Toll Gate down."

Despite all the fuss, however, the civic authorities were slow to buy the bridge and it was not until 1st April, 1924, that Mayor Solomon Stephens toured the toll gates at Millbridge, Laira, Embankment and here at Stonehouse and set them all free.

Photographs of these historic acts took up over half the front page of the following day's paper and an unspectacular memorial now marks the occasion and the position of the Ha'penny Bridge toll gate. Seen here to the left, in front of the railings.

To celebrate its freedom a new verse was struck . . . 'In Loving Memory of the Halfpenny Gate'.
"After the years I've bled you
Of halfpennies to pass my way,
It's no wonder you are all smiling
Over my demise today,
I've took toll of your grandfather's grandfather,
Your grandmother's grandmother, too,
Also their great great grandparents
As well as taking it from you."

Today the traffic whizzes over what is left of Stonehouse Creek and the bridge survives where so many of its neighbours have fallen by the wayside.

[WEH 9.6.84

Devonport Town Hall

Situated at the end of Ker Street this strange and sadly neglected view has changed little in more than 150 years.

There has been some change in the housing to the left, but otherwise the Crown and Column pub in the background looks much the same as does the Town Hall, the Column and the bizarre Egyptian style building on the right.

These last three pieces of architecture are all the work of John Foulston who at 38 was appointed Plymouth town architect in 1810. Foulston was also responsible for the Mount Zion Chapel in front of the Column, a Hindu style building which has long since disappeared and on the site of which was built, in 1904, the recently closed Ker Street Infants' School.

The Town Hall was built in 1823 to serve the thriving Town of Plymouth Dock. With a population in excess of 33,000 the Dock was the biggest town in Devon, the population of neighbouring Plymouth itself was then just over 21,000.

Such was the basis for the Dock's claim to independence, which was granted and received from King George IV with effect from the 1st of January, 1824.

From this day forward the town of Plymouth Dock was to be known as Devonport, to commemorate this event Devonport Column was proudly built.

Foulston's original drawings for the Column shows a statue of George IV on top. Over the years this has intrigued many who have seen the old print.

Today, however, we see the column as it has always been seen, for in the 1820s the money for the scheme ran out and the statue never materialised.

[*WEH* 15.5.82.

Scott Memorial, Mount Wise

Robert Falcon Scott—Scott of the Antarctic—distant descendant of Sir Walter Scott and father of the naturalist Peter Scott, was born in Devonport in 1868 at the family residence known as Outlands.

At that time Outlands was well and truly outside the main Plymouth—and for that matter Devonport—town development.

Today its site is occupied by St. Bartholomew's Church at the Milehouse end of Outland Road. Outlands House itself was pull down just after the Second World War, having sustained a great deal of bomb damage; it had been the Scott family home from 1819 through to 1894 when financial circumstances forced the family to let the property.

Scott, however returned to visit it when in Plymouth and on the last such occasion, in 1908, he carved his name on a tree in the garden. In later years when the tree was felled this piece, nine inches long and wide, was kept and mounted in a glass case in St. Bartholomew's Church.

As a child the young Scott, nicknamed Con by his family, went to school at Stoke Damerel, a journey he frequently made on his pony Beppo, which he also used to ride out to the lower reaches of Dartmoor and gaze out to the great distant ships at sea. By the age of 13 Scott had joined HMS *Britannia* at Dartmouth as a naval cadet, thereby beginning an illustrious naval career that inevitably brought him back to Plymouth from time to time. For three years in the 1890s Scott had himself transferred to Plymouth to the torpedo ship *Defiance* at Devonport in order that he might be at hand to help his sisters and parents.

The moneys from the sale of his father's Hoegate brewery business had disappeared and left them in difficulties.

In June, 1900, Scott was appointed to lead an Antarctic expedition and later in the same month was promoted to the rank of commander. The expedition of 1901–3 in the *Discovery*, with 38 men, 23 sledge dogs, 45 sheep, 150 tons of stores and 335 tons of coal, gave Scott a taste for exploration that never left him and the comparative success of the trip made him the natural choice to lead a second, private venture—the main object of which was 'to reach the South Pole, to secure for the British Empire the honour of this achievement.'

Around the turn of the century there had been several other Antarctic voyages of exploration—Belgian (1897–99), British in the *Southern Cross* (1898–1900), German (1901–3) and Swedish (1901–4), but the Pole itself had not been conquered and it was a big blow to Scott when he learned in 1910 in New Zealand that the Norwegian Roald Amundsen was going for the same goal.

In the event, of course, that appeared to be the Norwegian's sole concern. Amundsen's party of only eight men and 130 dogs made Scott's *Terra Nova* party of 65 men, 33 dogs, 15 ponies and three motor sledges, plus a huge amount of scientific equipment, look positively cumbersome and although for the final assault Scott took only four men with him—Oates, Wilson, Bowers and Evans—they made slow time.

Just beaten to the Pole, the small party failed to make the return journey. Evans had several falls and died. Oates, frost bitten and weak, walked out never to return and the other three, when they could go no further, simply stopped and waited for the end—it was March, 1912.

Although they failed to achieve the main objective, Scott's expedition furthered Antarctic knowledge considerably and the moneys that flooded in when the news broke in England almost a year later helped set up the Scott Polar Research Institute and Albert Hodge's marvellous memorial at Mount Wise.

Here Scott gazes forever south, surrounded by scenes from his epic journey and the likenesses of the four men whose names are also preserved in street names around the old Outlands site near Outlands Residential home today—Oates Road, Wilson Crescent, Bowers Road, Evans Place and the ship, too, in Terra Nova Green.

[*WEH* 30.7.83

The Old Chapel

Standing on the corner of Duke Street and George Street, the 'Old Chapel', Devonport, has been used as a place from which to sell wines and spirits, virtually since it was a new chapel.

Largely constructed in 1790, the building was opened as the 'New Unitarian Meeting' in April, 1791, and in an account of Plymouth Dock (Devonport) published the following year it was said that 'under the Name of a reformed Liturgy, they use a constant Form of Prayer'.

This Meeting then was one of the many nonconformist establishments that appeared in Devonport around this time. There had been a Unitarian Meeting in Plymouth since 1662, but Devonport was just fields and the impetus for the building here was the rapid eighteenth century expansion of Plymouth Dock, as it was known until 1824, together with the fresh wave of Unitarian thinking that followed in the wake of Theophilus Lindsey, 1723–1808, who, in London in 1774, established the first (so-called) Unitarian Church in England.

Unitarianism is essentially a form of Protestant Christianity that rejects the doctrines of the Trinity (Father, Son and Holy Ghost) and upholds instead the personal unity of God. The term Unitarian was first used to describe followers of Transylvanian Bishop Francis David in 1569 and Unitarian ideas were first formally put into print by Faustus Socinus at Rakow in Poland in 1605.

However, almost 200 years later these views and views of other religious nonconformists were largely regarded as being anti-establishment: 'One could give vent to one's wish to disregard squire, parson and local magistrate by going to a meeting house'. (Arthur Warne, *Church and Society in Eighteenth-century Devon*.)

In 1791 three Unitarians were executed after a riot in Birmingham, while in Plymouth Dock, Commissioner Fanshawe intimated that any Dockyardsmen who attended the New Chapel would be dismissed as disloyal subjects.

The chapel struggled, it closed and was then sold only ten years (or 15, according to which account you read) after it was opened. Either way, by the time Unitarianism was legally tolerated in England, just a few years later, in 1813, the chapel was already being used as a wine and spirits store. Another Unitarian chapel, however, was built in Granby Street in 1829.

Exactly when the Old Chapel became known as such is unclear but it would appear to be sometime around the turn of the century.

Throughout the 1800s a number of businesses operated here as wine and spirit merchants—Rundle & Cork, Bundle & Sons, Davis & Co, Jefferys & Co, Chubb & Co, Rickard & Co,—and it was not until the arrival of John Barnes in 1895 that there was a reference to the 'old wine cellars'. Here until 1901 Barnes was succeeded by Messrs. Wilson and Staton before in 1914 two more Barneses were running the 'Chapel Wine Vaults', which later became the 'Old Chapel Wine and Spirit Vaults'.

Today simply the 'Old Chapel', its licensee is Roy Sheen and although outwardly looking much the same as it always has done, this public house has in recent years undergone many changes inside. With a bierkeller downstairs it has one big bar on street level, the stage has gone from its temporary home above the bar and in its great quadrangle drinking area video and late disco are the order of the day. And now Servicemen and Dockyardsmen, who once upon a time might have risked their employment by coming to this chapel, today risk only a clear head in the morning.

[*WEH* 28.1.84

The Ballast Pound

Two hundred years old, completed several decades before work ever began on the Breakwater, scheduled as an Ancient Monument last year and thought to be one of only two such constructions on British foreshores today, the Ballast Pound just off Torpoint is a pretty unique piece of our maritime heritage.

It was completed soon after the end of the American War of Independence, when three times French and Spanish fleets had assembled in the Channel poised to invade us, indeed, at one time a rumour went around that the enemy had landed at Cawsand and the Commander of the Dockyard contemplated setting fire to the yard to render it useless to anyone.

Since then the 1¼ acre harbour with its marvellous old walls of well-laid dressed slate topped with limestone coping and granite sets has for over two centuries provided a safe refuge for shipping of various shapes and sizes.

It wasn't very old, however, when it had outlived its original use as a Ballast Pound.

From about 1810 onwards pig iron replaced the traditional and unwieldy sand and stone that had long since been used by cargo-carrying ships as ballast when empty.

Still with a fair amount of shingle and doubtless several old rotten hulks lying below its muddy low water floor, there was at one time—according to a report in the Naval and Military Record of 1905—a proposal to cover the Pound and use it as a submarine repair yard.

Needless to say this did not happen and from the 1920s the Pound was leased by W. V. Reynolds Ltd., who bought it in 1971 from the descendants of the original landowners, Reginald Pole Carew.

Remembered fondly as a seaside pool by many locals and used for a time as a sheltered moorings for tugboats and as an area generally suited to the repair and shelter of sailing craft, the Pound was sold in 1979 to Michael Lane. A former estate agent now dedicated to preserving this waterside wonder that he has made his home, Michael now manages the Pound from his boat *Firebrace* a fine vessel that from 1961 to 1979 was in the active service of the London Fire Brigade.

Named after the London firechief Sir Aylmer Firebrace and now berthed in the south easterly corner of the Pound, the Firebrace has a pumping capacity of 4,000 gallons per minute and from here off Torpoint could throw a jet of water about one-third of a mile, that's almost across to the 'Swan' which sits directly across the Tamar at the bottom of Cornwall Street.

Low, square, and with a narrow entrance, this unusual listed building is now complete with an electricity, water and phone supply and is enjoying a new lease of life as a yacht harbour, a life that hopefully will bring it enough interest, attention and funds to help stop its tough fabric from further crumbling.

Already partly restored, unlike a lot of ancient monuments, this is no great tourist attraction and short of mooring fees, lacks any ready source of income and it would undoubtedly be a shame after all these years to lose this early reminder of quite how unsafe Plymouth could be as a harbour before the Breakwater was built. A time when several senior naval officials would have preferred to have seen Torbay rather than Plymouth developed as the safe haven of the West.

[*WEH* 1.9.84

The Swan, Devonport

Ships had been built, repaired and refitted in and around Plymouth for many years before the building of the Dockyard was begun and the boatyards at Turnchapel, Teat's Hill and Saltash all doubtless played a part in fitting ships to fight the Armada.

It was around this time that Sir Walter Raleigh suggested to Queen Elizabeth that the land on the eastern shore of the Hamoaze would make a fine Dockyard, but nothing came of it; just as nothing came of the proposal, made during Charles I's time, to site just such an establishment at Saltash.

The advent of William III, however, saw many new proposals and in 1691, after Parliament had voted £2 million towards the project, the building of the Dockyard began and the town of Plymouth Dock (Devonport) started to take shape.

The first housing to be built for the new Dockyard workforce was at North Corner and then soon after, parallel to the north wall of the Dockyard, North Corner (Cornwall) Street appeared.

By 1731 it had been joined by Fore, King, Queen, Princess and Granby Streets and by 1733 some 3,000 people lived in 'the Dock.'

In the description that accompanies the 1736 illustration above we read this of the new town: 'From ye nature of its situation on a Rising Ground ye East Side of a Fine River, about a mile from its opening towards ye sea and from ye Freedom and Goodness of ye Air, ye Streets being regularly disposed and broad, it is generally Allow'd to be as Agreeable and Healthful, as any town in ye Kingdom.'

Of the housing that remains at North Corner, the 'Swan Hotel' stands proud by the cobbled roadside of Cornwall (formerly North Corner) Beach. At one time one of five pubs on Cornwall Beach, it is found today opposite the 'Steam Packet'.

Landlords of the 'Swan' can be traced back to 1791 when John Kelly was recorded as licensee of the 'Swan Inn'.

(The pub is believed to have taken the name *The Swan* from a 300-ton sloop built in the Dockyard in 1766–7 and the present pub signs, painted by yours truly, are based on an 1807 watercolour painting of this *Swan* in action against two French luggers).

The year 1791 was historically an important year for other reasons too, for this was the year the Torpoint Ferry service began and for many years all passenger traffic ran from here.

Since 1927 the Swan has been run by three families, from 1927–48 it was that of Alfred Sorell; from 1948–75 was in the hands of John, then Janet, Johnstone; and since 1975, when it closed for five months it has been run by Harry, Paddy, Jane, Tony and Loretta Hartop, during which time its centuries old cellars have become famous for the splendid range of traditional ales now kept in them.

[*WEH* 16.10.82.

Ferry Road convenience

Many have gone already and the convenience seen here is today boarded up. There are possible plans to remove it and store it in the museum, but this is nevertheless a sad fate for what is a DoE listed structure and for what Henry Aaron described in his 1982 book 'Pillar to Post' as 'undoubtedly a superb example of a fast disappearing class of street furniture.' Its roof at that time intact, Aaron begged the question, 'Is this Britain's finest cast iron loo . . .?' and went on to tell us that, 'it is painted green and the remarkable external decoration is in very fine condition despite its age.' 'Both patrons and the local authority,' he said, 'are to be highly recommended for having kept the place in such a good state of preservation.' Made by James Allen Senr & Co., of Glasgow, with six 'Adamant' stalls this convenience dates from the very early days of British conveniences, most of which were cast iron and made in one of the Glasgow foundries. Superb examples of 'Victorian craftsmanship, eclecticism and imagination' (Geoffrey Warren from 'Vanishing Street Furniture' 1978) the design of these conveniences like the one here, frequently included a sunflower motif, the symbol of the Arts and Crafts movement of the 1880s.

Designed to be admired and respected the thought given to their construction is reminiscent of the Romans who decorated their latrines with images of gods and hallowed emblems to discourage the potential graffitti artist. To hark back to the Romans, however, is to give a false impression of the history of sanitation, for although the Romans had 1,444 public latrines in their capital over 1,600 years ago and had set up many in London, Britain generally did not introduce a proper street relief system until the 1870s.

With so many other things, as the Romans disappeared from Britain, so did a good many of their civilized innovations and for centuries our ancestors lived in the dank dark ages.

Although the first Queen Elizabeth had the first indoor flushing privy it wasn't until 1778 that Joseph Bramah produced and patented a revised water closet design—even then it took the development of large towns and improved water supplies to make such things viable propositions.

It also took someone determined to persuade the authorities that such sanitation was necessary and in as much as it is possible to single out one man it was George Jennings who finally proved that 'conveniences suited to this advanced state of civilisation were both desirable and practical.'

In 1851 after overcoming great opposition from those whom Jennings suggested could never have been in great need themselves, he installed his conveniences at the Great Exhibition at Crystal Palace. People were charged a penny a head and the whole exercise was a huge success, so spending a penny was written into the history books and the local authority annual accounts.

With fewer people travelling on foot today there is, perhaps, less demand but that doesn't mean people still are not going to be in need from time to time and doubtless the penalty for being caught in the act is higher now than it was back in 1965 when three of those wild pop stars, the Rolling Stones, were fined £3 each in Romford for what was then called a public insult, but then, what do you call it when you've got to go and there's nowhere left to go?

'VOT,' asked George I courteously, 'is ze difference between a public nuisance and a public convenience?' A question posed by Caryl Brahms and S. J. Simon in 'No Nightingales' (chapter nine) and a question that our City Fathers may or may not have asked themselves recently—as in their wisdom they have decided to axe over 40 per cent of the city's public conveniences, more or less on the grounds that they are too much of a nuisance to maintain. Vandalism, neglect and an apparent lack of demand has brought forth a call for the demolition of 29 of the city's 69 'Halting Stations' including this one off Ferry Road, Devonport and two similar cast iron structures at Venn Lane, off Outland Road and at Pennycomequick.

[*WEH* 12.5.84]

Torpoint Ferry

The Torpoint Ferry service began in 1791 exactly 100 years after building had begun on Devonport Dockyard and apart from its obvious geographic link with Cornwall the development of Torpoint and the ferry service was largely in order to accommodate the growing Dockyard workforce.

Ferry fares at that time were set at one penny for foot passengers, two pence for horses; a horse and cart was one shilling and sixpence and a coach with four horses was five bob.

Two 'floating bridge,' steam and chain ferries were brought into operation in 1834 and 1835.

It was not long, however, before it was found that passing in mid-stream could be dangerous and so one 'steam-bridge' was kept in reserve. A permanent double-bridge service was introduced in 1932.

As well as having been in the past a danger to each other, the Torpoint ferries have had in their time quite a few brushes with the Royal Navy.

On one occasion in 1910 the excuse offered by the Navy for one of their destroyers colliding with the ferry was that the ferry was moving too slowly for the pilots to tell which way it was going. Indeed a naval lieutenant once claimed that the ferry was simultaneously moving in both directions! The ferries have since flown a red flag at the fore.

The warship is the Navy's latest anti-submarine frigate, HMS *Brilliant*, commissioned last summer.

[*WEH* 13.2.82.

Paddle Tug 'Faithful'

This year will see the 25th anniversary of the launching of RMAS *Favourite*, one of six sisters to the paddle tug RMAS (Royal Maritime Auxiliary Service) *Faithful* which was itself launched on the 14th of June, 1957.

The five others that made up this very distinctive and well-loved magnificent seven were the *Forceful*, the *Griper*, the *Grinder*, the *Dextrous* and, first into the water on the 11th June, 1956, the *Director*, the vessel which subsequently gave its name to the whole of this little class of identical tugs.

Originally purpose-built for the close-to handling of aircraft carriers in confined dockyard spaces these tugs had tremendous turning abilities achieved simply by driving full ahead with one paddle and astern with the other.

As a fleet they shared their work around the great naval bases of Portsmouth, Rosyth, Malta, Gibraltar and Devonport.

The *Faithful* herself spent some four years in service in Gibraltar. With 60 foot beam, 710 ton displacement and full time crew of 19 these Director-class tugs were, however, a bit big by most standards and so it was no great surprise that as the great old naval carriers, with their vast protruding flight decks, were being phased out, the role of these curious paddle vessels came under scrutiny.

From January, 1980 onwards their days were numbered and by the summer of 1981 the appropriately named *Faithful* was the only one left in British service.

It was, however, only a matter of months before the tug which had accompanied the *Eagle* and the *Ark Royal* on their last voyages was herself to make her last working trip.

On Friday, 4th September, 1981, at 12.05 in No. 4 Basin, the *Faithful*'s 2,000 horsepower engines were shut down. She had just helped to take up the river the 17,000 ton Dutch replenishment vessel *Zuiderkruis*.

Many dockers came out to salute her and many sirens sounded in her honour. It was a grey day for her local captain Dennis Jell who had been with her on and off for 20 years and a particularly sad one for Bosun Derek Lord who had been with the vessel since the day he collected her from the Yarrow Yard in Hull in 1957.

Believing the boat to be good for another 10 years, speculation among the crew as to her future was rife and the skipper suggested that the *Faithful* might possibly be saved as a museum piece.

Fate, however, had in store a much less dignified future and soon the *Faithful* had been stripped of all useful parts and then some months later was quietly towed out to sea and used for naval target practice.

[*WEH* 12.2.83

HMS Drake

Blocks of the Royal Navy Barracks at Devonport were first occupied on the 4th of June, 1889, thereby providing land accommodation for men who had previously been based in old ship hulks once they had been paid off a commissioned boat.

In the years that followed further blocks were added, a clock tower built (1896), and then in 1903, after four to five years' work, the Wardroom was completed.

Described at the time as being 'probably the most magnificent building yet erected for Naval purposes', the Wardroom is built of limestone with Portland stone dressings. It was constructed at a cost of £80,000 with a further £20,000 being spent on furnishings.

Although for the greater part of its history the complex has been generally referred to as the Royal Naval Barracks, Devonport, it was initially known specifically as 'Vivid'. HMS *Vivid* was the name of the Commander-in-Chief's yacht, and that was the name worn on 'inmates' cap bands until 1934.

On 1st January that year the Admiralty approved a new name and on the 24th of the same month some 3,000 cap ribbons were changed. The change arose out of a suggestion made the year before by the then Commander, Jack Egerton, at what was the first of many annual Drake Dinners.

This dinner was held to celebrate the victory over the Spanish Armada and to pay tribute to Sir Francis Drake and his men.

On this occasion, however, the dinner created its own place in history by being that night upon which the change in Barrack name was first mooted.

However, although the name of Drake has been linked with the Barracks now for nearly 50 years there has been another name that since the 1920s has been more popularly used to describe the buildings.

On the 1st of October, 1911, Alphonso Jago was appointed Warrant Instructor in the Cookery, where he remained until his death in 1928. During that time Mr. Jago was responsible for a major change in the serving of Naval nosh.

This change involved a move away from eating in messes and a move towards eating in dining halls.

It became known as the general mess system and was officially accepted in 1922. The system spread rapidly throughout the Navy and it earned for what was then Vivid the nickname 'Jago's Mansions'.

This nickname stuck so well that in 1961, when the function of the Barracks became primarily one of accommodation and accounting rather than training and the name HMS *Drake* was adopted for all purposes, thereby dropping altogether the title Royal Naval Barracks, local bus conductors had to be officially instructed to shout out 'Drake' instead of 'Jago's Mansions' or 'Barrix'.

[*WEH* 11.12.82

123

College of Further Education

Twenty years ago when the old Devonport Tech. building was then part of the Plymouth College of Technology it overlooked the King's Road Goods Yard just down from the Brickfields here in Devonport. In May 1966 the Government issued a white paper entitled 'A Plan for Polytechnics and other Colleges' and included Plymouth on their preliminary list of Technical Colleges to be invited to set up a polytechnic. Within 12 months the now familiar 8 storey poly block in Tavistock Road had been opened. Providing higher education degree and diploma courses for students of 18 and over the new Poly set up left a large amount of less advanced work uncovered. Consequently the College of Further Education was established in 1970. Originally operating from more than 15 annexes all over the City, it was not until 1974 that the major part of the development we see here was completed. Administered and organised completely separately from the Polytechnic, the C. of F.E., now functions mainly from here, although there are still a handful of annexes. One notable outpost is in North Road West where some 60 full-time students work on a three-year course towards a Society of Chiropody qualification. The old Tech. building meanwhile now houses the Commerce and Business studies departments.

The recently completed catering block on the right brought a welcome move to the erstwhile staff and students of the College of Domestic Science which had merged with the C. of F.E., in 1973. Previously housed in premises that were a little too small and rundown in Portland Square, the Catering Department now enjoys superb accommodation complete with excellent views of the City and Sound. Opened by an Italian E.E.C. Commissioner, the complex was part financed by the European Social Development Fund and there is already a healthy interchange with foreign colleges; some students studying on exchanges with a college in Arbois in the French Jura mountains.

The work of the catering students can be sampled and enjoyed by members of the public at most times. Lunches are served five days a week and dinners four. However it is generally necessary to book for these splendidly valued meals and services. The Coffee Shop is perhaps more accessible but certainly no less popular and is perpetually busy with breakfasts, light lunches and teas. With 2,500 full-time students and up to 8,500 part-time students per year the large refectory in the main block, also open to the public, is likewise kept very busy. Students vary in age from 16 to 80 plus, with around 2,000 part-timers doing short courses, some perhaps just half a day, others maybe one day a week over a period of months or years. Yet others may study without spending any time here at all. A little like the Open University, there is now an Open Tech. scheme. The Electronics department have in fact put together a learning package which consists of a box complete with books, information, components and part-completed computer software which is in great demand and looks as if it could soon be financially profitable for the department.

Employing around 800 people, including 270 full time teaching staff, the College is not only one of the City's major employers it is also one of its major assets. With a range of courses from mechanical engineering through motor vehicle maintenance to to leisure, recreation, travel and tourism, there may be many people in the area who would be surprised to find out what it could offer them whatever their age, whatever their time available and whatever their qualifications or lack of them.

[*WEH* 25.5.85

Devonport 'Tech'

Inside the heavy, high original wooden doors of this proud, largely unspoilt educational establishment are two beautifully preserved brass plaques.

Doubtless passed daily by many over the years without being read they each have a story to tell.

The right-hand tablet reads thus: 'The erection of this schoolbuilding was commenced in the year 1897 in commemoration of the 60 years glorious reign of Her Majesty Queen Victoria and on completion, was on the 25th Day of July 1899, duly inaugurated and dedicated to the public use and benefit by the Right Worshipful Mayor W. Hornbrook Esquire in the presence of and with the assistance of Sir William H. White KCB, LLB, Dr. Sce, FRS.'

So the Devonport Municipal Science, Art and Technical Schools building was the town's way of marking the Queen's Diamond Jubilee. Just ten years earlier neighbouring Plymouth had in the same way celebrated the Queen's Golden Jubilee with the building of the 'Victoria Jubilee Memorial Science, Art and Technical Schools'. Erected on part of an old cattle market site at the bottom of Tavistock Road immediately below the Poly it later made way for, this grand edifice was demolished in 1966.

Technical Schools, unheard of before the nineteenth century, were a development of the Mechanics Institutes founded in Britain in the 1820s (Plymouth 1825, Devonport 1825, Stonehouse 1846). One effect of the Industrial Revolution had been to make aspects of science and engineering too sophisticated to be merely picked up by young men serving apprenticeships.

Elements of the new sciences could not simply be explained by somebody in the job themselves, rather they required a full time period of explanation—a full time teaching course beyond the 3Rs. In 1889 an Act of Parliament empowered local authorities to levy a rate to provide Technical education.

In 1892 Plymouth Technical School was opened, Devonport's in 1899 and when in 1914 the three towns were merged, the two joined as the Plymouth and Devonport Technical College. As the twentieth century put further demands on higher technical and practical education so the college expanded eventually becoming in 1962 the Plymouth College of Technology.

Then in 1966 Plymouth was included in the Government's proposed Polytechnics and other colleges list. Thus in addition to the New Plymouth Polytechnic we had in 1970 the College of Further Education and today it is the commerce and business studies faculty of the C of FE that we find here in the old Devonport Tech. in Paradise Road. Apart from in the basement where the modern sciences of Hairdressing and Beauty Therapy have been taught since the mid sixties.

Opening official Sir William White incidentally was made a Freeman of Devonport on that day in 1899. Born in Devonport in 1845, White was a highly distinguished naval architect at the time when the Navy was changing from wood to armoured ironclads. His controversial design for the 'Inflexible' later became a standard for warship construction for many years. He was also largely responsible for the designs of the Mauretania and Lusitania.

From 1898 to 1936 Devonport Tech also housed the Devonport Municipal Secondary School for Girls which upon its move to its present premises in 1937 became Devonport High School for Girls.

The other tablet in the entrance hall refers to the clock and chimes presented to the town by Ald. John James and formally dedicated to the use and benefit of the public on 8th September, 1898.

Sadly, however, the clock stopped some 5 years ago and although repairable a lack of funds, and interest, has deprived Devonport of one of its little treasures.

[WEH 14.1.84

The Alexandra Maternity Home

Always a time surrounded by mystery, excitement and anticipation the circumstances surrounding birth have altered greatly in the last 100 years or so.

The natural process itself of course, has not, but nowadays we rather tend to take our knowledge of this process somewhat for granted.

We have come a long way from the tribe discovered by anthropologists in 1899 in Australia, who did not even relate the sexual act to pregnancy and the subsequent birth.

Indeed the Arunta allegedly believed that spirits of the dead entered women at the moment that the woman first became aware of her pregnant condition.

They also believed that where this event took place would determine of which spirit the child would be a reincarnation.

In Fiji, meanwhile, in certain areas where things are little understood and witchcraft prevails, a woman might go off into the bush towards the end of her pregnancy—build herself a shelter, deliver her baby alone and burn the shelter before returning to the village to avoid being bewitched.

In civilized society such ignorance is rare and few taboos attend birth, however, it wasn't until early last century that there was anything like the 'Schools of Mothercraft', largely inspired by the teachings of Florence Nightingale.

For the poor in Plymouth there was a lying-in charity attached to St. Andrew's Almshouses and every married woman in it was provided with five shillings and a suit of linen for the child.

Following Edinburgh obstetrician William Ballantyne's report 100 years later in 1901, 'Ante-Natal Pathology and Hygienes,' national authorities began to apply themselves more fully to the situation and some hospitals began to establish special clinics.

Around this time No. 1 St. Michael's Terrace, Stoke, was standing empty. Occupied at the turn of the century by John Goldsmith, between 1905–15 it was vacant. Then in 1916 it opened as the Alexandra Nursing Home.

The next 50 years saw the 'Alex' expand, within a few years it had taken over No. 2, and by 1932, the year my father became one of the many thousands of Plymothians first to greet the world from here, it occupied Nos 1, 2, 3 and 5 St. Michael's Terrace and No. 4 soon followed.

By now some 20 per cent of Plymouth babies were delivered here annually although still more than half of the new arrivals in the city were born at home.

It was not long after this that the older part of the Home was knocked down making way for the new St. Michael's Terrace accommodation.

The Alex, however, was furnished with new buildings adjacent to the old Stopford Place end of the site.

By 1970 'at home' births accounted for only 17 per cent of Plymouth new borns, but the percentage share had dropped at the Alex too and only ten per cent (526) were born here, while Freedom Fields accounted for almost 70 per cent of all local births.

To date a handful of babies have been born at the Alex this year and Freedom Fields now handles nearly all confinements, but with developments at Derriford still uncertain the crystal ball is looking very cloudy.

[*WEH* 13.10.84

The Lounge, Stoke

One hundred and forty years ago Flintoff's Local Guide described Stoke as a village 'of growing importance, situate about two-thirds of a mile from Devonport on the Tavistock Road'.

It went on to add that 'within a few years several rows of excellent dwelling houses have been built, which from their healthful situation and extensive prospects have become the favourite abodes of military and naval officers and persons whose engagements do not require their constant residence in town'.

A growing area it was indeed and as new streets sprang up their names reflected the patriotic fervour that existed among the new inhabitants.

Walking up from the main northern route from Plymouth to Devonport in 1850 you could reach this inn by walking along Wellington Street, turning left into Waterloo Street, then right along Trafalgar Row before turning left again into Stopford Place, finding what was then called the 'New Inn', on the corner with Napier Street. All names, including Nelson Terrace further on, associated with Britain's involvement in the Napoleonic and Peninsular Wars of 1800–15 and 1808–14 respectively. Trafalgar (1805) and Waterloo (1815) were battle locations; Stopford and Napier lesser known leaders.

Sir Charles James Napier was in action at the Battle of Corunna in 1809, while Rear-Admiral Sir Robert Stopford had together with Lieutenant-General Sir Samuel Auchmuty, completed the conquest of Java in 1811.

Arriving then here, at No. 7, Stopford Place, you would find a pub that for the last 130 years has never really looked much like a pub. Indeed, going through the street directories over the years it's not always obvious that it has been such a place.

The first recorded proprietor here was a man by the name of Jarvis Grills and appears to have been followed by James Leverton, in whose time the place was known as the 'Park Inn', as it was some years later when W. H. Gillman took over in 1867.

Before long, however, it was to become known as Gillman's Wine and Spirit Stores and despite many subsequent changes of licensee this was still the name by which the licensing magistrates recognized the place in 1960 when Winnie Board enjoyed a brief tenure here.

Previously at the old 'South Western' and subsequently at the 'Two Trees' and since 1966 the 'Queen's Arms' on the Barbican, Winnie recalls that this quiet village inn did not suit her taste for a busy town pub. Rather like a large domestic sitting room, 'The Lounge' acquired its current name more or less as a nickname during Frank Boxhall's 25 years behind the bar. Here throughout the last war and up until 1960 'The Lounge' had no bay window in Frank's time, this being an addition of the early sixties.

Extended back through the old store shop and snug since, 'The Lounge' is currently run by John Cannan. Here the transition from a bustling pub to a quiet one could hardly be more marked, as John arrived here in 1980 having spent seven years at the 'Ark Royal', during which time he gained the pub a reputation for heavy rock music—today at 'The Lounge' there isn't even a juke box.

One thing that will get louder in the next few weeks, however, is the external decoration and new 'Lounge' signs will consolidate a name it acquired rather than was given.

127

Mowbrays Railway Inn

In 1792 two London wagons left Devonport or 'Dock' twice weekly. By the late 1830s increased demand for speedy communications and improved roads now meant that several stage coaches left for London every day.

The Subscription and Defiance coaches left every morning and the Standard every day except Sunday. There was also the Quicksilver Mail which left Devonport at 6 a.m. and reached London by 6.30 a.m. the following day, making it one of the fastest coaches in Britain at that time.

The reign of these flyers was to be short-lived, however, as the great railways, arrived and rapidly ran the coaches off the road. By 1849, only 20 years after Stephenson's Rocket had first broken the 30 m.p.h. barriers, the railways reached the Three Towns.

On a national level there was a widespread outbreak of hotels, inns and taverns either adopting the name 'Railway' or changing their names to 'Railway'. Generally within close proximity of a station or crossing and sometimes taking the name of a particular engine, there are two surviving 'Railways' in Plymouth. One in Albert Road, formerly Navy Row and 'Mowbrays Railway Inn' here in Waterloo Street, Stoke (a third recently became the 'Mutley Tavern', off Greenbank Hill). Joseph Mowbray was born in Penzance in 1821, and, by all accounts, was a foreman working on the railways in the Stoke area. An iron footbridge by Stoke Church leads into Waterloo Street and doubtless Joseph Mowbray crossed it many times as he was such a regular at the 'Railway' (opened in 1852) that around 1870 he became the landlord there. The story goes that many of the labourers working in the area were unpopular with some of the pubs so Joseph Mowbray decided to run one for them.

Some ten years before all this Joseph had met a local girl, Emma, and married her and 100 years ago we find husband and wife living here with five daughters, Annie 23, Celia 21, Alice 18, Maud 13 and Kate aged 9. After Joseph it was Celia Mowbray who took over the 'Railway' and she ran it until the turn of the century.

Since 1900 the Mowbrays' 30-year stay has been surpassed by the Burts. Robert Burt arrived here in 1915 and just after the First World War was succeeded by his wife who was still here in 1951. Since then a number of licensees have held the place, but only to sell beer and scrumpy for, as the 'Railway Inn', it was the last pub in Plymouth to gain a spirit licence.

That was about ten years ago, just before Ivor Field took over. Here for eight years, Ivor, who has in the past worked on steam trains, extended the pub and two years ago, after looking through the deeds, picked out Mowbray's name to add to the pub's title to save confusion with other Railway inns. As 'Mowbrays Railway Inn' then it was purchased by Devenish Breweries, their first and, to date, only pub in Plymouth and on 23rd December, 1983, Margaret Hall, a barmaid here for several years became the new licensee.

Now with Devenish's impressive plans to refurbish the inn as a 'coach and horses' pub the future of this erstwhile little scrumpy house looks as rosy as the cheeks of any cider drinker. »Postscript

[*WEH* 3.11.84

Plymouth's Youth Hostel

Perhaps the finest example of architect John Foulston's work to survive in anything like its original context and outward appearance is this impressive edifice off Devonport Road in the middle of Stoke.

Known as Belmont House, it was built originally for the wealthy Devonport banker John Norman in 1820, who then lived here for many years. It subsequently changed hands a number of times, although it would appear to have been in the possession of Alan Bone (one-time recorder of Plymouth) and his descendants from the mid-1850s through to the 1920s.

In 1948, however, it was acquired from the St. Aubyn Estates by the Youth Hostels Trust of England and Wales and has since operated happily as Plymouth's Youth Hostel with the Regional YHA Office here in separate premises in Belmont's spacious grounds.

In as much as any one man can be regarded as the founder of youth hosteling, the credit goes to a German schoolmaster, Richard Schirrmann, who opened the world's first hostel in 1910. Today there are hostels across the globe from Poland to Pakistan, Japan to the Phillippines, and Australia to the USA. And Plymouth's hostel is one of over 400 in Britain and some 3,000 worldwide.

With a turnover of patrons that would be the envy of any hotel over 9,400 'guests' stayed here last year, over 5,000 of them foreigners, mainly the French, Dutch and Germans from Europe, and Americans, Australians and New Zealanders from the rest of the world.

Offering very inexpensive basic, but adequate accommodation, washing and catering facilities, the Plymouth hostel, like so many, is a happy place. Its services are available to the 'young at heart'—there are no age restrictions—and single travellers or even families are all made to feel at home. A feeling enhanced by the fact that all guests are expected to perform one minor household chore each day.

The YHA's simple aims then—'to help all, especially young people of limited means, to a greater knowledge, love and care of the countryside, particularly by providing hostels or other simple accommodation for them in their travels and thus to promote their health, rest and education'—while perhaps not what Foulston had in mind when he designed this Grecian-influenced building, is certainly well suited to the purpose.

And although the city doubtless enjoys greater spending on the part of the town's wealthier tourists, many young hostelers return in later years to places they remember with affection, so Plymouth must be grateful to the band of individuals who work full-time for the charitable YHA for less than commercial wages. Even more sad perhaps in this case is there is so little of Foulston's work around in such good condition and so open to the public.

Well patronized and nonprofit making as it is, Belmont House, with so many of its original interior features intact, nevertheless requires a lot of money to keep it in good order, and regional secretary Peter Mitchell, himself a keen member, finds it sad that local authorities in this country are so much slower and a lot more reluctant to support youth hostels than their European counterparts.

[WEH 26.1.85

Stoke Damerel High School

Stoke Damerel High School is currently enjoying its last few days solo occupancy of this impressive flat-roofed stone-built building in Keppel Place, as from next September through to July, 1986, the remaining girls will share here with the remaining middle three years of boys from Sutton High School, in Regent Street.

A move necessitated by the future educational policy of the city, for Sutton, temporarily at least, this represents a return to a situation that existed some 60 years ago, as it was from here that they moved, in 1926, to form the present school with the Regent Street Boys. That same year the girls became, for the first time, girls of Stoke Damerel, having previously been known as Keppel Place Central School.

Prior to that, the school had been called Stoke Public School, but this name referred to an earlier building which stood on this site. Founded originally in 1819, 'for the education of 40 boys of Stoke Damerel,' Stoke Public School 60 years later had 'accommodation for 350 boys and 220 girls' and one Alonzo Rider, FCS, as its head, a post he held for some 35 years.

Demolished in 1908, this earlier building was replaced by the current one, designed by Thornley and Rooke, and built by A. N. Coles in 1909.

After the changes of 1926, it later became Devonport Higher Elementary for Girls in 1932, Stoke Damerel Secondary School for Girls in 1935, finally settling on Stoke Damerel High School in 1937, the year Dr. Margaret Stimson arrived to take over the headship.

Used as a hospital during both wars, little pre-war information about the school survives. All the official records were destroyed during the blitz. However, from 1938 I did find a copy of the school magazine.

From it I learned that parents participated in two of the sports day events. Fathers in the thread-a-needle race and mothers in the potato race, and that on Wednesday, 18th May the head prefect, Audrey Hosier, along with representatives from many other local schools, presented Her Majesty, Queen Mary, at Greenbank, with a purse to endow the Princess Elizabeth cot.

Not long after leaving the school Audrey Hosier could be found teaching younger children in another Plymouth school—Hyde Park—and it was there some 20 years ago that she first introduced me to the delights of studying local history.

Retiring herself just a couple of years ago, Audrey Hosier's last head at Stoke Damerel, Margaret Stimson, remained at the helm some 15 years, a stint only surpassed by Doris Dixon. Here, from 1959–79, Miss Dixon always liked to keep her hand in with a bit of teaching and in her time taught one or two daughters of old girls she had known.

A feat and a sentiment echoed by the current head, Maureen Green, who refers to Stoke Damerel affectionately as 'a family school' with 'a great sense of belonging as past staff and pupils will testify'. Certainly, while neither my father nor I ever went to the school, we can add to the family tradition in as much as at one time or another in our adolescence we both had cause to wait outside the gates, and doubtless there are many who for any number of reasons will be sad that my son will not have that opportunity.

However, in the two years of life that the school has remaining, Mrs. Green and her staff are determined to see that the school goes out with its academic and sporting standards held high for all to see.

[*WEH* 7.7.84

The Pear Tree

There appears to have been an inn on or around this site for some 200 years or more and at the close of the eighteenth century, one John Moore was recorded as licensee.

Now it is believed that then and for many years thereafter a pear tree stood in the garden of the pub. Doubtless this was the reason for the naming of the pub (after all, Plymouth has several pubs owing their names to association with trees—'The Cherry Tree'; 'The Royal Oak'; 'The Olive Branch' and 'The Two Trees').

The decision was nevertheless probably encouraged by the pear tree reference in the 'Twelve Days of Christmas' folk song which even then had been around for over 600 years.

Emanating from France, the song is thought to have been derived from the French troubadours or folk poets and was written to be sung on the Twelfth Night, the traditional end of the midwinter festivities.

These festivities have been celebrated throughout the centuries and even for the Anglo-Saxons, we are told, it was an orgy of eating and drinking, dice and song.

In the ninth century Alfred the Great made laws decreeing that no work should be done during this time; legal proceedings should be suspended and everyone should live in peace. Legend has it he even lost Chippenham to the Danes in 875 because he would not fight during the Twelve Days.

Come the age of Puritanism this fine tradition began to be eroded and while many people may, this night, give voice to 'The Twelve Days Of Christmas' most of those in employment will have worked some time in that period.

But back to the pub itself where an incident that took place many moons ago gave cause for the place to be infamous rather than famous.

It was in 1827 when the village of Stoke was a short distance from Devonport and had 'rapidly increased in extent and population since the close of the late war'.

The impact of war has always made an impression on the city and then it was not just the Napoleonic Wars but the 1827 British involvement in Navarino against the Turks in Greece.

Returning troops caused much trouble in local pubs and one night 'during a revel held at Stoke, men and women were dancing in the Pear Tree Inn with utmost good humour when a body of marines insisted upon choosing partners. 'After a struggle they were ejected but, returning in increased numbers, they cleared the room at bayonet point. The majority escaped by jumping through the window but one petty officer was killed and several other persons wounded.' Similar incidents occurred elsewhere around the town and several others were badly or mortally wounded.

In more recent times one man who died here through natural causes was the pub's last landlord, Norman Pengelly, who passed away on Christmas Eve, 1981, just two days before his sixtieth birthday.

In this steadily run inn, for nearly 12 years himself, he was preceeded by Reg and Freda Summerell, who arrived in 1952, soon after Gordon and Hilda Tregenza—here from wartime through to 1951 and parents of Gordon junior who soon after took the 'Fortescue' where he still remains as jolly as ever today.

Meanwhile, the current 'Pear Tree' landlord, Bob Fisher, is just about to clock up his third year here having taken over on 18th January, 1982.

[WEH 5.1.85

Blockhouse Inn

The shops, inns and houses that line either side of what was, up until recently, Tavistock Road, Stoke and is now Devonport Road, were built in the first half of the last century.

Originally part of a separate development known as Higher Stoke, it was some years before it merged, first with Stoke itself, then Devonport, then Plymouth.

Earlier maps still show the area as Stoke Damerel, purportedly a corruption of the old term Stockes (fortified place) and d'Albermale after the Norman, Robert d'Albermale who was given the land in the post conquest handout—hence Stockes d'Albermale, Stoke Damerel.

Sitting just below the highest point of the old Plymouth there has doubtless been a fortification here from time immemorial but the construction which consolidated the current name for this defence post appeared in the reign of George II.

Nicknamed 'Pattypan' the blockhouse was erected to fortify the town of Dock—the old Devonport. Completed in 1758, the original buildings on top were destroyed by fire in 1855, since when the Blockhouse has been variously used, most recently as an air defence position.

In an area of public parkland and sometimes referred to as Mount Pleasant, the Blockhouse today affords marvellous views and Carrington's claims in his 1837 guide to the Three Towns almost remain true. 'The Blockhouse', he wrote, 'affords a place of refreshing and delightful promenade, from which is surveyed landward, seawards, and on every side, the most extensive and varied prospects, indeed the tourist will not find a more charming panoramic view in the United Kingdom.

Slipping down from the Blockhouse along Masterman Road we come to the 'Blockhouse Inn', which like most of its immediate neighbours has sadly been stripped of its original nineteenth century exterior.

Ale, nevertheless has been served from here for around 150 years. Perhaps the most significant change in that time, for the pub at least, was the acqusition of the shop next door and the subsequent extension of the façade, a development which one wouldn't readily pick up as being of just a couple of years standing.

The original half has the initial logo of the Ashes public house chain in its window. The other side was run latterly for a great many years from the late 1930s, by Mrs. Freda Cundy, as a wool shop.

Indeed Peter and Joan Phillips who ran the 'Blockhouse Inn' from 1976 until earlier this summer, ran it as such for a while before its incorporation into the pub premises. Premises now in the hands of three people—Neil Alker, Linda Keane and Gordon Winfield.

[*WEH* 24.9.83]

Plymouth Sound

Not many yards off Alma Road, sandwiched between De-la-Hay Avenue and Earl's Acre, stands this curious building which, since 1974, has been home to England's smallest radio station—Plymouth Sound. With only one smaller station in Britain—Moray Firth in Scotland—Plymouth Sound first hit the local airwaves at 6 a.m. on the morning of the 19th of May, 1975.

A year earlier there had been three main groups bidding for the franchise of Plymouth's proposed new independent local radio station and the leader of the successful group then and managing director from that day to this is the ebullient Bob Hussell.

Originally granted planning permission to lease and reconstruct the old Millbay Laundry the group decided instead to buy rather than lease premises so it was that in 1974 Hele's Organ Factory became Plymouth Sound Radio Station. The building had been purpose built as an organ factory in 1900 by George Hele. Born in the middle of the last century, George Hele had been a music teacher in Truro and organist at what was then simply St. Mary's Church, Truro, before moving to Plymouth in 1876 where he set up a small organ factory in Union Street's Octagon.

As the business grew premises were taken in St. Peter's Hall, Wyndham Square, before the building here was constructed. As well as expanding his business George Hele, in no uncertain terms, expanded his family and with his 15 children virtually guaranteed a family interest in the business over subsequent generations. Indeed John Hele, a great grandson, was still with the firm as the 1960s dawned.

Famed throughout the world and in its heyday with branches in Exeter and

London, the 'Hele and Co.' name is still in business today, operating out of Saltash in the hands of Maurice Eglington, who served his apprenticeship in the factory here.

With the specialized facilities required for organ production and assembly—all organs of course had to be tested before being 'broken down' to be transported to their destination—it is not surprising to learn that during both world wars factory production was either interrupted or amended. During the first war wings and fuselages were produced here for the famous Sopwith Camels and during the Second World War it was requisitioned as a joinery by the dockyard.

In the second instance the organ works temporarily moved to 4 Alma Villas where one of the Plymouth Sound presenters now lives.

In almost nine years of broadcasting the Plymouth Sound line-up has changed little and the continuity that marked the first 75 years' usage of the building appears to be rubbing off on its new occupants.

Not that wireless broadcasting is entirely new to the place; the small hut in the foreground with the partly shaded windows was, from John Hele's earliest recollections, the workshop for his uncle, Ken Hele, radio ham and wireless wizard extraordinary. One delightful unsubstantiated rumour that all concerned want to believe is true concerns a supposed visit to this workshop by the great Marconi himself, which resulted in the first public radio transmission in Plymouth. Although Marconi was often in the area no one seems to know how true this story is—however, one thing we do know, none of them could ever have guessed that the organ factory itself would one day give way to the wireless.

[*WEH* 14.4.84]

The Britannia

It was James Thomson (1700–48) who wrote those immortal lines, 'Rule, Britannia, Britannia rule the waves' and the Reverend Sydney Smith (1771–1845) who said: 'What two ideas are more inseparable than Beer and Britannia?'

Quite who was unable to separate the two ideas 150 years ago when this inn was built is, however, less certain. Apart from being the name of a pewter-like alloy, Britannia is first and foremost known as the name by which the Romans and maybe even the Celts, referred to this island of Britain.

The Roman Emperor Hadrian (AD 76–138) was the first ruler to have an armed female figure depicting Britannia on his coinage. Charles II re-introduced the figure in 1672 and thereafter, for some 300 years, our pennies bore the figure of Britannia.

The most likely clue to the naming of the inn, however, is perhaps provided by the ancestors of Robert Falcon Scott. In 1881 Scott went to the Britannia Naval College (which was superseded in 1905 by B.R.N.C. Dartmouth). Scott had been brought up in Outlands House, one of the few buildings here in the acres of countryside then surrounding this centuries-old crossroads.

Scott's family was traditionally a Services linked one and his grandfather had retired from the Navy in 1826, buying that same year the Hoegate Street Brewery with his brother. In 1830 grandfather Scott bought Outlands House, coincidentally only yards from the site of the inn built later that decade.

First opened then in the late 1830s the 'Britannia Inn' here at Milehouse (or Mile End as it was once known) has had, for the most part, a relatively steady run of licensees, at least seven of them staying more than ten years apiece.

One family alone ran the pub for almost 50 years between the 1870s and the 1920s, and old photographs from this period show the original pub building (which has since been much added to) bearing the legend Woolland's 'Britannia Inn'.

With ever-changing traffic at this ancient junction as horse and carriage has given way to cars, trams and omnibuses, the pub itself has witnessed many changes.

Most recently and most pertinently to this weekend have been the changes in the match day drinking and behaviour patterns of its patrons.

Gone are the days that landlord Brian Brown (now at the Cornwall's Gate) recalls from the 1960s when his doors would open to Cornish farmers and their families and this convivial bunch would consume a couple of bottles of Shrubs between them in one lunchtime.

All that began changing when Plymouth's rail links with Cornwall were cut back and the behaviour of the football fans generally began deteriorating.

For Brian Brown the turning point ironically was the F.A. Cup match against Everton in 1975 when much damage was done to the fixtures and fittings of the pub.

This, and subsequent troublesome match day lunchtimes often aggravated by coachloads of visiting fans being dropped at Home Park early in the morning, soured his attitude towards the place he had done his training in and had spent many years introducing functions, food, music and disco.

More recently, the 'Britannia' with its new landlord, Ray Smith, has closed on certain Saturday lunchtimes, as he and his wife Betty concentrate on making the inn a successful lunchtime roadside stop; a reputation not to be spoiled by its being the nearest pub to Argyle.

[*WEH* 10.3.84

135

The Home Park Public Call Office

There are well over 75,000 'Public Call Offices' in Britain and most of them look like the familiar Jubilee Box on the right.

Generally painted Post Office Pillar Box Red, the Jubilee Box or kiosk No. 6 as it's lovingly known in the trade, has been with us some 50 years now and like its slightly taller predecessor was designed by Sir Giles Gilbert Scott, he of the new Anglican Liverpool Cathedral and Waterloo Bridge fame.

Born into something of a dynasty of architects, Sir Giles's father and grandfather, both named George Gilbert Scott were also celebrated figures in the field and his brother, Adrian, was amongst other things, responsible for the restoration of Mount Edgcumbe House after the war.

Deisgned to blend in with the changing styles in architecture Kiosk No. 6 has become one of the few truly classic pieces of British street furniture—even in the late 1960s when fashion and the philosophy of change for change's sake was at its height the new kiosk No. 8 (there appears to have been no No. 7), with its single paned sides, retained the essential shape of the Scott box.

Only in recent years has the whole structure of the public call office been dramatically rethought. With open bottomed Swedish style booths and other such contraptions appearing partly designed to combat vandalism and their use as impromptu lavatories, the future of the familiar red phone box isn't so rosy.

Stylistic new external alterations are unlikely to be as impressive as the changes that have taken place inside kiosk No. 6. Gone are the days when you just lifted the receiver and waited for the operator to answer and connect you, gone the push button A or B (if no one answered and you wanted your tuppence back), gone too the necessity of calling the operator to make trunk calls.

STD, Subscriber Trunk Dialling reached Plymouth in 1965 and since 1979 it has been possible to call the world direct from Plymouth, this last development coming 16 years after it arrived in London, which is perhaps ironic as the first ever demonstration of the telephone in this country took place in Plymouth in 1877.

Indeed the first practical appliance was installed by Alexander Graham Bell himself in Robert Bayley's Torr House, Hartley; the house at which Bell was then a guest.

In the days before the metal cast box, free standing telephone boxes tended to be largely pre-cast concrete affairs and although superseded by the Post Office this remained as standard for the generally blue painted police phone boxes.

Complete with a flashing blue light on top, should it be necessary to summon the Bobby on the beat, Plymouth originally had just over a dozen such boxes, plus a further four watch houses and over 30 police phone pillars. The Plymouth police boxes, of which the one seen here, opposite the Lyndhurst Road—Outland Road junction, was No. 15, were slightly larger than the Metropolitan style box.

This latter box, of course, is the type featured in the 21-year-old BBC TV series 'Dr Who'. Otherwise known as the Tardis (Time and Relative Dimensions In Space) the doctor's machine was supposed to be able to change its shape according to its surroundings; however back in the very early episodes the Tardis' Chameleon Circuit was damaged and when recently the BBC contemplated repairing the circuit, effectively scrapping the police box, there was a great public outcry.

In real life of course the police box has ceased to be an important construction (since approx 1969, although one A1 roadside box was in service until 1980) and this one now houses 'no waiting' and other traffic signs.

In the days before walkie talkie sets and Panda cars, however, such boxes were bases for the Bobby on the Beat, both for desk work and the consumption of tea and sandwiches—and there was little vandalism here as there might always be a policeman coming around the corner. »Postscript

[WEH 31.3.84

Plymouth Argyle

Argyle Athletic Club played their first full game of football on 9th October, 1886 away to Launceston (then called Dunheved) College. Their captain F. Howard Grose was an old boy of the college and had been inspired to set up the team with another old boy W. Pethybridge. Both living in Plymouth they decided to round up other interested old boys from other schools in the area with a view to forming their own team.

They first met at Grose's home in the newly built Argyll Terrace off Houndis-combe (then Huntiscombe) Road, Mutley. After a couple of meetings it was decided that Grose should be club captain and the team at Grose's suggestion should be called Argyle Athletic.

'Plymouth Pickwick' was also considered but quickly rejected and there was already a Plymouth Town and a Plymouth United. It is claimed, apparently by Grose himself, that this naming was out of admiration for the style of play of the regimental team of the Argyll and Sutherland Highlanders (I'm grateful here for much information brought to my attention by Sam Rendell who in particular noted correspondence on this matter in The Western Morning News of 10th April 1934).

Even the familiar Argyle colours of green and black are believed to have been inspired by the Sutherland tartan which in turn was adopted as the Regimental colours for the Argyll and Sutherland Highlanders. Predominantly a large green and navy check (which appears green and black) overlaid with a few thin lines of white and green this tartan does indeed have certain similarities to the green and black quartered shirts that Argyle Athletic's football and rugby clubs both wore.

The name Argyll itself derives from the Gaelic 'Earraghaidheal' meaning The Boundary of the Gaels. The adoption of an anglicised version of Argyle was curiously enough echoed a year or two later as Argyll Terrace itself became Argyle Terrace, coincidentally around the same time as the houses in adjoining Sutherland Road were being built.

The development of Argyle Athletic football club was typical of so many clubs that had arisen out of public school old boys associations in the 1840s.

Later others were formed as works' teams and Service sides and by 1863 it was necessary to form the Football Association, primarily to standardize the rules.

Professionalism, resisted at first, was widespread by the time Argyle Athletic were formed.

Initially playing away games only, as they had no pitch of their own Argyle's early practice sessions were conducted at Freedom Fields and such was their enthusiasm that they even trained in the moonlight.

Their first regular pitch was at Mount Gould and it was not until 1901 that they took up residence at Home Park, which had originally been built for and home to Devonport Albion Rugby Club. For two years Argyle Athletic staged cycle racing, whippet racing and various levels of football before being admitted in 1903 to the Southern League.

It was then, for the first time that they took the pitch as Plymouth Argyle FC.

Home Park in those days was on the northern edge of town and was approached by a long lane from Pennycomequick, past fields and farms.

There was no terracing, no toilets and no crush barriers and the wooden stand was about half its present size.

A replacement stand built in 1930 was destroyed during the blitz and the present stand, floodlights and public address all date from the 1950s.

The lights themselves were first officially switched on one miserable night in October, 1953 for a 'friendly' against Exeter. The front entrance, erected in 1935, survived the blitz.

[WEH 18.2.84

Six Trees, Central Park

'. . . And then he (Piglet) had a clever idea. He would go up very quietly to the six pine trees now, peep very cautiously into the trap, and see if there was a heffalump there. And if there was, he would go back to bed, and if there wasn't, he wouldn't.' (A. A. Milne, Winnie-The-Pooh, 1926).

For more than 50 years now, these particular six trees (five pine and a *Cupressus macrocarpa*) have stood here on open ground as part of Plymouth's Central Park.

The word park comes from the Old English term used in forest laws for an enclosed area which could be obtained as a franchise from the Crown for beasts of the chase.

Situated just below the old part of Venn Lane and currently a little outside what is today called Pounds Park this was part of one of three plots sold to the corporation in the 1920s resulting in the 1931 opening of the 241-acre Central Park.

Outside the three town boundaries for the greater part of the nineteenth century, as Plymouth, Devonport and Stonehouse merged in 1914 and city status was conferred upon Plymouth in 1928, it became increasingly apparent that for health and social reasons a green area would need to be set aside for the benefit of all Plymothians.

Indeed the development of the park helped some locals in other ways too, for it was even then, part funded as a project of approved work to help relieve unemployment.

Prior to 1931 this area, called Hunscomb's Hill in an 1814 map, had sported a couple of farms, a site for events (the Bath & West Show was held on Exhibition Fields in 1922), a few tennis courts, Plymouth Cricket Club and since 1903, Home Park Sports and Athletic Club, home of Plymouth Argyle FC, it also included the last remaining strip of what had been the 500-acre site of the Pound's estate.

Pound's House, the top of which is just visible between the trees, had its heyday in the middle and later part of the last century, as the home of the Chapell Hodges. In 1851 they had inherited the estate (and the Devonport Bank), from William Hodge, founder and last surviving partners of the same.

Built by 1830 the house was sadly empty 100 years later when the park was opened and in 1937 it was even suggested that the house should be pulled down—'because of its dilapidated condition'.

There was of course an ulterior motive, the education committee had put a minute before the City Council to the effect that following the arrival of Devonport High School for Girls at Montpelier, the Boys School should follow them here to Pounds.

Of course it never happened and the house was saved and today after housing for many years the Town Clerk's Department it operates in a variety of roles—including, as a library, as a baby clinic, as a home for Plymouth Camera Club and as a meeting place.

Furthermore its future and that of the land around it and the six trees looks today to be a healthy one, for, if the recommendations of the 1981 Central Park report are followed Pounds Park will expand slightly and together with the whole east side of the Park will be subject for development as a passive recreation area with more trees and walkways, as the more athletic sports move to the other side of the park.

Pounds Park will then become more of a magical woodland area, free perhaps of dogs but maybe not of heffalumps.

[WEH 21.1.84

Plymouth Cricket Club

One of the city's senior sporting clubs, the exact age of Plymouth Cricket Club is uncertain as almost all of its pre-war records were lost in a town bank vault during the Blitz.

However, we do know that by 1862 it had moved out from the Hoe to a new ground opposite South Devon Place where the Astor Playing Fields are today at Prince Rock.

Furthermore, according to a report in the *Western Daily Mercury* of 11th February 1863 'the Club' was by this time 'beginning to obtain the notoriety in the cricketing world which it so well deserves' and 'Already the knickerbocker Club comprising some of the first gentlemen players in England has challenged it . . .'

Cricket always has, of course, been a gentleman's game and the notion of fair play being synonymous with cricket and any sporting unfairness or cheating being simply 'not cricket' has been around since the middle of the last century.

But this was only after a period in the eighteenth century when there was a certain amount of bribery and corruption associated with some matches, caused by great landlords and noblemen and even one Prince of Wales wagering as much as 1,000 guineas on a game.

A practice only curbed after one heated incident at Lords many years ago soon after which in the 1820s the MCC banned all bookmakers from the ground.

Originally a game played with a cricc or staff and perhaps similar to the criquet used in the French game of bowls, cricket has altered little since the acceptance, after much fuss, of the overarm bowling law in 1864 which permitted bowlers to bowl with the hand at any height provided that the ball is not thrown or jerked.

In its earlier forms the game had been played with two stumps, a bail and a hole between, one stump and a hole and just a hole on its own—then you could only be caught or run out—by someone popping the ball into the popping hole before the batsman could put his bat in it.

This potentially dangerous situation was replaced by the popping crease sometime later.

Long since established as the English summer game, Plymouth has never been particularly famous as a cricket city but many clubs play the game at a reasonable level.

Plymouth Cricket Club, after moving from Prince Rock, enjoyed a brief spell at Beacon Down where Civil Service now play before moving to Central Park in the 1920s.

The present Peverell Park pavilion, which boasts a panoramic view of the city was designed by a subsequent club chairman, E. G. Catchpole and was built in 1935, its wooden predecessor being pulled down in the early 1970s to make way for new squash courts.

Known today as Plymouth Cricket and Sports Club, tennis, hockey and pool teams also have their base here, as well as an offshoot of Plymouth Cricket Club itself—the Plymouth Queeries.

Captained for over 30 years by the ever youthful septagenarian Larry Lusmore, the Queeries were formed when a desire to play Sunday Cricket was thwarted by objections on religious grounds.

Collected by a coach outside the club gates each Sunday the team would be whisked off to some mystery ground for a fixture where Larry would, and still does, contrive to win the toss.

Still playing a handful of matches each season the Queeries tie with its plain question mark on a navy blue background is, I'm assured, one of the hardest ties to get in the game.

[*WEH* 18.8.84

Devonport High School for Girls

As we see it today, here off Outland Road, Devonport High School for Girls was begun in 1936 and completed in 1937 when 500 girls arrived under their headmistress, Miss D. Moore, to undergo their secondary education.

Now only three years from celebrating its 50th year in these buildings DHS for Girls has, over the years, enjoyed several birthday parties. Daisy Moore herself presided over the school's 21st birthday in 1930.

The school was then housed in the building most Plymothians know simply as Devonport Tech and one old girl, writing in the school's magazine of that year, stated that 'the thought of a new school building, though filling us with joy, nevertheless gives a pang to those of us who feel that another home can never be "ours" in the same realistic way.'

Several years later Miss B. M. Weedon in the school's 1957 magazine wrote of the impending 50th birthday celebrations and how in September 1908 the school had opened with ten scholars. 'We are proud' she added 'to trace back the links to that small beginning, although the school did not then bear its present name.'

It didn't indeed, as it was then known as Devonport Municipal Secondary School for Girls, later becoming simply Devonport Secondary School for Girls.

Its status as a secondary school followed the abolition of the School Board in 1902, after which many of the dozens of schools in the Three Towns were either phased out or taken over by the local education authority.

One or two schools remained 'private' but there appeared to be no clear programme of school building and it would seem that Devonport Municipal Secondary School was a development of the girls' school that had been in the old Tech building since it opened in 1898.

Known by a variety of names it appears that this earlier school moved to the Tech after 20 years in Albert Road and before that two years in No. 1, Tamar Terrace.

First opened in 1875, this was Devonport, Stoke and Stonehouse High School for Girls and followed hard on the heels of Plymouth High School for Girls which had opened the year before (Plymouth High School for Boys, later Plymouth College, opened in 1877).

In the wake of the 1870 Education Act School Boards were formed to take control of local public education and the Devonport, Stoke and Stonehouse High School Company met on 25th May, 1875 to sort out a financial basis upon which the new school could be established.

A decision was made to raise £5,000 by means of 1,000 £5 shares and it was not long before sufficient money had been raised to proceed with the building—a 'handsome' construction, which stands today in Albert Road. Built at a cost of £6,000 a Miss McCallum was its first headmistress.

Known for a while locally as the 'New High School for Girls' or simply Devonport High School for Girls, there seems to be little doubt that this establishment is a genuine forerunner of the present school.

What prompted the girls to move to the new Tech building in 1898 is uncertain but in 1899 we find the newly-formed Devonport High School for Boys in Albert Road and the girls apparently overflowing their allocated space in the Tech for we also read of a High School for Girls under a Miss Raymond operating around the same time in the nearby St. Michael's Lodge. Was this perhaps a junior annexe?

Whatever, while still in the Tech building we find that the school had already adopted its familiar lily emblem and motto—Sine Labe Decus—Honour without stain, a legend it shares with the London borough of Wimbledon.

Miss Moore, head for more than two decades, succeeded Miss A. Hill and in turn has been followed at Peverell by the Misses Vale, Weedon and Edwards. The present head, Mrs. A. A. Clayton, has been at the school since 1977 and for the time being can look forward to a healthy future for what has long been one of the city's most successful girls' schools.

[WEH 27.10.84

St. Boniface's College

I cannot remember ever feeling as sad while drawing as I did when sitting opposite the strange and imposing frontage of the buildings known for the last 50 years as St. Boniface's College.

Although they are of no special architectural importance and certainly of no particular emotional significance for me it was, nevertheless, quite unnerving to sit and draw as the sound of heavy machinery, bending metal, falling timbers, breaking glass and cracking slates resounded around the pitifully overgrown playing fields.

In a matter of weeks if not days from now this hotch-potch of buildings that was until recently operating happily as a school for almost 800 boys will have vanished forever. The fortunate souls who will come to live in the housing that will appear in its place, however, will not be quite so melancholy; after all, the views from this site around the city and beyond are quite wonderful.

Indeed, they are doubtless what prompted the owner of the fine house, that we see on the right, to name it 'Prospect'.

Prospect House stood here alone for many years at a time when Weston Peverel or Pennycross, the village of which it was part, was a chapelry with a population of less than 400. Here lived, in the middle of last century, James Bryant and later, exactly 100 years ago in 1883, Lord Francis Horace Pierrepont Cecil, JP, RN.

By this time the house had been renamed 'Beaconsfield'. In Elizabethan times there had been a fire beacon near here, Penny Crosse Beaken, hence the name Beacon Park.

In 1884 'Beaconsfield' was sold to the Basilian Fathers, who had recently taken over the running of the Catholic School in North Road in Plymouth, which had grown out of an earlier (1863) college in Melbourne Street.

The cost of the land and buildings of 'Beaconsfield' in 1884 was £10,000. In 1983 the site, with a great deal more building upon it and five acres of playing field, fetched around one million pounds. While this is 100 times more in as many years, given inflation and the increasing demand for a large inner city school with grounds and the prohibitive cost of building the same, it also seems like a pretty good buy, even as it stands, or rather, stood.

In September, 1884, then the College of St. Mary Immaculate or the College of the Immaculate Conception opened here as a boarding school. In 1900 it closed down. Ironically, later in 1900, St. Boniface's College was founded in its place in Wyndham Square by Bishop Vaughan, the then Catholic Bishop of Plymouth, and it was to be 30 years before the school moved 'back' to 'Beaconsfield'. When it eventually did so it was as a result of a generous move by the Sisters of Nazareth, who had bought the place in 1930 from the exiled Ursuline Sisters.

The Ursuline Sisters from Brittany had been at Beaconsfield since 1906 and in 1911 had built onto the house (if not into, as it looks as though the one has been shunted into the other) the grand limestone building in which they operated a successful girls' high school.

The Sisters of Nazareth, who bought the school from them, in turn passed it over to Bishop Barrett, who installed the Irish Christian Brothers to run a school in accordance with the Sisters' wishes for the education of Catholic boys. And so, on 7th September, 1931, after yet more alterations, extensions and repairs, the College was reopened with 142 pupils under the Rev. Brother J. H. McDonald.

St. Boniface himself, incidentally, was born with the name Winfrith in the year 680 in Crediton, Devon. Boniface (which literally means 'the man who spoke well') is regarded by some as the greatest Englishman who ever lived and his name has been put forward as the ideal patron saint for a United Europe. He was murdered by heathens in Erisia in 754.

Official government recognition for St. Boniface's was applied for in 1932 and after an inspection made in July, 1933, the College was declared 'Recognised' and 'Efficient'. From then on until very recently the school continued through a series of ups and downs (including a four-year shutdown and evacuation to Buckfast Abbey during the war) under a steady succession of heads, Brothers Dowling, Dolan, Curran, Grice, McHugh, Colemand and Sreenan.

[*WEH* 27.8.83]

St. Pancras Church

The contemporary visitor to St. Pancras will know well the marvellous views afforded from the churchyard; from Manadon College down around past the valley carrying the new Plymouth through road out towards St. Budeaux then over to the west looking past Weston Mill and on into Cornwall.

Although well inside the Plymouth boundary today, much of this surrounding land has yet to be built upon; however, much of it is now developed, so consider back to when Plymouth's boundary was over two miles from here and Pennycross or Weston Peverell had a population of under 300—only 20-odd of whom were able to vote.

Writing in 1830, Henry Carrington describes the Pennycross 'Chapel of Ease' thus—'It was perhaps the smallest in the kingdom and of great but unrecorded antiquity.

'In its pristine state it had an air of age and seclusion about it . . . The western end was clad with very luxuriant ivy and, enveloped in this solemn and appropriate vesture could just be seen the bell, which tolling occasionally, called the inhabitants of the hill and valley to prayers.

'It was such a lovely spot—so luxuriant the hedge—so green the grass—so sweet the intertwining wild flowers—so quiet the aspect of the whole . . . seated in the midst of fields and streams so beautiful.

'No lover of the picturesque ever thought of passing by Pennycross Chapel without lifting the humble latch of its little gate and straying awhile in its green burial ground.'

Carrington went on to acknowledge that the greater part of this chapel was torn down then enlarged in 1820, work accomplished principally under the direction of George Collings, Esq., of Ham.

Re-opened on 26th August, 1821, the 'new' chapel was further enlarged and repaired between 1866–70.

Although there has been a religious building on this site for several centuries (indeed it is believed that the church may be of early Saxon origin) it was not until 1898 that the separate parish of St. Pancras was created, the Rev. William Waddington being the first vicar.

Dedicated to St. Pancras, who was martyred in 304 AD, it is not known for sure whether Pennycross takes its name from a Devon corruption in pronunciation of St. Pancras or whether perhaps Pennycross comes from the Celtic. 'Penny-cross', meaning 'hill of the cross'.

Whichever, this little chapel has survived the years and today is being extended again with a new vestry, coffee bar, kitchen and octagonal meeting room, which now joins St. Pancras to the church hall, built on the site of the old school building in 1964.

This latest development will be opened on 21st January, 1984, by the Bishop of Exeter.

Probably the smallest parish church in Plymouth, St. Pancras has ironically the largest parish in Plymouth (20,000) if not in the whole of the Exeter diocese.

Its size and cruciform shape, however, works, according to Lawrence Denny, vicar of St. Pancras since 1973, to the church's advantage for the church is more intimate and strangers are more readily made welcome.

[*WEH* 24.12.83

St. Budeaux Church

According to legend St. Budoc came to Tamerton creek in the year AD 480. This celebrated Celtic Saint had arrived from Brittany and it is believed that for some time he settled near Warren point forming a sanctuary there, erecting by a natural spring in Ernesettle Wood a rude cross in order that he might baptize his flock.

Whilst the exact form and whereabouts of any of the early religious buildings in St. Budeaux are uncertain, there appears to be little doubt that the area took its name from St. Budoc, correctly pronounced the French way rather than the literal English rendition St. Buddocks.

This latter version, however, gives us insight into the local name Budshead as it is the logical corruption of the suffix 'hide' or land measure, in the possession of Budoc; hence Budoc's hide and any number of different spellings of the family who held the land for many centuries.

Thus in 1241 we find the manor held by Alan de Buddekesid and more than 400 years later by one Roger Budockshed, the latter being responsible in 1566 for granting the 2,000 year lease of two pieces of land and the edifices thereon. The most notable edifice is the present church which had been completed just three years earlier.

This extremely long lease was not, however, without its conditions, for the parishioners were to pay, 'if demanded, one penny of lawful English money at the south door of the church, between one and three o'clock at the Feast of the Birth of our Lord God.' This Christmas Day penny was regularly paid well into this century.

Visible above the south door is a splendid sundial, placed there in 1670 and still there today. It bears the motto 'Ex hoc momento Pendet Aeternitas' from this moment hangs all eternity . . .' Also in fine condition today are the churchyard trees, many of which were planted there in 1753.

Looking westward the fields of Cornwall can just be seen. This is the view that the St. Budeaux Newman family would have known well as they assembled outside the church on the 4th of July, 1569 to witness the marriage of Mary Newman to undoubtedly the most famous of the grooms to sign the church's register, Francis Drake.

[WEH 18.9.82

Cornwall's Gate

One might easily be fooled by the appearance of this public house into thinking that it must have been a thirst-quenching stop for travellers into and out of Cornwall for well over 100 years—however, while the building is of sufficient antiquity its use as an inn isn't.

Indeed, its original purpose could hardly have provided a greater contrast. Around 1860 the British Government had a mild panic about the safety of the country's two greatest naval ports and commissioned a ring of forts to be built around both Plymouth and Portsmouth.

Prompted by Napoleon III's imperialist ambitions, these forts came to be known as Palmerston's follies after the Prime Minister of the time and evidence of those completed can still be seen today—Picklecombe, Tregantle, Bovisand, Staddiscombe, Crownhill, Laira . . .

One which was mooted but never came to pass was to have been built at Higher St. Budeaux by the parish church and the then 'St. Budeaux Inn', better known now as the 'Blue Monkey'.

Plans for this proposal were set in motion and to compensate for the vicarage to be lost in the scheme the Government built this impressive house overlooking the Brunel bridge.

At that time there were very few other buildings in the area. Barne Tower stood just below it towards the river and there were a number of dwellings at Saltash Passage, all of which were then in Cornwall, for it was only at the end of the last century (1895) that the 120-acre area, Little Ayshe Barton, known also as the 'Cornish Patch', became part of Devon.

The road on which the vicarage had been constructed subsequently became known as Vicarage Road, for centuries part of the main road from Plymouth to Saltash, it was renamed Normandy Way sometime after the last war in the mid-1950s.

Home then for the Vicar of St. Budeaux in the late 19th century, the Rev. William Watson was here during World War One and his son, the Rev. R. L. Watson has been back to the house since its conversion.

Now 83 and with memories of walking down from the house through the fields to St. Budeaux Station to catch the train to Mutley and school at Plymouth College, the Rev. Watson and his two sisters remember the lounge bar affectionately in its former role as drawing room.

Sadly for such memories today the grand view offered from this window has recently been much restricted thanks to the seemingly unreasonably high sound barrier that has been constructed to shelter the premises in Normandy Way from the noise that will be created by the new Plymouth through road that runs below.

Opened in 1962, the year the Tamar Bridge was completed, the 'Cornwall's Gate' is then no longer quite the roadside gatehouse it was then. However, two ancient boundary stones, neither bearing any decipherable markings today, just a few yards down from the inn are a reminder that this once was a real border post.

In private hands for many years before it was acquired by H. and G. Simmonds, now Courages, the 'Gate' has had only three landlords—George Cox, Robbie Roberts, now retired, who was here 19 years and currently the dynamic duo of Brian and Val Brown, who came here after many happy years together at the 'Britannia' at Milehouse.

[*WEH* 22.9.84]

Royal Albert Bridge Inn

Quite how long there has been an Inn on this site is uncertain. Until 1961 and the building of the Tamar Road Bridge, a regular ferry service had operated across the river here from Esses Torre or Ashtorre (Saltash) dating back to medieval days at least. The ferry itself was once known as Ashe-Torre Passage and the road that runs behind the Inn was for centuries the main road from Cornwall into Plymouth. (Indeed until this century this part of St. Budeaux was in Cornwall.)

Perhaps the earliest documented record of the inn is from 1822, when as the Dock Inn it was sold to Francis James, victualler, for the princely sum of £295. Doubtless dating back in its present form to the eighteenth century the Inn underwent a name change in 1823 in keeping with the town of Dock itself which was given its charter and became Devonport that same year. In those days the ferry ran along the line now taken by the Royal Albert Bridge and it was only when work began on Brunel's masterpiece that the ferry's path moved down by what then became the 'Ferry House Inn'. Although Brunel and his engineers had begun work in 1848 it was not until 1859 that the bridge was completed. The following year the 'Devonport Inn' became the 'Royal Albert Bridge Inn'. Meanwhile one of Brunel's engineers, Bradford Leslie, later knighted and responsible for many bridges in India, and who had been staying in the Inn, had married landlord William Honey's daughter Mary. In 1896 John Stoneman took the pub. While previously at the old 'Post Office Inn' in Market Street, Devonport, John Stoneman's son had run away to pursue a career on stage. Achieving success with his wife as 'Conley and Carew, refined comedy duetists, singers and sand-dancers' they appeared in variety shows around the world but came back to Plymouth and took over the 'Royal Albert' when his father died. Another John Stoneman himself, the first of his sons was born in the Inn in 1906. For many years after the family lived in the cottage next door, part of which around the time of the last war became the lounge bar and present toilet area. Chris Stoneman, the eldest son, still drinks here and lives close by and supplied fascinating turn-of-the-century photographs of the Inn to his contemporary, Marshall Ware, for his two very readable books on old St. Budeaux. Chris also makes half boats, models mounted on mirrors, some of which hang in the lounge. John Cooper, a retired butler, succeeded the Stonemans in 1919.

Meanwhile another son of a former landlord, Tom Wales, the ex-metropolitan and dockyard policeman, here in the late 1920s early 1930s, also still drinks here and lives nearby. Still in St. Budeaux too is a son of the Inn's longest serving family of licensees, the Smiths (Charles, Ada, Jasper then Florence), here between 1941–73. Prior to them Tom Grozier, the former Argyle striker who scored 57 goals for the Pilgrims in 210 games between 1926–36, was here for a couple of years. Today, however, it is Cornishman Eddie Shannon and his wife Lyn who run the 'Royal Albert Bridge Inn'. A genial no nonsense host who has fulfilled a long ambition in running a pub, Eddie is the only tenant landlord in Plymouth whose kitchen and facilities merited one of the Corporation's recent E.A.T. awards. Meanwhile the lack of adjacent ferry has not stopped him and his regulars pushing out into the river. On their infamous 'Royal Albert Bridge Inn' raft they have negotiated two trips to the Eddystone and the whole of the Cornish coastline, raising many worthwhile funds in the process.

The memorial in the foreground incidentally honours the Americans of the V and VII Corps for whom Normandy Way had been U.S. Army route 23 and this had been their departure point back in June 1944.

[WEH 8.6.85

Royal Albert Bridge

An old drawing of the Railway Bridge, by Thomas Gilks, appeared in the 1879 'Illustrated Handbook to Plymouth, Stonehouse and Devonport,' written by W. H. K. Wright, public librarian.

The book was divided into walks and this drawing came at the end of the walk that began at Millbridge and went via Stoke and the Dockyard along the banks of the Tamar.

As Wright approached the bridge he wrote: 'Away in the distance may be discerned the picturesque little town of Saltash, and the immense tubes of that masterpiece of Brunel—the Royal Albert Bridge.'

The bridge had been completed in 1859 and opened by HRH Prince Albert. Brunel could not attend. He did, however, come to Plymouth some time after, and resting on a mattress tied to a railway truck, he saw for the first and last time his finished creation.

Brunel's Bridge cost more than £225,000 to construct and although we think of such problems as being peculiar to the twentieth century, it took some 10 years to complete, work having been held up for four years because of financial difficulties.

For more than 100 years the bridge stood alone, then in 1962 the wife of Prince Albert's great-grandson, Queen Elizabeth the Queen Mother, opened the Tamar Road Bridge, the bridge which at that time had the longest single span in Britain— some 1,100 ft. The new bridge had taken just over two years to erect and cost around £2,000,000 to construct.

[WEH 27.3.82

Brunel's Bridge from Saltash

In the early 1800s, Marc Isambard Brunel was asked by a body of Saltash merchants if he could devise some way of bridging the Tamar. The civil engineer, an exiled Frenchman, replied that he thought that the river, 1,000 feet across at that point, was too wide to bridge.

Some years later, in 1846, when an Act of Parliament gave the go ahead for the Cornwall Railway Company to construct a railway line between Plymouth and Falmouth, the problem arose again. This time though the situation was more urgent and the engineer approached was of a more ambitious school; his name, Isambard Kingdom Brunel, son of Marc and his English wife Sophia Kingdom.

Isambard Brunel's first inclination however echoed his father's thoughts and he proposed a steam train ferry running across the Tamar further down the river near the current Torpoint Ferry.

Fortunately for future generations the 1846 Act only allowed for a fixed, rather than a floating, bridge over the river and so this plan was rejected, as were Brunel's two subsequent proposals for a seven, and then a four, span wooden bridge.

With an estimated working life of perhaps some 50 years the Admiralty vetoed these proposals and further added to Brunel's problems by stipulating that the bridge should have only one pier in the river and that the water should be cleared by at least 100 feet.

Brunel then produced another two designs, the first although feasible was a very ambitious single span wrought iron project and was prohibitively expensive; the second, for a two span wrought iron bridge, met with the approval of the Admiralty and with the Cornwall Railway Company, so it was then that in 1848 the great engineer, now in his 42nd year, began planning one of his finest works.

Details of the planning and construction of the bridge can be found in the pages of Thomas Bowden and Bernard Mills's well laid out recent publication 'Brunel's Royal Albert Bridge, Saltash'. Held up for several years by financial difficulties work was eventually completed on the bridge in 1859.

Huge crowds had attended the positioning of the two great sections of the bridge and the first floating in September 1857, supervised by Brunel himself, attracted some 30–40,000 excited persons, many from as far afield as Exeter and London.

For the residents of the Three Towns, the day was treated as a public holiday, indeed such was the interest that the railway company issued special tickets for the viewing of the floating of the second section the following July.

The first train ran from Plymouth to Truro on 11th April, 1859. The official opening took place 'amidst much public rejoicing and festivity' the following month, on 2nd May. Prince Albert, having consented to his name being used for the bridge some years earlier, was there and completed a thorough inspection of the construction.

Brunel was absent, lying ill in Switzerland. Before the end of the summer, however, he did manage to see the finished bridge, but, sadly, soon after his return to London the great man died at the age of 53.

As a mark of respect, by way of making the bridge a fitting memorial to him, however, the directors of the Cornwall Railway Co., had 'I. K. Brunel, Engineer 1859' boldly painted on either end of the bridge.

Repainted every six years at a cost not allowing for inflation well in excess of the cost of its original building, the bridge stands firm today and looks set to keep its 'new' (1962) neighbour company for a good many decades yet.

[WEH 3.9.83

Southway School

Southway School was opened 21 years ago, just six years after the first settlers of this modern large estate had moved into the area. Previously a part of the parish of Tamerton Foliot, reached via Southway Lane, this area contained land belonging to some seven farms, including Langley, Clittaford, Southway and Birdcage, none of which was eager to surrender its status.

However, in the wake of the blitz, demands for accommodation were acute and this area north of Plymouth was earmarked for such housing development as early as 1943. Although the local farmers argued and appealed they met with little success; in 1947 an Act granted powers of statutory purchase and by 1950 the land had been secured.

No housing was completed until 1956 by which time some 300 residences had been furnished and occupied. Bit by bit the estate, named Southway because of the area's position in relation to the ancient Southern Way into Tavistock, grew, as first families, then facilities, then factories appeared.

In 1958 Southway Junior School was opened and the starting of the secondary school was approved with proposed opening date of 1960. Almost inevitably, the project was delayed and the completed school built on the site of the Old Barn Park, was opened in 1962 with Swiss-born P. M. Bindschedler at its helm.

With a keen sense of the school's position within the community Mr. Bindschedler remained in office until his retirement last year, now Mr. E. H. Goddard heads the 1,500 strong school and is anxious to further develop the school's local role.

Of the original 1962 staff line up only two teachers, Diane Evans and John Ellis remain today.

In 1971 Southway became a parish in its own right, breaking away from the old parish of Tamerton and reducing the size of the same by about a quarter. The school badge incidentally derives in large part from the family arms of Copleston; this family acquired the parish of Tamerton by marriage in 1472.

Reputedly they moved here from their ancestral home of Coplestone near Crediton in order to enjoy the views of Cornwall, the Tamar Estuary, the Moors and the Sound—views nowhere better appreciated today than from here in the top floor of the main school block.

[*WEH* 17.9.83]

The Seven Stars

Fool: The reason why the Seven Stars are no more than seven is a pretty reason.

Lear: Because they are not eight.

Fool: Yes, indeed, thou wouldst make a good fool.

A few lines from Shakespeare's King Lear (Act 1, Scene V) which throws no light whatsoever on the derivation of the name of this ancient ale house in Tamerton Foliot.

Situated some way along Seven Stars Lane, this public house, possibly the oldest in the Plymouth area, almost certainly dates back to the thirteenth century and so Eric Delderfield's comments in one of his books on inn signs and names are interesting— 'Seven Stars,' he writes, 'was a popular religious sign in the Middle Ages.'

'The sign represented the seven-starred celestial crown usual on figures of the Virgin Mary. Some signs show a constellation of stars.'

Certainly the signs we see on early photographic records of the pub depict star constellations and in a recent article on the inn Chris Wood put forward the popular local theory; 'The Seven Stars,' he wrote, 'were used to inform the local inhabitants who could not read that the seven sacraments were available and administered there.'

Another account suggests that the sign indicated that the seven sacraments could be obtained at the church nearby. The fact that the monks from Plympton Priory are believed to have used the building as a hostelry while preaching locally in the fourteenth century, lends some weight to the first idea.

Seven has long been a mystic or sacred number and the seven sacraments (or sacred mysteries) are Baptism, Confirmation, the Eucharist, Penance, Orders, Matrimony and Extreme Unction.

The Seven Stars, on the other hand, formerly applied to the five planets known to the ancients—Mercury, Mars, Venus, Jupiter and Saturn plus the Sun and the Moon.

Uranus was discovered in 1781, Neptune, which is invisible to the naked eye, in 1846 and the near invisible Pluto in 1930.

In later years the seven stars referred to a group of stars in the constellation Taurus, of which six are clearly visible. These are also called the Pleiades, the Seven Sisters, so named after the seven daughters of Pleione and Atlas who, in classical mythology were transformed into stars.

Could it then be these out of the 6,000 odd stars visible to the naked eye, give their name to the pub?

Whatever the story there is little doubt that there has been a building here since around the time of Domesday.

In 1066 the Manor of Tamerton Foliot was the richest, most valuable and most developed in the area and today Tamerton, more than most local incorporated villages, has an almost timeless quality about it.

Stepping into the 'Seven Stars' with its centuries old exposed walls and low ceilings this feeling is not readily dispelled, particularly as its current landlord, Ken Stout, has successfully avoided such modern pub contrivances as video machines, a TV, jukebox, pool table and even a dart board.

Instead he concentrates on traditional inn fare—food and drink, and every now and then there's even a bit of Morris dancing in the garden.

[WEH 8.10.83

The Tamar Hotel

A map drawn up by the Royal Engineers in 1856 depicts the heart of Knackersknowle just prior to the building of Crownhill Fort in the 1860s.

One of Palmerston's ring of 'follies' built to defend the three towns against the supposed threat from the French under Napoleon III the fort was named Crownhill after a pair of cottages called Crown Hill which were demolished during the fort's construction.

In the years that followed as the village grew to accommodate the increased traffic, population and interest, partly generated by this development, so the old name Knackersknowle or knoll, which appeared in a 1765 survey as Nackershole, was dropped and the name of the fort assumed in its place.

Appropriately enough too, as in 1765 there appeared to be only one major building on the crossroads and even in 1856 the village was still very small.

With its farms sprawled out to the east and the west, Knackersknowle was at that time divided between the parishes of St. Budeaux and Eggbuckland (it didn't fall within the Plymouth boundary until 1939).

The main settlement around the fort however was in St. Budeaux parish and within it were two inns, the 'First and Last' and the 'New Inn'.

Quite how long they had been there is difficult to say; however Kelly's 1857 Directory tells us that James Pengelly was licensee of the 'First and Last' and Servington Lethbridge licensee of the 'New Inn'.

In 1850 only the 'New Inn' is shown, run then by James Pengelly and clearly the older of the two. The 'First and Last' was, I believe, built soon afterwards next door to the 'New Inn'.

For some 20 years it appears that William Pengelly—wheelwright and beer retailer ran the 'First and Last'; in 1870 we find James Pengelly back in the 'New Inn'. However around 100 years ago we no longer find either of these men in Crownhill.

Instead it is George Pengelly who is listed as the village wheelwright while William Raymond is in the 'New Inn' and William Henry Cudlip appears to have taken over as the other local beer retailer.

The 1889 Directory suggests that Cudlip had changed the name of the 'First and Last' to the 'Tamar Inn' and a contemporary photograph shows the Inn with a sign bearing that name along with his own.

In 1891–92, however, the building of the new military barracks above the crossroads prompted yet more development in the village. It was then, it would seem, that both the 'Tamar Inn' and the 'New Inn' were knocked down and replaced by the much larger 'Tamar Hotel' which we see today in their place.

The first manager of this grand new establishment was William Henry Worth, who was here until 1900 when he was succeeded first by James and Beatrice Bennett, then James and Hilda Ponsford, who between them saw the 'Tamar' through the two World Wars.

With many changes since, both inside and out; notably the neighbouring police station there since the 1890s making way in 1967 for the new road, with the traffic mainly running now behind the 'Hotel', the most recent change has been in personnel.

Last year Donald Vellacot moved to the 'George' at Roborough after seven years here and David and Diane Lovell moved in after 15 years spent in the trade, exiled on the other side of the Tamar, in Saltash, Dobwalls and Falmouth. »Postscript

[WEH 19.1.85.

Widey Grange

Various acts of corporate and non-corporate vandalism coupled with grand modern planning schemes over the last 30 years have seen the disappearance of most of the splendid Widey Court Estate.

First to go was the grand historic mansion. Used by Prince Maurice as headquarters for the Royalists laying siege to Plymouth during the Civil War, Widey housed Charles I for some time in 1643, thereby earning its regal 'court' title.

Substantially rebuilt down the centuries on an original Tudor dwelling, Widey, after some 300 years in the hands of the Morshead family, was at the beginning of World War II occupied by two naval gentlemen, Commander William Evelyn Cavendish Davy and Lt. Cmdr Geoffrey Dennis St. Quintin Marescaux, and there were plans to convert the mansion into a first-class hotel.

However, in 1941 it was requisitioned by the City Police, then in 1945 turned over to the City Stores Officer. Some rooms were let privately but all tenants were out by 1950 when a compulsory purchase order was slapped on it.

After a few years of wanton neglect it was eventually demolished to make way for Widey Primary School in 1954.

Originally approached by two carriage drives, much attention was recently given to the destruction of the second and only surviving lodge to the 53 acre Widey Court estate, and in particular the moving of its famous gateposts.

However, similar unmoved gateposts survive here today at the entrance to Widey Court's Dower House at Higher Widey—Widey Grange.

Built to house relatives of the occupants of Widey Court, the Grange was similarly much added to over the years.

Described in 1921 as a handsome Georgian residence the building as now seen, was built early last century on to the front of a seventeenth century construction which would have been erected about the same time as the adjoining barn—the same barn which reputedly once sheltered the fugitive Charles II while he attempted to escape from England.

Today the barn, like the Grange itself, is in safe hands and in recent years much work and a lot of money has been spent privately keeping the buildings in good shape.

Earlier this century, rurally set with neighbouring cottages, this was the heart of Higher Widey farm and was occupied by Sydney Hannaford of the local farming family. 100 years ago William Luke, another farmer, was here, while a Major Letts lived in the Grange itself.

Described 60 years ago as a 'Cow House for Thirty with loft over' and an adjoining cider cellar the barn has in recent years been sympathetically converted by architect Francis Bush—when he first acquired the place it had planning permission for its destruction and a bungalow to be built in its place.

Meanwhile the Grange today is a listed building and in it John and Pam Dryburgh run a residential home for elderly ladies.

Taking over some years ago from the late Mrs. Prentice, John Dryburgh has since done much to restore this home to its former glory and he clearly enjoys living here in these pleasant historic surroundings at Widey.

Mentioned in Domesday the name Widey is thought to come from 'Withey' from the withies or willow trees growing around the spring at the heart of the manor and still to be found in the small section of Widey Woods that has so far resisted encroachment as Eggbuckland, Crownhill and Plymouth itself have relentlessly developed the land around, which unlike Edgcumbe or even Saltram had little in the way of natural defences.

[WEH 17.3.84

The Church of The Ascension Crownhill

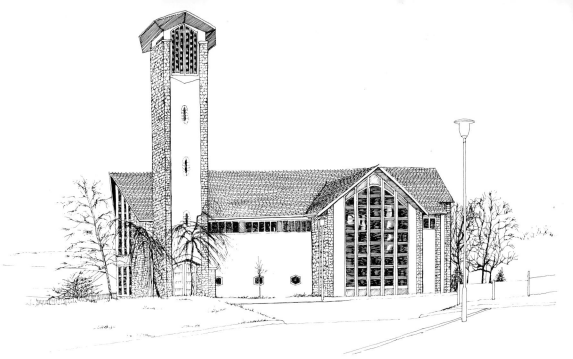

One of Plymouth's more recent religious buildings, the Church of the Ascension at Crownhill this year celebrates its 25th anniversary.

Dedicated on the 6th December, 1958, the church provided a welcome home to those worshippers who, in the earlier part of this century, had been housed variously in the church of the Holy Trinity in Budshead Road, a small, unsatisfactory building which the congregation rapidly outgrew.

They then moved into St. Christopher's in Crownhill Road, which had formerly served as their church hall and then as that was outgrown they joined forces with the Crownhill Garrison Church, St. Alban's. Today only the Budshead Road building still stands.

The new church, called the Church of the Ascension, and appropriate to Crownhill as it sits at the top of a hill (and the Biblical reference to the Lord's Ascension mentions the top of a hill) brought with it the creation of a new Anglican parish and it was largely thanks to the effort and enthusiasm of these parishioners that the church was ever completed.

For, as fate would have it, the first contractors to be given the job of building architect Robert Potter's church went into voluntary liquidation not long after Princess Alexandra laid the foundation stone in 1956.

Then, as if that were not enough, the second contractors hired for the job followed them in the summer of 1957. The vicar at the time was quoted as saying: 'It is to be expected that where the Devil sees the Lord's work being done, he naturally puts his greatest forces to work.'

The Parish Church Council however soon solved the situation by taking the bold step of themselves employing the same men and the same sub-contractors that the last firm had been using, thereby becoming the first parish church in the diocese in over 300 years to have been constructed by 'direct labour.'

Built with substantial financial assistance from the War Damage Commission in respect of St. George's Church at Stonehouse, which was destroyed during the Blitz, the Church of the Ascension 'inherited' pews from St. Catherine's, demolished in the post war rebuilding of the City Centre; an organ from St. Mary's Cattedown, another bomb victim and a bell from old Widey Court.

Although in most other respects a very modern church the building does in fact follow the traditional East-West alignment in cruciform shape. The congregation faces east and therefore looks towards the rising sun, symbolic of the resurrection of Christ and the second coming.

The east wall itself symbolizes death and through its 12 stained glass windows shines the light of Christ's 12 'I am' sayings, contrasting starkly with the solid bare-stoned wall and symbolic of the light of heaven and life beyond.

Behind the congregation, along the foot of the east wall can be seen a narrow bed of plant life, symbolizing growth, a beginning and the Garden of Eden.

The altar is positioned in the centre of the church's cruciform shape in the natural position from which to conduct the work of Christ.

In its 25 years the church has seen four vicars, the first, Eric Turnbull, had been at Crownhill since 1954 and was followed in 1962 by Maurice Bickley; in 1974 by John Metters and then in 1979 the present incumbent, Michael Malsom.

[WEH 5.2.83]

Blindman's Wood

Just over 30 years ago some £400 was paid to the St. Aubyn Estate to secure this 4½-acre woodland site that sits a little to the south of the new Manadon roundabout.

Distinctively named Blindman's Wood, perhaps because of an earlier association with Tor Home for the Blind nearby—although no one is quite sure this land has, over the years, been moulded into the impressive headquarters of the Plymouth Scout Association.

The foundation stone to the warden's accommodation, the Scout shop and the administration block was laid in 1957. Completed within three years, a store, washhouse and garage were added in 1962 and then, on Saturday, 12th June, 1965, the main hall was opened.

Previously based at Buckland House, Millbay, for many years after brief spells in Frankfort Street and before that, at 7A or 7½ Regent Street, Plymouth's scouting movement was first registered at Scout HQ in London on 4th July, 1908, the year Robert Baden-Powell's *Scouting for Boys* was first published.
Two years later Baden-Powell visited Plymouth and carried out an inspection of 14 local troops with a membership of about 300 Scouts. Today there are nearer 3,000 Scouts, Cub Scouts, Sea Scouts, Venture Scouts and leaders and 61 different local groups for whom this is HQ—it's also used at times by local Guides and Brownies.

Appropriately enough, the architect for the main Blindman's Wood development was one of the 300 Scouts to have turned out for Baden-Powell at Millbay in June, 1910. A member then of the Torpoint Troop, Lionel Vanstone, who has designed a great variety of buildings in and around the city, remembers Blindman's Wood as one of his most enjoyable projects, although the bright octogenarian is quick to point out that it was his son, Laurie, who worked up the rough plans and did a lot of the work.

A long established architect himself, Laurie, too, was a Scout in his youth, one of the 19th Emmanuel, a troop that I was also a member of some years later. Indeed it was with that cub pack that I sat my only ever art 'exam' to get my Artist's Badge and it is only recently that the lady who awarded that badge, 'Akela' Jane Adams, has left the 19th Emmanuel after more than 21 years.

Scouting in Plymouth then, had survived through several generations. Now in its 78th year its principles and pleasures are still much the same. Sadly the 'Gang Show' has gone, however, jamborees are still with us and next year the local jamboree will be making a welcome return to Mount Edgcumbe, scene of so much Scouting activity in the 1950s and before.

Meanwhile this summer the National Scoutcar Races will take place on Plymouth Hoe and will doubtless come as a mixed blessing to current City Commissioner Tom Blagdon, whose long involvement in local Scouting—he was a wartime member of St. Andrew's Troop—has made him well aware of the headaches and the fun associated with big events.

During these activities Blindman's Wood will, as it does all year round, play host to many visiting Scouts and keep Scouter-Warden Peter Johnson and his wife, Trisha, more than just a little busy.

[*WEH* 12.1.85

Golden Hind

It must be difficult for Plymouth's postwar generations to imagine now that less than 50 years ago not only was the 'Golden Hind' not built, but the site on which it stands was well outside the Plymouth boundary.

This then was the north-west corner of Compton Gifford, a separate parish, with roads and houses lit by gas, that stretched down to Mutley Plain and Compton Village and which until the early part of the nineteenth century had grown little from the fourteen or fifteen households in the area recorded in the Domesday Survey.

An old house called Redlands, which survived into this century, was the only Compton Gifford building near this location in 1801.

Yet today the 'Golden Hind' stands almost plum in the middle of the great sprawling city of Plymouth—a situation that places it right next to the mammoth earthworks heralding the arrival of Plymouth's mini spaghetti-junction on the new A38 Marsh Mills to Manadon section of the London to Penzance trunk road.

It was in 1938, when Plymouth won a boundary extension that meant an instant city growth from 5,711 acres to 9,595 acres, that the 'Golden Hind' was built.

At the same time housing estates here and elsewhere inside the new city limits sprang up and another two pubs appeared.

'The Golden Hind', the neighbouring 'Cherry Tree', and the 'Fellowship' at St. Budeaux are clearly very similar in many structural respects and were all originally owned by Plymouth Breweries and have all since been passed to Courage.

First landlord of the 'Golden Hind' in 1938 was a gentleman called Bob Warren. He saw the pub through the war years during which time the garage was used as an ARP post.

Altogether the first twenty years here saw a succession of licensees and following on from Bob Warren came Don Coxwell, Roy Medland, Peter Trimm and Don Thomson.

Since 1958, however, one man, Bill Shortt, the ex-Welsh international goalkeeper who made 361 appearances for Argyle, has been its host. Bill came to Argyle from Chester, in 1946—a great favourite at Home Park he retired in 1956 and came to the 'Golden Hind' after a couple of years at the 'Duke of York' in Tavistock.

One of several ex-Argyle publicans, a list that includes Jack Chisholm ('Penny-comequick'), Alec Govan ('Hyde Park'), Billy Strauss (the old 'Octagon Tandem' and the 'Standard') and Fred Titmus ('Cherry Tree').

[WEH 11.6.83]

Tor Boundary Stones

Hundreds, maybe thousands of travellers must pass these boundary stones each day, many will probably not even notice that they are there and many others may wonder at their significance.

Bearing the legends Tything of Western Peverell and Tything of Compton Gifford, the two stones sit either side of the head and arms of a late medieval cross and are undoubtedly among the oldest man-made objects openly visible to Plymothians inside the city boundaries (although the level of tar in which they stand is rising).

Boundary stones as we know them appear to have been in use for some 7,000 years and often we find references, until comparatively recently, of such stones being used as measuring points or meeting places. Early stones are commonly known as pudding stones as their shape and texture is often reminiscent of Christmas plum puddings.

The two stones here at Tor while like a handful or so of other pairs around the city are simply boundary markers, together with the cross they do indicate the point at which the Iron Age road from Sutton Pool to Roborough Down (now the Tavistock Road), was crossed by a trackway from Plympton to Saltash.

Currently sited in a wall on the Eastern side of the road between the two sets of traffic lights immediately to the south of 'Sungates' and before Hartley Reservoir, here then is the boundary between what was the Tythings of Compton Gifford and Western Peverell.

Both these manors appear in the Domesday survey when Judhel of Totnes acquired both from their Saxon owners, Westone from Ulnod and Contone or Contona from Osulf. Originally the smallest unit of Anglo-Saxon local government a Tything was simply a collection of ten households where each was responsible for the behaviour of the rest.

Ten Tythings in turn made up a hundred and Westone, the area we now know as Pennycross, was part of the hundred of Roborough.

Meanwhile at the time of Domesday it is thought, by the nineteenth century local historian R. N. Worth at least, that Compton or Contone included within its Tything territory 'all that is now called Plymouth'—(he was writing in 1896). This gives us some idea of the population of the area over 900 years ago.

However, whilst the population of Plymouth or Sutton grew rapidly from the middle ages, Weston Peverell and Compton Gifford were believed by Worth not to 'vary materially from the conquest to the beginning of the 19th century'.

Indeed although there was substantial growth last century it is really since 1900 that both areas have mushroomed as the Plymouth boundary itself has pushed out well beyond this point leaving it today almost in the geographic centre of the town . . . and it is no small irony that less than half a mile away is the soon to be completed through road that will virtually divide the city into four quarters as the old North–South road is crossed by the new East–West route.

Boundary markers on all new roads, however, are tailored to suit modern traffic and are situated above ground and at right angles to the traveller's path of vision.

Boundary stones and milestones such as those we see here could only be read when people travelled by foot or by horse, and of course when they weren't blackened by dirt or grime as to many ancient roadside stones in the area are today.

[WEH 21.7.84

Emmanuel Church

At the beginning of last century less than two dozen families in some 18 houses made up the entire population of Compton Gifford, a small village a mile and a half outside of Plymouth.

It had neither church nor chapel and had probably altered little over many hundreds of years.

Today, of course, it has been swallowed up by the ever expanding city of Plymouth and is several miles in any direction inside the town's boundaries.

The expansion of Compton Gifford began in earnest in the 1820s when wealthy individuals from the Three Towns began looking for suitable sites on which to build themselves a big house with a bit of land.

The architect John Foulston selected a position just off the present Wilderness Road and Capt. J. G. Bremer, later Sir Gordon Bremer, selected a site in Compton Village itself.

Soon after his move Bremer made a site available for the building of a chapel and offered £200 towards the cost of building it. Licensed in 1836 it was not long before this chapel itself was recognized as being too small for the rapidly expanding community it served.

In 1866, the year the Reverend George Fletcher became curate-in-charge at Compton, a meeting of Mannamead, Compton and other local inhabitants was called, by Fletcher and the Rev. Henry Greaves (vicar of the mother parish of Charles Church), to adopt measures providing the erection of a proposed new church at Mannamead.

Once again a private site was offered, this time by Mrs. Betsy Revel and her daughter Elizabeth. The impetus for this offer came from the late Rev. Revel, Elizabeth's brother, who had, on his deathbed, been anxious that something be done for the church.

Accompanying the subsequent offer of the land was the wish that the church might be named after the Rev. Revel's college at Cambridge—Emmanuel. This college was founded in 1584 and Immanuel or Emmanuel is of course the symbolical name of the child announced by Isaiah (Isa. 7.14) and applied to Jesus as the Messiah in Matthew 1, 23 . . . 'Behold, a virgin shall be with child, and shall bring forth a son and they shall call his name Emmanuel, which being interpreted is, God with us.'

Built from the designs of a Mr. Reid, a local architect, who made no charge for his services, the first corner stone was laid by the Rev. Greaves on 17th June, 1869. Work on the nave and aisles began immediately; unfortunately, however, so did some other work right in front of the church. The Revels had given the site for the church but had kept, and let, the strip of land between it and Tavistock Road to a certain Mr. Marshall who started building three villas here.

From the walls alone it soon became apparent that such development would spoil the roadside views and cramp the church itself, so two men, Mr. C. T. Bewes and Mr. W. Luscombe, took it upon themselves to buy the land, pay off Mr. Marshall and pull down the walls.

In time this land was conveyed to the church and so it still has today this marvellous open space in front of it with its great variety of trees and bushes.

Further church developments were sporadic; the initial work was finished by September 1870 and in 1887 a second corner stone was laid for the building of the transepts, chancel, vestry and completion of the nave. Then in 1895 a third foundation stone marked the beginning of work on the tower.

Both of these later developments are identifiable by the regular as opposed to mosaic-style stonework.

Today of course Emmanuel still looks unfinished, and describing the church in 1896 historian R. N. Worth said 'this year the church is being provided with a tower, eventually to be surmounted by a spire'.

However as time ran on, money ran out and such aspirations were in vain. It seems unlikely now that current incumbent the Rev. Peter Stephens (12th Vicar of Emmanuel) and his successors will ever move to change the tower, however, for those who wonder what it would have been like there is an original artist's impression—inside the porch.

[WEH 29.10.83]

BBC Plymouth

At the end of the 1930s the BBC began its move out of the city centre, a prudent move in the light of the 1941 bombing which forced a complete withdrawal from their premises in Athenaeum Lane.

The new home of broadcasting in Plymouth thus became a grand Victorian villa, called at the time it was purchased from its owner Mrs. Douglass, 'Ingledene'.

Mrs. Douglass was a relative of Sir James Douglass, designer of the Eddystone Lighthouse built in 1882 that we see at sea today.

'Ingledene' formerly Stamford House is perhaps unique among current BBC premises in that the corporation actually own, rather than lease, the property. Situated today in Seymour Road, its address 100 years ago was simply Second Avenue and, indeed, prior to that all dwellings in the area went under the one collective address of Mannamead.

Broadcasting began in Plymouth with station 5PY on 28th March, 1924, within 12 years, however, Plymouth's function as a regular broadcasting centre was cut back with only occasional programmes and the odd series being sent out from here.

Johnny Morris was one of the many to cut his broadcasting teeth down here in that era and during wartime itself Frank Gillard was one of several regular war correspondents who somehow secretly made it across from France, transmitted their reports and then slipped quietly back across the Channel.

True local radio, however, was still a far-off prospect when ironically a buzz of activity in 1961 saw the introduction of a regular ten-minute television spot—'News from the South West' read by Tom Salmon. Although television had been seen in the Westcountry since 1954 this was the first time that there had been a genuine local contribution and within a year the slot was doubled in length, becoming at first 'South West at Six' and then, in 1963, 'Spotlight'. This long-running programme has launched many illustrious media careers and among its celebrated presenters the programme can count, David Smeeton (1960–3), David Lomax (1963–7), Hugh Scully (1963–78), Sheila Tracey (1963–73), Angela Rippon (1966–70), Jan Leeming (1968–9), Sue Lawley (1970–3), Kate Adie (1976), Linda Alexander (1977), and Fern Britton.

Whatever local BBC Television's claim to national success, however, and yes Don Hoyle's Breakfast TV contibutions came from these grounds, it is in local radio that the biggest steps have been made in recent years.

In February 1970 the regular five-minute local news bulletins were greatly extended with the introduction of 'Midday Parade' which finished exactly ten years ago and was superseded on the 1st of March 1973 by 'Morning Sou'west'.

Incidentally, 1973 was also the year of the building of the major new extension and studios to make way for the introduction of local colour transmissions in August 1974.

Morning Sou'west itself didn't quite run a full ten years ending with the arrival of BBC Radio Devon and Radio Cornwall, which effectively increased overnight local BBC Radio coverage from 2½ hours a day to the present 12 hours a day.

For the local BBC Radio headquarters, this new venture heralds for the most part a move away from Seymour Road up the A38 to Exeter.

[*WEH* 26.2.83

Hyde Park Hotel

On page 127 of his 1879 Handbook to Plymouth, W. H. K. Wright provides us with one of the earliest literary references to this Mutley Plain landmark:

'Passing over the Plain, we reach the foot of Townsend Hill, opposite the Hyde Park Hotel.'

Townsend, we are told, is a corruption of Tongue's Land, the original name for this area of land.

Ironically, however, it wasn't that many years earlier that Townsend Hill would have marked the actual Town's End of what we know today as Plymouth.

But, 100 years ago this area was not even part of Plymouth; rather it was a part of Compton Gifford.

Furthermore, while earlier directory references to the 'Hyde Park Hotel' go back to 1867 there was mention made in 1866 of a 'Townsend Inn', run by one Servington Lethbridge, at Ford Park, Mutley.

This inn was not heard of after 1866 and indeed its location suggests that it was the 'Hyde Park' under a different name.

Directory references to the 'Townsend Inn' go back as far as 1856 and certainly this is a likely enough time for the hotel to have been built as the development of that end of Mutley was then well under way, having grown from only a handful of people and dwelling houses in 1801 to several thousand people by the end of the century.

In 1823 one guide had written: 'from North Hill a path across pleasant fields leads to Mutley, a small village with several genteel dwellings.' An earlier writer tells us that this little village was 'much frequented in the summer by the inhabitants of Plymouth to drink tea at.'

Change however, was brisk and soon after the appearances of 'some very neat villas and the plantation of several young elm trees,' local cottages, then terraces, appeared,

Hyde Park Terrace itself dating from 1849.

The name Hyde Park first occurred in Middlesex after the Norman *hida* (a hide is also an old term for a measurement of land).

Development beyond Mutley also became conspicuous around this time and the Parish of Compton Gifford expanded dramatically off its Bronze Age backbone, Tavistock Road, which had been greatly improved some years earlier by the Tavistock Turnpike Act, during George III's time, when both Hartley and Townsend Hills were much levelled and other sections raised, including Mutley Plain, prompting the nineteenth century Plymouth Historian R. N. Worth to note that 'The original ups and downs were far more considerable than is now apparent.'

Tavistock Road at this time ran up from the side of the 'Hyde Park Hotel' that we see here, there then being stables at the back. At the turn of the century horses were always kept here, at Hyde Park Corner, to help trams up Townsend Hill.

Always at the side of a busy thoroughfare, the 'Hyde Park' has had a fair flow of landlords—from Victor Walker, its first recorded licensee as the 'Hyde Park', through to more recent years with Len Irish who spent a couple of years there in the early 1950s before moving on to the 'Rising Sun', and Alec Govan who is perhaps better known to locals as the Argyle forward who played 145 games scoring 35 goals for the club in two periods between 1946–60.

Today, with its revitalized Folk Club upstairs and its unique road island views the 'Hyde Park' appears to be enjoying its most successful phase to date.

Since August 1981, when they took over from George Ashley, Rod and Maggie Hillman have invited all comers to what they've appropriately dubbed their 'Island of Hospitality'.

[*WEH* 21.5.83

Hyde Park School

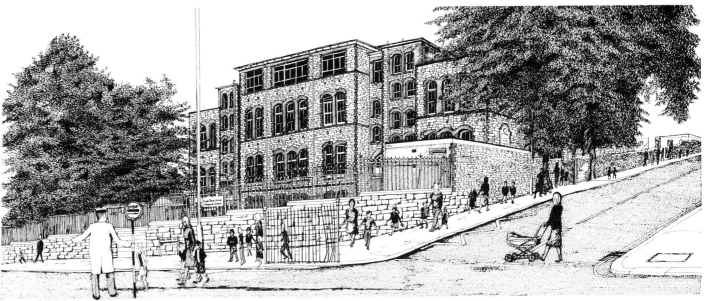

When, two or three hundred years after the Domesday Survey, lower Mutley became part of Compton, the Manor House for this estate moved from Compton village to here where Hyde Park School now stands.

In the days of Elizabeth I the building that was here had a very famous tenant as proclaimed in the tablet on the wall . . . 'On this site stood Thornhill House, which, in 1592 was the property of Edmund Parker and in the occupation of Sir Francis Drake.'

From this house Drake would have had the pleasure of seeing what was subsequently called Drake's Leat flowing past his windows, for he was its champion.

Built to supplement the towns' already inadequate supply of fresh water the scheme received Royal Assent in 1585, however, thanks to the war with Spain and the Armada, work did not begin until December 1590. By the 24th April, 1591, the 17-mile long 6-foot wide, 2-foot deep ditch was complete and legend has it that Drake rode from the Head Weir at Burrator to Plymouth followed by the first flow of water and the Lord Mayor of Plymouth and his retinue.

Some 300 years later again all was different as, not long after its architectural twin in Salisbury Road, Hyde Park Road School was opened in 1904.

Used as a hospital during the First World War the school suffered major structural damage during the Second World War which accounts for the low flat modern roof we see on the building today.

The rebuilding of Hyde Park took a long time. Initially just after the school had been bombed classes were evacuated and conducted in the neighbouring churches; by the time the war had ended classes had been brought back although not all were in the school building itself. Two groups found themselves in the British Restaurant Hut that had been set up during wartime in the front playground and another took lessons in the school dining room. With the large halls in the middle of the building

also damaged the only way from one side of the school to the other at this time was down the stairs and around the front or back. This, combined with the taking of assemblies in individual classrooms, meant that communication around the school was often less than efficient.

In 1948 when radio personality Richard Dimbleby arrived with the rest of his 'Down Your Way' team to interview the head boy and girl about the school's marvellous 'Paper for Salvage' efforts, it was not until the next day that Audrey Hosier and her class in the dining room learned about it. A teacher at the school until 1981, Hyde Park owes a lot to Miss Hosier for her successful fight to keep the wonderful old trees around the school today.

Back in the mid-forties the school had a radio star of its own in the shape of teacher Ruby Luscombe, who regularly made trips up to the BBC in Bristol to take part in plays and other broadcasts. Geoffrey Cowley, the ballet choreographer, was a pupil about then and of course in later years dancer extraordinaire Wayne Sleep completed his junior school education here.

As the 1950s dawned, the rebuilding of the school was virtually completed and the only major upheavals after Mr. F. W. Buckley arrived as Headmaster in 1951, took place outside the school walls as the tramlines in Hyde Park Road with their great granite sets were pulled up. Well liked and well remembered, Mr. Buckley saw a complete generation through the school in his 25 year stay and many are they including myself, who can remember waiting nervously outside his office to receive a reprimand for some typical junior school offence. Today that office is occupied by his 1977 successor, Richard Jordan who now has anxious parents waiting outside.

Happy with their children's Hyde Park junior and infant education, they want to know when this large Plymouth school is going to have a satisfactory secondary school counterpart.

[*WEH* 25.6.83]

Plymouth College

Exactly 100 years ago Plymouth High School for Boys, which had been founded a few years after Plymouth High School for Girls, changed its name to Plymouth College.

Originally founded in 1877 the College joined forces in 1896 with Mannamead School, the latter having been started by the Rev Peter Holmes in 1854.

Disillusioned with the 300-year-old Plymouth Grammar School where he had been headmaster for fourteen years, Holmes decided to set up his own school for 'A limited number of Young Gentlemen preparing for the Public Schools or the Naval or Military Colleges or the Universities.'

Initially a great success, numbers of this school in Seymour Villa began to decline in the 1880s as Plymouth College started to establish itself in the City.

The eventual amalgamation of these two schools gave rise to an expanded old boys' organization whose members have since been known as Old Plymothians and Mannameadians—OPMs.

Celebrated for their local prowess in the Rugby Sevens, the OPMs and the school have not always been rugger playing institutions and indeed up until 1906 football was the school game.

In the 1880s and 1890s both the school and the Old Boys enjoyed a wide variety of football fixtures with strong links being formed between the school and the newly constituted Argyle FC who regularly played on the Ford Park pitch before their move to Home Park.

Many games were played between the various teams and on one occasion in 1885 the OPs, as they were then, beat the pre-professional Argyle FC 10–0.

Whilst the OPM colours of magenta, chocolate and light blue were officially determined the year the OPs and the OMs first teamed up, it was to be another 30 years before the now familiar green of Mannamead School was added to the original Plymouth College colours of red and black, the school cap and blazer consequently being redesigned in 1926.

The main school building as it stands today is but part of the original plan which save for financial restrictions would have seen a much extended and grander version of this impressive old edifice, a structure which itself was saved from devastation by fire during the blitz by the quick reactions of the various 'watches' set up by the then headmaster H. W. Ralph. Mr. Ralph was at the school's helm for 16 years from 1929 and all but one of his post-war successors are alive today, B. H. Garnons-Williams (1945–53), C. M. Meade King (1955–73), J. L. Goddard (1973–4) and the current head R. H. Merrett who retires this year. F. W. Lockwood (1953–5) died in office, occasioning the long-serving John Dufton to step in as acting head for the second time in his career.

Meanwhile in its hundred years as Plymouth College the school has grown more than tenfold from its 60-odd in 1880 to its total of well over 600 today; with perhaps the biggest single change being the introduction of girls into the sixth form which began in 1976.

[WEH 19.2.83]

The Belgrave

Meanwhile, elsewhere in 1911, Guy Prance was busy getting the Ford Palladium (now Palladium Timbers) off the ground. Guy Prance was one of the big names in local entertainment in the early part of this century and although primarily a cinema man he spent a number of years managing the Palace Theatre in the 1920s. In 1931, together with William Mumford (of Mumford Motors) he built the 3,254-seater Regent Cinema in Frankfort Street and in later years still well ahead of his time, his plan to build a great Embassy Cinema, Restaurant and Dance Hall complex at Milehouse was only thwarted by the Government restrictions on steel availability.

Nevertheless, the Embassy Cinema Plymouth Ltd. company had been formed and in 1951 added the Belgrave Picture Theatre to its acquisitions and from that date until the present day the Belgrave has been run by the charming quietly spoken man with the pipe and trilby, Guy Prance's son, John.

Like his father John has spent all his working days in the cinema and for a while ran the Plaza just after its pre-war opening.

Prior to 1951 Ernest Bertram (Bertie) Hoyle ran the Belgrave for some 25 years, and, like John Prance, his father was also a one-time manager of the Palace Theatre.

Tommy Hoyle really left his mark at the Palace by having his initials plastered all around the auditorium. Legend has it that Tommy Hoyle bought the Belgrave for his son as a wedding present.

Situated at the top of Belgrave Road, the cinema (or Picture Theatre as it used to say under the cinema sign above the front canopy) was for a short time used as an auction hall.

Before that the site enjoyed several decades of horse business—100 years ago it was known as Harry Bickell's Horse Emporium; in the 1890s it became Major R. Woods & Sons Horse Repository and then after a brief period as a tramway stables, it was, until the building of Belgrave Hall, the Devon and Cornwall Horse Bazaar.

The HQ of this building No. 2 Belgrave Road was incorporated into the frontage of the Picture Theatre in the 1920s, the original entrance being approached by the black-and-white tiled path that runs up from the front gate.

Before Belgrave Road was re-numbered No. 2 was No. 76 and in its earliest days it was No. 76 Middleton Street.

One of local history's nice little coincidences was discovered when outgoing owner John Prance was looking through the early deeds to the site and found the witnessing signature of his great grandfather, a local solicitor, at the bottom of one of the documents.

Easily the oldest surviving picture house in Plymouth, the Belgrave opens its doors to local cinema goers tonight for the last time.

The Belgrave was opened in 1912 and at that time was one of seven such houses in the area.

An outing to the pictures then would cost anywhere between tuppence and sixpence and tea was generally served free to ladies between 3 o'clock and 4.30.

Cinematograph pictures were still fairly novel then, however, and a 1911 advertisement for the Theatre Elite in Ebrington Street proudly proclaimed that this medium was now 'recognized as ideal family entertainment.'

[WEH 26.3.83

The Fortescue, Mutley Plain

Mutley Plain has been a comparatively busy local thoroughfare for several thousand years now and for the Bronze Age person this natural ridge formed part of the northern route from Sutton Pool to Dartmoor.

By the time of the Domesday Survey, Mutley or Modlei had been developed up to the extent of two small manors worth five shillings each.

Both of these were at the northern end of the ridge and between them they comprised a manor house, three farms and a couple of smallholdings.

Inevitably, however, the population grew and as the village of Mutley evolved it did so, half as part of Compton Gifford and half as part of Plymouth.

Indeed, the 1866 Directory of Devon described Compton Gifford as a 'small village and tithing a mile-and-a-half from Plymouth in the southern division of the county ... but not within the borough of Plymouth ... It includes the pleasant villages of Mutley and Ford Park.'

The Plymouth boundary was then marked by the railway line west of the Plain, the pavement on its western side and the lane above Connaught Avenue. Just inside this line and first mentioned in 1867 was John Dickenson's 'Fortescue Hotel'. Variously referred to as numbers 16, 14 and 19 Mutley Plain, the 'Fortescue' finally became No. 37 Mutley Plain in 1896, the year Plymouth's extension bill was successfully put through Parliament. Thereafter Compton, together with Peverell and Laira were brought inside the city boundary, thereby eliminating the anomaly whereby people who lived at one end of the Plain paid only half the rates of those who lived at the other end.

1896 also saw a change in the licensee at the 'Fortescue' as a Mrs. Wright was succeeded by a Mrs. Lavers. Orlando Wright had run the 'Hotel' from 1870 to 1890 and the Lavers family subsequently held the place until 1904.

In that year in the tenancy of S. M. J. Hodge, 37 Mutley Plain and the first two houses of Moor View Terrace were knocked into one as the 'Fortescue' stretched outwards and upwards, this work being completed in 1905, hence the two dates on the corner facia top and bottom.

In 1907 A. J. Bidway took over at the bar and since that day only two other landlords have run the 'Forte'. Albert Dyer succeeded Bidway in the mid-twenties and shortly after Dyer's death in 1951, his wife handed over to the ebullient Gordon Tregenza, who has been there ever since.

In 1954 Gordon says he opened Mutley's first licensed restaurant downstairs and but for one or two other fairly minor changes, the 'Fortescue' and its landlord have not greatly altered since.

With 32 years *in situ* under his belt and still going strong, Gordon Tregenza must surely be well set to complete the record stint as a licensee in one place in Plymouth, should anyone ever happen to know what such a record is.

[*WEH* 9.4.83

Royal Eye Infirmary

Situated only yards away from the site of the old Mutley Railway Station, the Plymouth Royal Eye Infirmary has been here in this purpose built building since 1900. Prior to that it had been based for over 50 years in converted accommodation on the corner of Millbay Road and the old Buckland Street where the Continental Hotel now stands.

This in turn was the third premises that infirmary founder Dr. John Butter had worked from. The Plymouth Eye Dispensary, as it was first known, began life in No. 16 Cornwall Street and opened to the public on Christmas Day 1821.

This dispensary at last superseded the limited ophthalmic work that had been carried out since 1799 under the umbrella of the Plymouth General Dispensary. Deemed to be operating at a level well below what one would expect of an area the size of the Three Towns in 1821, it was only after a vigorous campaign that Dr. Butter established this separate body.

In 1822 the 'Plymouth Eye Dispensary' became the 'Plymouth Eye Infirmary' and then five years later, thanks to the patronage of the Duke of Clarence (later William IV), it changed again to the 'Plymouth Royal Eye Infirmary', a title it still has today. That same year, 1827, there was a move from Cornwall Street to Westwell Street.

The foundation stone for the present site for sore eyes was laid in 1897 to commemorate Queen Victoria's Diamond Jubilee and although patients were admitted here before the end of 1900, Victoria's death in January 1901 delayed the official opening until 30th October, 1901.

The total cost of the building, including fences, furnishings, laying the grounds, the architects' fees and the land itself— £18,613 15s 4d.

In May 1939, just two months before the 90 year-old Mutley Station closed, the infirmary's east wing extension was offically opened, since when, apart from war damage, the building has altered little externally. Inside, however, developments, surgical and technological have continued apace.

Some 80 patients are dealt with here each day with on average over 11,000 new patients presenting themselves here each year, with one in ten likely to be operated on.

Most common operations today are squints in infants and cataracts in older patients, while still one of the most common causes of casualty cases at the infirmary is the head-through-the-car-windscreen crash victim. While ophthalmic techniques may have changed greatly over the last 100 years or so and lasers have replaced leeches as the unusual items in the surgery, one element has remained constant—the human one.

Talking with some staff members in the light of Monday's Herald headline about a proposed move to Derriford (which they, too, first learned about when reading their paper) one is reminded of John Butters's original 1821 circular.

Commenting on their break for 'independence' the pamphlet stated . . . 'the numerous and extended services annually rendered by the General Dispensary are not forgotten. These sister institutions would not be opposed to each other but allied as members of one family of which the public are parents. But they must be separate and distinct here as elsewhere, in order to give the utmost efficiency and certainty to the treatment of ophthalmic cases.'

Different staffing arrangements and not Derriford premises are seen by many here at Mutley today as the step towards greater efficiency.

[*WEH* 3.3.84

The Baptist Church, Mutley

With the arrival of the railways in Plymouth in the middle of the last century, the South Devon Railway Co. dug a large tunnel under Mutley Plain. On its west side soon after appeared Mutley Station, which remained open until 1939. In recent years this tunnel has been extended a little by the building of Mutley's multi-storey car park.

The view as seen here is taken from almost directly above this tunnel upon which has also stood since 1869 the impressive Mutley Baptist Church. It was built from the designs of Messrs Ambrose and Snell at a cost of nearly £8,000, and fronting as it does onto one of Plymouth's main thoroughfares, few people ever manage to take in all of this grand structure in one glance.

As far as the West Country is concerned the design of this church is believed to be unique and certainly the only other type of building I can think of where 'the front elevation consists of a pediment over a large arched recess flanked by two quasi-towers with high pitched truncated slate roofs' is a Toytown one made of children's wooden building blocks.

Here, however, the main structural features are of Portland Stone, the front steps and slabs are Cornish granite, while blue Pomphlett limestone makes up the walls.

Opened on Thursday, 11th November, 1869, the church was Plymouth's second Baptist Chapel and for several years it was jointly ministered in the shadow of the earlier George Street Chapel.

In 1876, however, it was decided that Mutley, originally designed as a kind of overspill chapel, should go it alone.

Consequently in July that year the Rev. Benwell Bird, of Birmingham, became the parish's first pastor.

A popular figure, Mr. Bird remained in Plymouth until his death in 1920 and although he had long since retired (1900) he did return for a brief period during the Great War when the Rev W. Vaughan King served in France for two years as the United Army Board Chaplain.

Mr. King was the third minister at Mutley, having taken over in 1914 from Rev J. Bell Johnson. Messrs. Franklin (1923), Grey (1932), Gladstone (1955), and Wright (1960) followed, and then in 1966 the present incumbent, the jolly Philip Withers, was called to the ministry.

During the Second World War the time came for Mutley to play host to the George Street parishioners as their chapel sadly fell victim to the bombing, and indeed on more than one occasion Mutley itself was only spared from destruction by the efficient handling of incendiaries. However, survive it did and today the church, having successfully celebrated its centenary, has only pigeons to contend with.

167

[WEH 9.1.83

Bowyers

The old Bowyers factory in Alexandra Road was always many things to many people. To hundreds, if not thousands, it was a place of work but to many more it was a reminder to those coming back to Plymouth by train that the station was just a tunnel away and it was time to put your coat on.

The factory was a landmark that all Plymothians were familiar with. Most people knew it as the Beechwood factory and indeed if my experience is anything to go by there are more than a handful of people in Plymouth today who think it's still there.

However, it's now more than two and a half years since this strangely wonderful pile of little red bricks came crashing to the ground.

Almost a hundred years had passed since the buildings had gone up in the 1880s. Built originally as a brewery it began life as the New Bedford Brewery, Mutley. Here they bottled, among other delights, Oatmalt Stout, Devon Stout, the celebrated Dinner Ale, Brown Ale and even for a time Guinness.

Established in 1824, the Bedford Brewery was later taken over by Allsops and in turn Ind Coope. The Brewery moved from Alexandra Road to Weston Park Road in 1921.

The same year production lines inside the walls were introduced to churn out something completely different—sausages.

Brown, Wills and Nicholson became the new owners in 1921 and although they had started out almost 150 years earlier as tea blenders and grocers they initiated a change in use of the premises which remained constant to its close, despite several changes in ownership.

In 1957 a subsidiary of Cow and Gate, the Yeovil-based Aplin and Barratt, bought the place; two years later, however, Cow and Gate merged with United Diaries to become Unigate and then just as everything seemed settled Bowyers, at that time a separate concern, bought up the Beechwood Plant.

It was now 1960 and 350 people were employed producing a wide range of goods that included sausages, pasties and pies and packing bacon, gammon, frankfurters and ox-tongue.

At peak times this sun-baked sausage factory could produce some 20,000 pounds of sausages and twice as many pies per day.

In addition to this, tons and tons of ox-tongue were tinned and taken out and indeed today the new Bowyers plant can produce 3,000 cases of ox-tongue per week.

The Beechwood factory was demolished in 1980, the chimney itself tumbling down on the morning of 15th May.

Bowyers, of course, moved out to the Newnham Industrial Estate at Plympton and the massive Texas Homecare shed now occupies this site, but the memories, if not the pong, linger on.

[*WEH* 18.12.82]

Compton Inn

Of indeterminate age the building that houses the 'Compton Inn' is known to be centuries old and believed to be the oldest surviving building in Compton.

With walls that are in places up to four feet thick the 'Compton' was thought to have once contained a granary, tannery and cobbler's shop, and Worth in his 1896 paper on the Tything of Compton Gifford tells us that the building was 'the farmhouse of Kelway's (or Callaway's) tenement'. However since 1857 at least part of it has been the 'Compton Inn' and was run last century for over 30 years by Thomas Moule. It is likely that the 'Compton's' life as an Inn began with Thomas Moule a little before 1857.

Although, according to Worth, Compton (Contone or Contona) was probably 'the most important Domesday manor within the Three Towns area (Stoke Damerel excepted)' it nevertheless appears that there was little change in its population and development until the dawn of the nineteenth century. When the first census was taken in 1801 there was a population of 92 made up of 16 families in 15 houses and the 1086 Domesday Survey had accounted for fourteen or fifteen households in the area. Within 40 years however the population had all but trebled, the 1841 census listing 271 inhabitants. Thomas Moule was one of them and in 1858 we already find him to be one of the Tything's more substantial landowners, and, come 1849, one of the 22 men in the area entitled to vote. Incidentally in 1838 we find reference to a beershop in the area run by someone called Stapledon, and in 1841 William Rendle, described as a Plymouth Gentleman, is shown as owning a beerhouse. From these records, however, it is not clear whether the two are the same or whether either of them could be one of the three Compton pubs here in 1857—the 'Compton', 'Rising Sun' and 'Townsend Inn', which later became the 'Hyde Park Hotel'.

Whatever the case, once Thomas Moule acquired the premises, the 'Compton' was to remain in the family until 1938, throughout which time the Compton was an attractive little thatched free house. Back in 1885 when Compton was still a village outside Plymouth, there were several Moules living here; John Moule was the sanitary inspector to the local board, his wife a draper and Robert Moule, who took over the Compton in the early 1890s, was the local grocer. Mary Moule succeeded him 20 years later and then, after ten years being run by Fred Parkin, Charles Moule became the last of the family to own and manage the Inn. Plymouth Breweries bought the pub in 1940 and Bert Squires, an ex-metropolitan police sergeant, became their first licensee here. Like so many of his predecessors, Bert's stay was a long one; as is that of the 'Compton's' current hosts Dick and Jean Cardey, who arrived late in 1967. A former Royal Hampshire's man, this is Dick's first pub and, he says, it will be his last. He took it over from Emma Clarke who left the 'Compton' for the 'George' in Plympton.

Meanwhile Compton Village itself has seen a good many comings and goings with a great deal of development and re-development taking place all around. Thus while still to be found 'where two shallow valleys meet round a sharp spur of higher ground at the head of a steep coombe (hence Coombe-ton)', Compton Village is not quite the 'somewhat picturesque coombe . . . shrouded in trees' that Worth knew and loved all those years ago.

[*WEH* 27.4.85]

Rising Sun, Compton

Few public houses inside the Plymouth boundary look more like a country pub than the 'Rising Sun' here in Compton.

Not that this is particularly surprising for the 'Rising Sun' stood for almost 200 years as a wayside inn in the country before being enveloped in the Plymouth housing sprawl in the late 1930s, since when it has changed very little externally save for a bit of decoration here and there, some shuttering and some signwriting.

All round, however, apart from Hillside House and the immediately adjacent buildings, the changes have been major and widespread.

Gone are the acres of market gardens that stretched out towards Abrahams farm at the top of what is now Efford.

Gone is Tremlett's farm and his dairy on Mutley Plain; gone is Harry Knapman's farm from where this drawing was taken and where, once upon a time, people on their way to church could witness the farmer ending the life of some poor fatted pig.

Gone too is the old Dingles slaughterhouse a bit further down the road at the head of the ancient public right of way from Sutton Pool to Eggbuckland.

Still dubbed Slaughterhouse Lane by some of the locals, this part of the old throughway has sadly been allowed to grow wild and unruly, a mess to most people but a paradise to dog owners.

Long gone too the Barrashalls with their horse and cart refuse collection business.

Meanwhile, as the streets sprang up so the main road, Eggbuckland Road, was widened and a pavement constructed outside the pub. The old stone wall though remains much the same, only today you're unlikely to see any horses impounded here.

In the days when the stage coach used to stop at Hender's Corner two fresh horses would be brought down from here having earlier been brought up Chapel Way from Compton Village.

In those days when Mrs. Folkes ran the 'Rising Sun' it would not have been unusual to see ducks and chickens clucking around the bar.

Very much a simple beer and cider only pub then, it is very different today. The various structural changes since the last war, however, have not been marked by a great number of personnel changes behind the bar.

Only three landlords have had the place in that time, Harry Fernley, Len Irish and Jack and Pat Woodford, who arrived here six years ago and intend to retire from here.

Starting out as a team back in 1958 they were then the first licensees of 'The Falstaff' at Southway, subsequently enjoying spells at the 'Royal Naval Arms' and 'The Prince Regent' before coming here.

A common enough name nationwide, there have been several other 'Rising Suns' in Plymouth, the last changing its name to 'The Roundabout' a few years ago.

The name 'Rising Sun' itself is thought to derive from the badge of Britain's fourteenth-century monarch Edward III.

Simple and sensible as 'Rising Sun' sounds the 'Rising Moon' seems like a very silly name for a pub; there is one however—in Cheshire and no doubt it keeps the cat smiling.

[WEH 11.8.84]

Eggbuckland Church

Eggbuckland was mentioned in William the Conqueror's Domesday Book.

It was listed as an estate owned by Judhel and held by deed in the time of Edward the Confessor by a Saxon lord called Heche, and it is from Heche that the name Eggbuckland as Egg Buckland derives.

In 1068 it was known as Hecke's boke londe or Heche's book land and by 1385 this had become Ekebokland.

Until medieval times this estate was, via Plym Bridge, the natural halfway stage between Plympton Priory and Sutton Prior.

At this time Plympton Priory had jurisdiction over Eggbuckland, as indeed it also had over Sutton, and although the Priory's clerical patronage ended with the dissolution of the monasteries in 1538 it was not until 1939 that the Parish Council of Eggbuckland ceased to fall under the control of Plympton Rural District Council and instead found itself, albeit very reluctantly, inside Plymouth's ever-expanding boundary line.

Long before this, however, among the estates that fell within the Parish of Eggbuckland itself, were those of Leigham, Efford and Widey.

This latter estate became a source of trouble for the village during the Civil War, for it was here that the Royalist Prince Maurice made his headquarters and it was here during 1644 that he was visited by King Charles.

By way of punishment for showing such sympathy to the Royalists the Plymouth Sectarians some time after the war in 1653 took vengeance on Eggbuckland and vandalized the church 'by the authority of Parliament'.

Windows and woodwork were damaged and the 80-year-old vicar turned out. The main fabric of the church however was untouched.

Indeed, today the tower, the nave and the porch are all original and date from about 1430. The northern aisle and the chancel were added last century. The site was probably once occupied by a Saxon church and doubtless replaced by a Norman one. The first recorded vicar of Eggbuckland, Walter, was initiated on 17th April, 1275.

The clock in the tower commemorates one of St. Edward's longest serving vicars, Charles Turner, who died in 1901, having taken up his post in 1861. Charles Whitfield the present vicar of this delightful old church (dedicated to Edward the Martyr, King of the West Saxons) took up his post in 1968.

[*WEH* 4.9.82

Plym Bridge

'The scenery of the banks of this river is very little known—even to most of the natives, and therefore rarely attracts the notice of strangers, deserving of attention . . . it should be visited on horseback as the roads will scarcely admit of any carriage!'

The first half of this description could almost apply today, only the latter, and perhaps the phraseology give away the fact that it wasn't written this century but rather the beginning of last, in 1812.

A few years later in his 1830 guide to the Plymouth Area Henry Carrington gave us a somewhat fuller, more timeless account of this view . . . 'Plym Bridge' . . . he wrote, 'is situated in a kind of grand natural amphitheatre formed by wooded hills, rising on every side but one to a great height. The river above the bridge spreads into a mimic lake, and fine old trees stand on the margin . . . with their green faces fixed upon the flood.

'The stream is so still that the dip of the smallest insect creates little ringlets on the surface. The water is here and there darkened by the overhanging limb of some gigantic forester; and frequently may a speckled trout be seen jealously darting along the weedy margin.

'Below the bridge it is pleasing to remark the stream, which was so tranquil above, bursting into foam as it descends the inclined floors of the arches, saluting the ear with all the delightful associations attendant on falling water.'

Sitting drawing for several sunny days beside this bridge it's hard to imagine that 150 years worth of water have flowed under its arches since that was written. Hard that is until the unpleasant roar of a small but disproportionately noisy motorbike shatters the gentle sounds of the birds and the bees and the wind in the trees.

Today of course as well as bikes Plym Bridge also accommodates light motorized carriages and Plym Bridge Lane as it runs down from the new Leigham estate must be the prettiest road in Plymouth.

Plym Bridge itself is of uncertain age, its first known reference is in the 'Devon Feet of Fines' which recorded an agreement in June 1238 which mentioned 'the highway leading to Tavistock, as far as below the old pond of the mill of Bocland by the Bridge of the Plyme'.

This road between Eggbuckland and Plym Bridge together with Forder Valley and the Plym itself marked the Domesday Manor of Leigham (Leuricheston). A two-farmed, one-manor-house estate which changed little between 1086 and 1966 when the new housing estate programme began in that area.

The estate's Domesday name however highlights another question, one raised in recent years in Crispin Gill's very readable Plymouth Histories. Could Leurichestona be a reference to Leurie's Stone, the stone by the leurie from which the local farms Mainstone and Rock perhaps took their names; and if so was the Leurie or Laira the original name for the Plym, for there appears to be a general consensus that the name Plym is a back formation from Plympton, a name several centuries older than that of Plymouth itself, but a name by no means as old as the Tamar for example.

The Laira of course is not the Plym's only named estuary for the river has yet to pass through the Cattewater before it reaches the Sound.

However, suggestions that the Cattewater tooks its name from a land formation, in other words as with Leurie's Stone there was possibly once a rock which looked like a cat, here by the water, doesn't seem quite as plausible as the simple one offered by Brewer's nineteenth century dictionary of phrase and fable which refers to the common spelling of Catwater and states that this is a 'corruption of chateau; as the castle at the mouth of the Plym used to be called'. As even most people who claim to know no French will know chateau is French for castle, chat is cat and eau is water.

[*WEH* 9.7.83]

Plympton St. Mary

Plympton St. Mary Church was built in the ancient cemetery of Plympton Priory; it is believed to have been dedicated or consecrated on 29th October, 1311.

The Priory itself had been founded in 1121 by Bishop Warwist (or Warelast) a nephew of William the Conqueror and cousin of Henry I.

Bishop Warwist was apparently not satisfied with the secular clergy in the Saxon college at Plympton, possibly, it has been suggested, because there had been the odd and at the time forbidden marriage contracted by the incumbent clergy.

Whatever the reasons, the arrival of the Norman Augustinian canons spelt the end of the Saxon Monasticism that had prevailed at 'Plymentum' since at least 904AD, and the old church and house were soon replaced by more ornate Norman buildings.

The priory church completed in 1176 was later ravaged as part of the wholesale dissolution and destruction of religious houses ordered by Henry VIII.

St. Mary's Church escaped unscathed. Early Perpendicular in style it was apparently begun in the later part of the thirteenth century. In 1806 and 1858 restoration work was carried out, chiefly inside the church and little has changed in the outward appearance of the church in at least 140 years.

The grounds have been extended a little and a clock and boiler house added; otherwise it's much the same as it was when Henry E. Carrington wrote in 1828: 'Plympton St. Mary Church is an edifice of venerable aspect standing close to the London road.

'The tower is handsome having pinnacles at the four corners and contains a good set of bells.'

[*WEH* 24.4.82

The George, Plympton

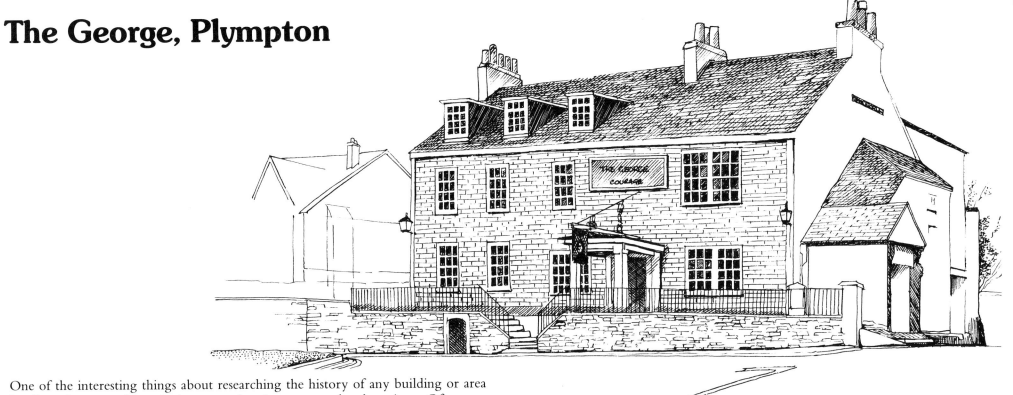

One of the interesting things about researching the history of any building or area locally is that you seldom find a comprehensive account already written. Often you find only brief glimpses into the past with a line or two of information in one old journal or another.

Such is the case with the 'George' at Plympton. From the Universal British Directory of 1798 we learn that Ridgeway was a village 'A quarter of a mile distant from Plympton (St Maurice),' with the turnpike road running through it and further than that, 'the post formerly went through Plympton (St Maurice,) but, since the institution of the mailcoach, the post goes through Ridgeway and the postmaster waits at the 'George Inn' to take the bag.'

Doubtless then the postmaster William Eveleigh (who was also the local bailiff and whose son William Eveleigh Jun. was the local serjeant-at-mace) would have whiled away his waiting moments with the landlord Richard King, who acquired a nine-year lease on the building in 1797.

It is from another deed that we glean the information that in 1837 the 'George' went from the hands of William Moor to those of Samuel Woollacott of Crediton, who was still there in 1850 when from a contemporary directory we find that 'every alternate Tuesday petty sessions are held in the 'George' by the magistrates of Ermington and Plympton Division, to whom Mr T. Kelly of Yealmpton, is clerk.'

The next name we find associated with the inn is one which will be familiar to longstanding Debenhams customers for in 1857 a John Yeo was licensee. Whether or not he was related to the original store boss I do not know.

Similarly one wonders if Harry Earle, landlord 100 years ago, owed his surname to the other name by which neighbouring St. Maurice was known, that is Plympton Earl, or Erle. Whatever, Harry Earle was there some 20 years during which time he operated a cab business from the 'George'. These would, of course, have been the original horsedrawn hackney carriages.

Despite an inevitable long list of changes in licensees the 'George' has managed to retain an aura of bygone days and the changes effected during the recent tenancy of Alan Lee have if anything added to this.

By coincidence rather than design another change takes place today as the landlady of the past few years, Gill Skelley, hands over to the new licensees of the 'George' — Mr. and Mrs. George.

This in turn begs another question: After which George is the pub named? Known to have been built sometime in the eighteenth century and thought to have been named after the reigning monarch the situation could hardly be less clear as between 1714 and 1830 there was an uninterrupted succession of Georges on the throne; George I from 1714 to 1727, then George II until 1760, George III till 1820 and finally until 1830 George IV.

Never before or since has one name so dominated the monarchy (closest were the first three Edwards between 1272 and 1377). However the most likely candidate is probably George III.

[WEH 8.12.84]

London Inn

Believed to be over 200 years old, early records of the 'London Inn', Church Road, Plympton St. Maurice, are scant to say the least. However, there is one early reference to the pub that is as interesting as it is unusual. On the 8th March 1817 a duel was fought near Plympton St. Mary bridge between two officers of the Royal Marine Light Infantry, Lieutenant William Hindes and Lieutenant Gilbert Conroy. In the event Conroy emerged the victor and the injured Hindes was brought here to the 'London Inn'. Unfortunately for Conroy his adversary survived only one night and William Hindes died in the London Inn on the 9th of March, subsequently becoming one of the first three bodies to be buried in newly (1812) consecrated church ground, west of the church path and known as Ribbon Field. Had Hindes lived longer Conroy would perhaps have been spared Coroner John Boger's verdict of wilful murder that was returned against both the officer and his second. 150 years later there is still said to be a door upstairs in the Inn which has a habit of opening by itself . . .

Whilst we have little other record of the 'London's' history, it would appear to have been owned by members of the Treby family in the early 1800s. From the middle of last century however, to the present day, it is possible to find a fairly comprehensive list of licensees of the 'London'. William Toop had the Inn in 1850 and was succeeded by George Brook. Thereafter came two men, William Kingsland and John Handcock, in whose time the Inn also housed the local excise or inland revenue office. John Handcock himself was succeeded by another two Johns— Messrs. Banks and Luxon—who took the pub through to the beginning of a 50-year reign by the father and son team of James 'Tin Whiskers' (on account of his silver moustache) and John or Jack, Gardner. Between them the Gardners saw the pub through two World Wars and a great many changes and innovations in transport, technology and entertainment. However few, if any, of these changes were reflected inside the 'London' and when Vic and Vera Knight arrived here on 1st October 1951 they found the place just a little bit run down. Over the next 21 years they tidied the place up, swapped the lounge with the bar, closed the Bottle and Jug and brought in a great deal of cosy fixtures and fittings, including an interesting collection of ships' crests, some ships' lamps, a wheel from a Suez vintage Jewish emigrant ship and a fine set of old handbells.

These bells originally came from Buckfastleigh and were bought by 'Tin Whiskers' Gardner in 1901. At some point they left the pub and Vic bought them back off Bert Webber just before Christmas, 1951. Bert's wife was not too keen on his playing of them at home and it's perhaps no coincidence that Vic himself, who now keeps them at home, is in turn looking to sell them. A popular feature in Vic's days, the bells were once recorded for an Alan Gibson BBC radio programme in a series on entertainment in pubs, in the days before the juke box and the rock group. Not that the 'London' is particularly famous for either of these today. Nor is it likely to be under its new licensee Tony 'Rip' Kirby and his wife Frances, who took over from Roger Seldon earlier this month. A well-known local rugby player, Rip is another going into the business for the first time and, like Vic before, intends to play down gimmicks and rely on the traditional Inn fare of food and drink to keep his customers satisfied.

[WEH 16.3.85

The Old Grammar School, Plympton

Built between 1663–71, the Old Grammar School at Plympton was in fact initially known as Hele's School in honour of the man, Elize Hele, who had left monies in his estate for the construction of such charitable institutions.

Trustees of his estate, Sir John Maynard and Elize Stert allocated money for the building of this and two other schools—Hele's and the Blue Maid's School (now the Maynard School) in Exeter.

The Reverend Samuel Reynolds was an early headmaster there, and his seventh child, Joshua, (1723–92) went on to become the school's most illustrious pupil and the first of four consecutive notable artists who studied first at the school and then under their predecessor.

After Reynolds came James Northcote (1746–1831), Benjamin Haydon (1786–1846) headboy in 1801 and Charles Locke Eastlake (1793–1865).

Joshua Reynolds, perhaps Britain's foremost portrait painter, became the first President of the Royal Academy in 1768. In 1769 he was knighted by George III and in 1772 he was chosen as Mayor of Plympton, an honour which he told the King gave him more pleasure than any other he had received, saving of course that which the king himself had bestowed upon him.

Jack Russell, breeder of the terrier and celebrated hunting parson was another former pupil of this grand gothic structure, which closed in 1905 after the state had taken over responsibility for secondary schools in 1902.

The school, which had had many problems during the nineteenth century, was reopened in 1921 as a co-ed.

Within ten years the growth of the new Plympton grammar school required that it expand into the old schoolroom and soon after that, in 1937, the school was moved wholesale to its present Stone Barton location.

Still leased by the Hele Trust, the school was again re-opened in 1980, this time as an independent with a new name—the Sir Joshua Reynolds School. »Postscript

[WEH 19.6.82

Plympton St. Maurice

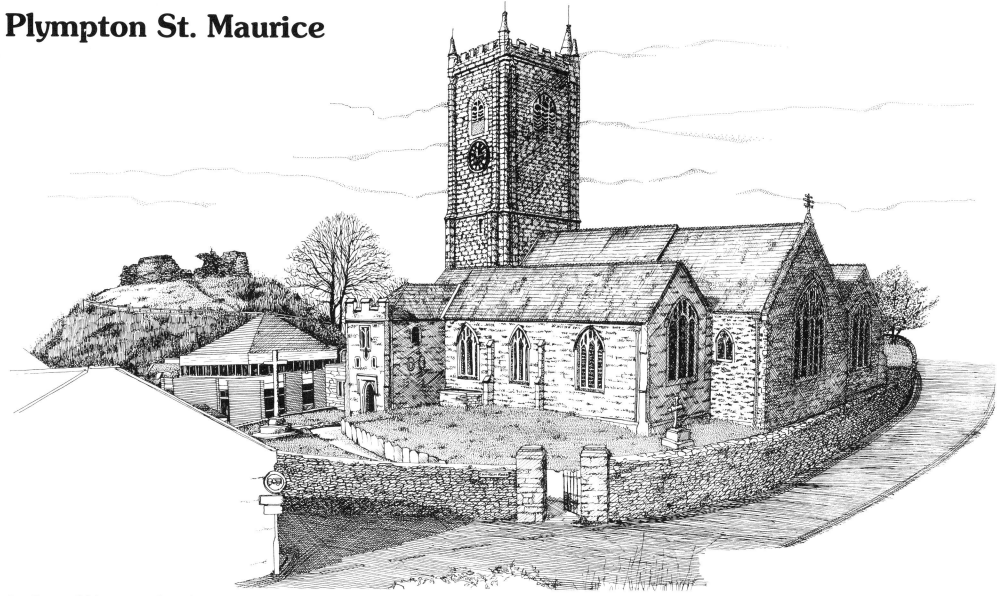

An 'impossible' view, taken from an upper window of what was known as Plympton Grammar School and has now been renamed the Sir Joshua Reynolds school in honour of its most celebrated pupil. I say impossible because houses have for centuries prevented such a full view of the rear of this late thirteenth century church.

The church was originally dedicated to St. Thomas but this was changed after 1538. It is not clear why St. Maurice was chosen. Maurice was commander of a Roman legion around the year 290, who, along with his men, was slaughtered in Switzerland for not taking part in a solemn sacrifice.

St. Maurice Castle, has been a ruin virtually since it was built. In the early 1130s Baldwin, son of Richard de Revers (the Norman lord who probably completed the castle) quarrelled unreasonably with King Stephen.

Needless to say the King fared best, for while Baldwin fumed in another of his castles at Exeter, Stephen sent 200 men and a large body of archers to Plympton where they arrived unexpectedly around daybreak and almost entirely destroyed the fortress.

[*WEH* 20.3.82

The Guildhall—Plympton St. Maurice

For many hundreds of years Fore Street was at the very heart of life in the ancient Borough of Plympton St. Maurice.

After all, Plympton as J. Brooking-Rowe tells us in his definitive study of the area, 'had no broad thoroughfare or open space or market place and the Fore Street or High Street, through which all the traffic of the town passed, had also to accommodate the stalls and the standings for the oxen, sheep and pigs for the great markets held four times a year, beside other smaller ones.'

Such commercial activities would have also included the weekly tin court held here. Plympton, so designated in 1328, was one of four stannary towns in Devon, which meant that it was, along with Tavistock, Ashburton and Chagford, a town where local tinners could go and have their tin (stannum in Latin) weighed and stamped.

Throughout this time, 'when Plympton was a flourishing market town, the Guildhall was its centre and its most important secular building,' Brooking-Rowe again who later suggests that 'there is no doubt that the present Guildhall building occupies the same site which the earlier building (erected probably in the 13th century) did.'

The present Guildhall, the front of which is little changed from its original 1688 appearance, stands proud as one of the finest old buildings around today in the Plymouth area. Much altered and improved in 1788, the whole building was, save for the granite arcade and council chamber above, completely revamped another 70-odd years later.

In 1860 the Court of Aldermen and Common Council in Plympton decided to refrain from electing a new mayor. The Guildhall became neglected and a company was formed to revitalize and reassess the function of the building. By 1862 a large hall, capable of seating about 300 people had been created at the expense of the old court, cells and some small rooms above.

The front entrance to the Guildhall was brought forward at the same time to be level with the other buildings in the street. Suitable now for large meetings and concerts (a musicians' balcony has been constructed at one end) further alterations were carried out to the building in 1903 and then in 1973 major restoration work was done, culminating, four years ago, with the re-roofing of the main hall. Sadly, due to a breakdown in administrative communications the roof was retiled with new tiles despite the old ones having been carefully kept for that purpose. However, the old tiles on the council chamber roof serve as a reminder.

Here it was in this chamber that Sir Joshua Reynolds sat in 1733 as Lord Mayor of Plympton and doubtless would have looked out over the same hill and seen Fore Street curving round to the right, following the line of the old castle moat.

St. Maurice House and the stone rubble garden wall of Cedar Lodge that it stands beyond would perhaps also have met the westward gaze of the celebrated local artist. Beyond that the lodge was built a little later, around 1840, on the site of an old farmyard. Further up the slope towards the Guildhall is Cedar Lodge itself, where it is believed that an old inn, 'The Three Mariners', once stood.

Crossing over the road here are yet more buildings dating from the 1700s and right next door to the Guildhall we find another inn—the 'Forresters'. This one, however, is still very much in use, only gone are the old bay windows and side entrance that used to connect it directly to the Guildhall in order that the local civic dignitaries might seek immediate refreshment.

[*WEH* 6.8.83

Tudor Lodge

Number 63 Fore Street, Plympton St. Maurice, is undoubtedly one of the oldest dwelling houses in the Plymouth area still being lived in today.

Known nowadays as Tudor Lodge this charming high-roofed, gabled and wooden fronted building in fact only dates back, according to parish records, to 1682 when it is mentioned that Thomas Lux was the owner of this newly erected house. The name Tudor Lodge is a recent one appearing first in the 1950s. Nevertheless, the house is considerably older than its neighbours, numbers 57 and 67 which whilst built on the sites of earlier constructions can only claim standing of a mere 100–150 years.

The apparent discrepancy in the numbering in this part of Fore Street is a reference to other neighbouring dwellings, through the old snicket behind the door on the left as we see it and down the alley under Tudor Lodge, known to older residents of the area as Brewery Lane. It was through this lane that the main part of a large local brewery was reached up until the middle of last century and with it Nos 1–14 Brewery Cottages, of which all that remains now are the old numbers 1 and 2, forming Brook Cottage, and the outside walls of some of the others, the last of these being demolished in the mid 1950s. The cottages behind and including 57 Fore Street are however still referred to as Brewery House Cottages.

On the other side of Brewery Lane at the back of the impressively fronted 67 used to be an old laundry where servants would clean among other things the larger linen items from Saltram House.

Plympton St. Maurice is an area of great historical interest, designated a conservation area in 1968. Many locals spend a great deal of personal time and effort chasing up its social history and indeed in No. 67 Painswick House, can be found Audrey Mills whose guide to the area was published recently, whilst down the lane in Brook Cottage, Sally Luscombe has copies of all the parish records up until 1817 and has produced several long and fascinating local family trees.

Being of a manageable size and fairly self contained certain families have played a great part in the history of Plympton St. Maurice and indeed Tudor Lodge has had living within its walls many local notables. Edward Sparke, attorney and one-time town clerk, bought the house from Thomas Lux and he in turn sold it to Simon Hele whose ancestor, Elize Hele earlier in the seventeenth century had been, upon his death, responsible for the setting up of what is now the Sir Joshua Reynolds School. Hele was followed in the house by another attorney and town clerk William Woollcombe who together with his descendants held the house for a great many years. Indeed, the place was known for a long time as the Woollcombe House. An early Woollcombe had been a constable at Plympton Castle and the family has had within its number over the years a great many solicitors and men of legal matters.

Strangely enough the current master of the house, John Haythorn is also a local solicitor and, even more strangely, he is a partner with the firm, established in 1728, of Woollcombe and Yonge.

[*WEH* 12.3.83]

Saltram House

Described in 1788 by writer Fanny Burney as 'one of the most magnificent houses in the country,' Saltram still merits such a description today.

Apart from the entrance porch (added by John Foulston in 1818) the mansion as we see it here was largely completed by 1750 and had been built around the earlier seventeenth century house erected by James Bagge.

Bagge was a privateer from Poole who was twice Mayor of Plymouth (1595 and 1605) and returned as MP for the Borough in 1601 and 1603.

An aggressive man, Bagge once threatened to break the neck of Mayor Thomas Fownes (1610 and 1619), he called John Scoble (Mayor 1613) an insolent knave and Thomas Sherwill, who the town replaced him with as MP in 1614 'a seditious fellow'.

In 1615 Bagge was 'clean removed from the bench' and despite successfully suing and being restored, he bought himself a farm at Saltram and retired seeing before his death in 1624 the building of his great house.

Bagge was succeeded in all his posts by his son James, a young man every bit as corrupt as his father, who before his downfall in the 1630s embezzled a fortune, creaming off monies meant for the fleet to fight the Spanish, causing untold suffering and death amongst the plague-ridden press-ganged troops. Despite the eventual public disgrace of 'the Bottomless Bagge' as he was once referred to in Parliament, his family managed to hold on to Saltram.

In 1661 it passed into the hands of the Carteret family and fifty years later it was bought by a local squire, George Parker, with whose descendants it remained until 1957 when it was acquired by the National Trust.

Extensive alterations were carried out in 1768 by Robert Adam, and his magnificent interiors still exude splendour today as do the many fine paintings in the house, particularly those by the celebrated family friend of John Parker, Sir Joshua Reynolds.

[*WEH* 12.6.82

185

The Morley Arms

Exactly two hundred years ago, yesterday, John Parker of Saltram was created Baron Boringdon of Boringdon, Devon. Just over 30 years later his son, John, was further elevated to the title Viscount Boringdon of North Molton and Earl of Morley.

Today a great great grandson of this first earl, another John, holds the title, the 6th Earl of Morley, and while his brother still lives at Saltram, administered since 1956 by the National Trust, the Earl now resides in Yelverton.

Meanwhile the family arms have adorned the signs of this Pomphlett inn for some 150 years. Built on the edge of the Saltram estate it is clearly marked on Pringle and Greenwood's Survey Map of Devon as an inn in 1827.

This was the year in which the first earl's iron bridge was completed at a cost of £10,500. Built by the young engineer James Meadows Rendel, work had begun on the project four years earlier and when completed it was one of the largest such bridges in the country.

Upon its completion, in a paper published in the Transactions of the Plymouth Institution, Rendel concluded his account of the work with respectful praise for his patron, stating that aside from his own personal gratitude . . . 'for the advantage derived from the bridge itself the Earl of Morley has laid the public of Plymouth under lasting obligation.'

Doubtless since many grateful travellers have drunk the earl's health here under the sign with the silver stag, buck's head, sable greyhound and horses head—the last two being particularly apt in the light of the sporting activities witnessed at Chelson Meadow before the last war.

Although quite what the punters would have made of the family motto—'Fideli certa Merces,'—'to the faithful man there is assuredly a reward'—is anyone's guess.

Rendel's impressive five arched construction stood for 134 years and although sold by the 3rd earl to the corporation of Plymouth for £43,000 in 1897, it continued to be a toll bridge into the early part of this century.

In 1961 the present, much wider Laira Bridge was built, its access road still running hard past the Morley Arms. Although long a passing stage for travellers (the iron bridge itself was preceded by a variety of ferries that operated under Lord Morley's guidance) it would appear that the inn began life as such with the opening of this metal construction and indeed it wasn't until 1903 that the building was leased from the Saltram estate. Twenty years later it was sold outright to the Octagon Brewery for £2,000.

Today a tenanted Courage house the last fifty years have seen a steady succession of licensees—Bill Crinks, Fred May, George Cocks, Stan Bates and since 1976 Maurice Moore.

A lively Bristolian Maurice Moore came to Plymouth partly to retire, having spent some 40 years in the trade and latterly running one of the biggest pubs in the Bristol area, the 'Good Intent' in Brislington.

However, in addition to the day-to-day running of his inn, the building of a sea wall, setting out of a garden with an interesting if not motley collection of animals and the re-styling of the inside of the building, to give it something of its original period flavour, has kept the man more than busy.

A recent fire in his kitchens did little to ease his load, however it wasn't long before business was back as usual—and among his customers last week, a coach load of regulars from the 'Good Intent' paying an annual visit, although whether or not these particular travellers ever intended or managed to cross the Laira Bridge is not so clear.

[*WEH* 19.5.84

Elburton Hotel

Situated on the main south-eastern route out of Plymouth, Elburton Road was constructed in the 1820s in the wake of the building of Laira Bridge (1823–7). Established by Lord Morley of Saltram, who had earlier (1807) instituted a flying bridge—a boat capable of carrying horses and carriages at a supposedly higher speed than other ferries—both constructions were the work of James Meadows Rendel.

As one would expect, the increase in traffic at this point and along the roads made busier by this improvement soon led to the appearance of new wayside inns. The 'Morley Arms' was open as early as 1827: meanwhile further along in the slowly developing farming hamlet of Elburton the 'Volunteer Inn', a much smaller ale house had been set up in what are now just Greystone Cottages by the middle of the century. In 1851 John Avery was listed as its licensee and his apparent short tenure was followed by Mrs. Elizabeth Rowse and then William Rowse, from the early 1890s. By the turn of the century it had passed to John Hobbs. Here then travellers in Victorian times would call between 6–10 a.m. and drink ale at tuppence a jug and perhaps watch the locals playing rings or dominoes in the tiny bar. In 1904 the 'Volunteer' closed and its licence and licensee moved to the newly constructed 'Elburton Hotel'. George White had only been at the 'Volunteer' for a couple of years when local builder George Turpin demolished what was left of Dixs' farm and built the 'Elburton Hotel'. Dixs' farm had been the first of Elburton's ten farms to stop working, apparently back in the 1850s (see Arthur Clamps *Ten Farms of Elburton*); it had taken its name from the Reverend Samuel Dickes who had been at Mary's and All Saints Church, Plymstock, between 1673–81. Dickes had then owned the farm and its land and had let it to an Elburton family.

Although the farm land was worked throughout the nineteenth century, the farm itself seems to have been unoccupied when Turpin bought and developed the site thereafter selling it to Messrs. C. W. Blundell and Co., Wine and Spirit Merchants of Kingsbridge in 1904. For the White family, however, all this meant was a move to bigger premises with consequent opportunities to expand services and the 'Elburton' started to offer Bed and Breakfast accommodation. George White was succeeded by Frederick and Lavinia White and their son Charles and between them they ran the 'Elburton' for 45 years.

Since 1949 there have been more than ten different licensees here and the continual changes inside have been mirrored by the changes outside and indeed in the links between the two . . . As Elburton itself has expanded so have its telephone numbers. Back at the end of the First World War the Hotel's number was 13; twenty years later a 32 prefix had been added and more recently a 4 so now it's the five digit 43213 and doubtless likely to grow again soon. In 1967 Elburton and Plymstock were absorbed by Plymouth's new boundary lines and then in 1975 Elburton Road was widened, with the consequent loss of some shops and the petrol station which had stood opposite the Hotel.

The Elburton's greatest period of post war landlord stability occurred either side of the 1967 boundary change. Wilf Phillips, here since 1958, left that year and in April 1968 Harry (Nick) Nicholls, now at the 'Cherry Tree', began a five-year stay here. Current licensee, Mike Edwards, took over from Robbie Selway in 1982 and, despite all the changes, he has found an ale house which is still very much a village pub and one in which darts and pool have superseded rings; but euchre (dominoes) is still very popular among the locals.

[*WEH* 30.3.85

Plymstock Church and Inn

Seventy-two years ago in the Royal Hotel in Plymouth, 211 lots were up for sale in one of the more unusual sales of this century.

Lot 23 was the 'Plymstock Inn' and the occasion of this particular auction was the selling up of the estate of the Duke of Bedford.

The Duke was one of the biggest landowners in the area and at one time, during the nineteenth century, the Duke, Barry Buteel Harris and Edmund Rodney Pollexfen Bastard between them owned more than half of the entire Plymstock area.

The 211 lots in the 1911 auction included 'Desirable farms, choice and well-placed residential properties, valuable smallholdings and numerous cottages.'

One such cottage was Barbara Stanley's Littlecote from the garden of which this current scene was drawn.

Situated in one of the oldest parts of Plymstock, Littlecote is at one end of Holland or Hollands Road, a name which owes its derivation to Hollins Well which used to be at the eastern end of Cob Lane, near Amberley House.

At its western end, Hollands Road meets with Church Road and the old 'Church House Inn' which from 1902 onwards has been known as the 'Plymstock Inn', one of the establishments in the old 'People's Refreshment House' (PRHA) and an inn where until recently one could find a bed for the night.

Among the customers today in Keith De Bruin's greatly revamped centuries-old pub are the bell ringers from St. Mary and All Saints' across the road. A fine body, their success is echoed in the sign outside the pub and the many trophies that they've won in recent years, including the much prized Devon Association for the encouragement of Round Ringing Shield, the Reg Champ Cornwood Ringing Shield and the Eight Bell South Devon Trophy.

Quite an achievement considering that until recently the tower had only six bells, although four of these are almost 250 years old.

Much younger than these bells, but nevertheless giving them a good run for their money is 77-year-old ringer Wilf Weeks, whose grandfather used to run the 'Plymstock Inn' and who was himself born there in room number three.

Wilf has seen many landlords come and go and last year pulled the first pint when the pub with its new layout was re-opened.

Whilst restructuring the pub may have been a relatively straightforward, albeit expensive, move, the internal layout of the church has been a much more controversial affair and the fate of the marvellous fourteenth century rood screen has been the subject of much debate.

Saved from Cromwell's men by being buried in the churchyard this marvellous piece of wall to wall wood carving is an awe-inspiring artefact which has done well to survive the various attempts at restoration, notably the work done almost 100 years ago when Arthur St. Quentin Sproule, M.A., was the local incumbent. Sproule was one of a long chain of Plymstock vicars who stretched back to the sixteenth century when the church was greatly extended and its status raised from that of being merely All Saints' Chapel belonging to Plympton Priory.

Today the church and the vicar, Geoffrey Sunderland, are at the centre of a Plymstock community which has grown from 3,000 odd in 1881 to around 20,000 today.

[*WEH* 2.4.83

King's Arms, Oreston

There was a time when the only way to obtain a view such as this of the pub on the Quay at Oreston would have been from the top deck of the local ferry boat at high tide.

Sadly, however, the ancient Oreston ferry service has long since stopped running and perhaps sadder still the water no longer laps against this old sea wall.

A combination of objections about the unsightly muddy beach here and the need to shift a lot of rubble from the building of the neighbouring gas works saw Oreston Quay filled in, grassed over and provided with a promenade.

Still very much a village today, however, Oreston, or 'Osun', has enjoyed a long history as a working waterside community. Marked as Ostun on a 1640s Civil War map, showing the deployment of 'enemy' troops, it appears to have been a strong Royalist position.

A strangely appropriate situation in the circumstances as the only pub left in Oreston today bears the name 'The King's Arms'.

Originally there were some four or five inns here; the 'Forrester's Arms', the 'Ferryboat', the 'Old', the 'King's Arms' and one which later became known as 'Minniards House' and which still stands on the Quay today.

It is on the wall of this house that we find a plaque commemorating the brief stay in Oreston of one Alexander Selkirk, who on 12th December 1720, married Frances Candish, a spinster 19 years his senior, who herself kept an inn in Oreston.

Selkirk was a sailor and was back at sea eight days after his marriage and ironically he died at sea, of yellow fever, on his first wedding anniversary. Better known as the man who inspired Daniel Defoe to write 'Robinson Crusoe' (first published in 1719) Selkirk spent four years and four months in a somewhat self imposed solitary stay on Juan Fernandez Island in the South Pacific between 1704–9.

Whether Selkirk drank in the 'King's Arms' and whether there was even a pub on this site at that time is uncertain. Whitbread, who now own the building, generally take great care to base such 'King's Arm's' signs around those of the King at the time the pub began business.

On this basis, then, the pub would appear to date from between 1801–16, for the arms depicted are a version of those George III had at that time.

George III had three coats of arms during his 60-year reign. He began with those of his predecessor, George II, but they changed substantially in 1801 to the form that with slight alterations has continued to the present time. The change was brought about as the Union of Great Britain with Ireland (passed by both Irish Houses of Parliament in 1799) took effect and at the same time it was at last decided, in the wake of the French Revolution and at Napoleon's insistence, to drop the outdated claim of the English Monarch to be King of France.

George III's 60-year reign has only ever been surpassed by Victoria (1837–1901). However, another reign equally impressive in its own terms, and slightly longer, began at the 'King's Arms' in 1857.

In that year John Pile became licensee and after being succeeded variously by Caroline, Samuel, Emma and Harold, the Piles held sway here through to the 1930s ... a record surely seldom if ever surpassed and one which current landlord Horace Purvis is unlikely to contemplate challenging.

The pub, however, greatly extended around the time of Harold Pile (the roof line shows its original extent), looks set to face another century or so yet.

[*WEH* 22.10.83]

Royal Oak, Hooe

A common enough name for an inn most 'Royal Oaks' take their name from the famous historical incident following the battle at Worcester on 3rd September 1651 when Charles II was defeated by the Parliamentarians.

Taking flight he and a Major Careless eluded capture the following day only by hiding in what later became the Royal Oak tree at Boscobel, near Shifnal, Salop.

Subsequently remembered—by a 1664 Act of Parliament—every 29th May (Charles II's birthday and the day on which he returned to London for the Restoration) as a day of thanksgiving thereafter known as Oak Apple Day or Royal Oak Day, hundreds of commemoratively-named pubs have since appeared across the country.

There are half a dozen or so in Devon and Cornwall and there used to be one a long time ago in Southside Street on the Barbican. Quite how old the inn here at Hooe is however is uncertain, but several of the buildings nearby date from the early 1700s.

Alongside the inn's new beer garden is an old boat builder's cottage from where before the cottage's garden wall was constructed, boats would be built and launched from an almost natural mud and grassy slip.

While water still laps this cottage wall and the beer garden it did, of course, used to come up a lot further and only 20 years ago this view as drawn would only have been possible from a floating vantage point.

Infilled to make way for a large village green, Hooe Lake has gradually been encroached upon but for over 20 years now plans have been afoot to build a splendid marina here. Something that would doubtless please both the brewery and the new licensees here when they arrive after the extensive refurbishing work, currently in progress, has been completed.

A popular village inn for a hundred years and more the 'Royal Oak' was here at least in 1850 when it was run by Thomas Ryder and the 'Victoria Inn', around the corner, run by Abraham Ryder.

Succeeded here by another Ryder, Henry, a few years later by 1878 the inn was managed by one Thomas Cole, a man who was responsible locally for collecting rates and assessing taxes. Whether this made him unpopular or not we will probably never know but a publican's job isn't always conducive to making a lot of friends, despite the obvious appearances.

Some here however have made their mark. At the end of the first war a Mr. Pine ran the 'Oak' and after him Jim Furse enjoyed a long spell here.

After the second war another long stay was that of Charles Wiltshire who was followed in the mid 1950s by William Knight.

A very popular husband and wife team Maurice and Em, were most recently succeeded in the mid 1970s by the mother and daughter team of Betty and Pat Burrows who were the last licensees here before Courage decided to upmarket the whole place.

Now refitted with a great deal of wood around the place, the future of the 'Oak' looks very sound indeed.

Radford Castle

This early nineteenth-century folly which is still without gas, electricity, or even running water inside, has witnessed many changes in its local environment over the years but one aspect that has remained unaltered is its unusual status as a gatehouse to a weir that separates a fresh water lake from a salt water one.

Threatened with demolition and a victim of neglect in recent years, when originally constructed this 'castle' was part of the magnificent Radford Estate which dated back to 1206 since when it was owned by various members of le Abbe family who at some point assumed the name Redford, apparently after the colour of the local soil.

The Redfords or Radfords held the place for several generations before it passed into the hands of the Harris family in the late fifteenth century.

Soon after this we first find reference to the house which was later expanded into Plymstock's largest house, the imposing 50-room Radford Mansion which later passed to the Bulteels before being sold just before the First World War to a Mr. Mitchell. Tenanted for some years afterwards it stood unoccupied for five years before its demolition in 1937. A sad end for a building steeped in history with echoes of Drake, Raleigh, Howard and Hawkins and the English Civil War.

Daunting though the financial proposition of maintaining such properties is, it is nevertheless unfortunate that the city has lost so much of its history in this way.

However, while Radford disappeared before the last war, and all the devastation that accompanied it, Widey, demolished in 1953, could possibly have been saved as could perhaps Boringdon Hall which now appears to have passed the point of no return.

All water through the weir now, at least we do still have this odd piece of architectural nonsense, one time gatehouse and later home to the Edwards, the Onions and since 1973, after a period of inner emptiness and decay, home of the art studios of local sculptress and screen printer Frana Favata and her fellow craftswomen Sue Morris and Jean Merrett.

A fine setting for aesthetic pursuits, the area around is regularly visited by enthusiasts in other fields as botanists, ornithologists and arborists come to study the often rare and exotic plants, birds and trees which have been encouraged to flourish and grow here, particularly since the establishment in 1974 of the Radford Park arboretum, a development that grew from an idea of the late Eric Hawtry who was founder chairman of the Radford Heritage Group. At a time when so much of our parkland is being 'improved' by being provided with indoor facilities it is heartening that the great outdoor delights are being encouraged in this way.

[*WEH* 15.9.84

St. John's, Hooe

It appears to have been a last minute decision back in the 1850s that saw this little church in Hooe dedicated to St. John the Evangelist and not St. Anne, the Mother of the Blessed Virgin Mary.

The original plans for the church, drawn up in 1853, referred to it as St. Anne's, the original vicarage (now in the hands of the MoD) was St. Anne's House and the earliest recorded religious house in the area, a small chapel at the head of Hooe Lake, was dedicated to St. Anne.

Believed to have been built around 1100 this earlier building no longer stands whole, however its name, while not preserved in the present church is believed to survive in the name of the neighbouring village that grew up later at the other end of the lake.

Thus St. Anne's Chapel became Tan Chapel thence Turn Chapel and today Turnchapel.

Consecrated in 1855 in the name then of St. John the Evangelist, the parish of St. John, Hooe was constituted the following year. Designed by the Cornish architect W. H. White the building is based largely on a fourteenth century design. The adjoining school and schoolmaster's house, also designed by White are more firmly rooted in the nineteenth century.

Now used as the church hall, the school operated as such for some 75 years before being superseded in the early 1930s by Hooe Junior School. Likewise obsolete is the English noun 'lich' meaning a body, living or dead, however we still have 'lichways'—paths by which the dead are carried to burial and 'lich' or 'lychgates'—roofed churchyard gateways used to rest the bier under until the priest arrives.

The one here at the entrance to St. John's with its stone cattle grid is a particularly fine example.

Son of Zebedee and brother of James it is somehow quite appropriate that this church, that overlooks Hooe and the mouth of the Plym, should be dedicated to John, a fisherman and more appropriate still that the longest serving incumbent at this church to date should have been christened James John.

Here from 1870 through several decades into this century the Reverend James John Tapson MA, saw in 1893 a stone bell turret replace the original wooden one and earlier, in 1885, an organ placed at the top of the side aisle. In 1968, not long after the arrival of the present vicar, the Rev. A. B. Robinson, the organ was moved to the back of the church. This was done at the suggestion of local architect Frank Crowe who was generally responsible for the internal restructuring which took place then.

A simple if not unimpressive church from the outside, St. John's has a great deal of charm inside and has an unusual and attractive oak 'linefold' panelling around its walls, carved by Plymothian Violet Pinwell and installed together with her figure of the boy Jesus, in the church in 1916.

Also seen to their best advantage inside the church are the numerous stained glass windows the bulk of which were installed between 1932–58 and designed by W. Cooper Abbs.

[*WEH* 28.4.84]

New Inn, Turnchapel

One of a handful or so of Plymouth pubs offering a view of the water, the New Inn here at Turnchapel, was 'new' over 200 years ago.

It was not then housed, however, in its present home but in what is now Mandela House at No. 1, The Hill—a building immediately behind the pub that used to have a seaward entrance and now fronts onto the single track road that leads into and out of this little known quarter of the city.

Even the affable Gerry Hunston who now runs the pub and his wife, Shelagh, Plymouth-born and bred, admit that they had never been there until they were offered the inn, and I know many other well travelled Plymothians who would have trouble finding their way to Turnchapel.

Delightful and unspoilt as this waterside village is, it sadly lacks many of the facilities it enjoyed in recent years.

Serviced by the London and South Western Railway Company until 1951 on a line direct from Friary Station and by ferry by the Oreston and Turnchapel Steamboat Co., until 1957, even the local retail commercial interests have dwindled.

Gone is the 'Shipwrights Arms', gone the local dairy and Post Office, gone the bakery and L. T. Mutton's butcher's shop which stood opposite the pub; gone, too, the Prince of Wales Café and all but one of the local shops.

While not exactly a ghost town, Turnchapel is but a shadow of its former self and long since removed from the thriving shipbuilding hamlet it was in 1770 when the Earl of Morley set up a landlady on a peppercorn rent to run the 'New Inn'.

With substantial financial interests in the whole Plympton, Plymstock area, Lord Boringdon, the Earl of Morley, is also remembered in the name of the other surviving Turnchapel inn, the 'Boringdon Arms' and the main sea front road, Boringdon Road, in which the present 'New Inn' has stood for some 100 years now.

Believed to have moved down in the 1880s during the stay of landlord William Hine and while George Hine ran the 'Castle Inn' around the corner at Mount Batten (which was demolished in 1962 to make way for the present Sergeants' Mess), the 'New Inn' originally occupied the current pool room and corridor of the pub as presently constituted.

The large part facing us as we see it here was the local dairy and prior to that the bakery.

For well over 60 years between 1850 and 1910 at least, the Kelly family operated a bakery here as Robert handed down to William, then Elizabeth, then John Kelly in turn.

Soon after the beginning of the century, however, this building was incorporated into the 'New Inn'—an inn run by, among others since the first war, Harry King, Bill Warren, Dick Newman, Bill Luckie, Jim Lumsden, John Hayes and since December 1982, Gerry and Shelagh Hunston.

New to the trade, Gerry has made it his business to look after his beer and his locals and feels fortunate in being in one of the most pleasantly situated inns in the city.

[*WEH* 8.9.84

View from Turnchapel

Believed to have taken its name from the little chapel that long ago stood at the head of Hooe Lake—Turnchapel and the areas around it have, for centuries, afforded visitors the best and most panoramic views of the heart of the City of Plymouth.

These views inspired the great J. M. W. Turner himself to stay and produce drawings, one of which was later (1817) engraved by Will Cooke. In it the tower of Mount Batten predominates.

Mount Batten, or Howe Stert as it was known until the Civil War of the 1640s, was the scene of some of the most vigorous local encounters between the Roundheads and Royalists and upon his restoration in 1660, Charles II ordered the building of a tower at Mount Batten along with the Citadel on the Hoe, which is seen larger than life in Turner's drawing with old Emigration Depot, Biscuit Factory and Victualling Warehouses at its foot.

To the right of Turner's view can be seen the Tower of St. Andrew's Church and the spire of Charles Church, landmarks that still break the skyline today. This contemporary view doesn't take us quite so far around as Charles spire—it does however show us how Mount Batten has been developed in recent years, primarily as an RAF station from as early as 1913.

It is perhaps worth noting that evidence suggests that Mount Batten was occupied by man some 2,000 years before Plymouth.

RAF Mount Batten (or RAF Cattewater as it was known until 1928) is possibly best known nationally as a base for World War I and II flying boats, particularly the distinctive Sunderland and Southampton series.

The station's most notable RAF orderly, however, was undoubtedly Aircraftsman T. E. Shaw, who served there between 1929 and 1933.

Designer of the Squadron's crest, T. E. Shaw was the humble identity assumed by the man better known to the world as Lawrence of Arabia.

Further around the waterline, in Turnchapel itself, we see the sadly dilapidated pier, now in its last year, having been first opened in 1889 with many thousands making the ferry crossing to Plymouth from here until the service closed some 20 odd years ago.

[*WEH* 10.7.82

Postscript

Rather than attempt to collate all the information in this volume so that it is all correct up to one particular point in time I have decided rather to let the pieces stand as of the date they were originally published. Below are a few notes concerning one or two major changes, original inaccurances, obvious omissions and points of interest.

Fish Quay   The *Pelerin* in the foregorund of this picture sank in Plymouth Sound two weeks after the drawing had been completed.

Plymouth Castle   An attempt was later made by the Council to clean up this relic and the surrounding area.

Island House   Early in 1985 a new plaque, commissioned by the Barbican Association and including the names of all the female pilgrims, was unveiled in place of this earlier one.

Barbican Arms   George Rowe the signwriter from Southside Street (who has painted several signs for me) subsequently wrote to the *Herald* to state that he had not only painted the new Barbican Arms sign but had also devised the Arms himself. Long-established in the area with a keen interest in it, George had given the project much though and said I had mostly got his reasons right.

Kings Head   In the preface to the second edition of his History of Plymouth, Crispin Gill pointed out that his suggestions that Billbury marked the original settlement site that grew into Sutton, then Plymouth, is just a theory.

Plymouth Gin   A tasteful conversion in the early part of 1985 saw the opening of the 'Distillery' public house here with a Beefeater Restaurant upstairs. An enormous glass partition has been constructed under the arch; the area in front of it is now a sitting-area for the 'Distillery' whilst behind the glass it is business as usual for the huge stills.

Prysten House   This was the first article in the 'Time Draws On' series and the one which to date had got me into most hot water. Within days I was called into the Editor's office to read the letter written by James Barber, Director of the City Museum and Art Gallery. Whilst I had referred to the popular speculation about the building Mr Barber drew attention to Jennifer Barber's work on the Finewell Street property. This proves 'that the building was erected as a town house by. . .Thomas Yogge' and that 'the real Prysten House, home of Plymouth's Chantry priests, stood a few doors further down Finewell Street', Jennifer Barber's work appears in volume 105 of the Transaxtion of the Devonshire Association and is available as a separate pamphlet from Plymouth Museum or Merchant's House.

Plymouth Guildhall   I had been commissioned to do an artist's impression of how the Airdomes would look if brought to the City and located outside the Duke of Cornwall. This I did and the Airdomes duly appeared; ugly to look at and uncomfortable to work in. I was not unhappy when one 'blew away' and they were later sold.

Theatre Royal   Written to coincide with the opening of the New Theatre Royal details of the new theatre appeared elsewhere in the *Evening Herald* and in a special supplement, consequently I omitted them from my piece. Designed for the City of Plymouth by the Peter Moro Partnership work began on the 4th April 1979 and was finished on 16th April 1982. It was officially opened by HRH Princess Margaret on 5th May 1982.

Derry's Clock   In 1984 the 'Lockyer Tavern', despite being the older building, was demolished in order that the old bank building could be redeveloped as a public house. Now known as 'The Bank' the conversion is extremely effective and it is perhaps now the largest and most impressive of the town pubs.

Hoe Promenade   My first Plymouth pen-and-ink drawing, Smeaton's Tower has since been repainted in its original colours; however the top of the bollard eighth from the left is still missing.

Cross on the Hoe   One of the problems in producing any sort of history is that often popular myths, by dint of appearing in print at one time or another will at a later date be taken as the truth. Despite making great efforts to avoid any myth perpetuating it doubtless occurs now and then, indeed, it would appear to be the case with the Cross on the Hoe. Stanley Goodman, of the Old Plymouth Society, tells me that the cross is in fact believed to be a war office boundary marker and that the actual site of the execution was probably a little nearer the Citadel's Sally Port Gate.

Greenbank Horsetrough   Stanley Goodman wrote to me following this article pointing out that on the upright ends of the trough are two monograms 'EJ' at one end and 'JJ' at the other. These refer to the James brothers who provided the trough and lived in Greenbank House, a large mansion which formerly stood behind the wall behind the trough.

Lipson Milestone   Ted Masson-Phillips subsequently wrote to confirm that the milestone built into the wall of 17 Brooklyn Terrace at Camel's Head in fact still stands. He added that two other recent survivors, one near Milehouse and one beyond St. Budeaux Square, were believed now to be missing. I have to thank Ray Bush, however, for showing me that the Milehouse milestone also still stands.

Oxford Street School   Just as an 'ordinary' picture can be much enhanced by an attractive frame so a building can be made to look more impressive if it has a pleasant setting. The open playing fields do much for Plymouth College. Given the same treatment perhaps the decisions to axe Sutton, Stoke Damerel, Public and Plymouth High as school buildings altogether may not have been so readily taken. Having said that though, clearly St. Boniface did not survive with its wonderful disposition and here Oxford Street apparently only got its new playing fields on condition that the old school building was pulled down.

The New Palace Theatre   Since closed and reopened again, this time as 'the best disco in the country'—'The Academy'.

Artillery Tower (Firestone Bay)   Plans for the premises now have been realized and the Artillery Tower Restaurant was opened early in 1985. All wood and original stonework inside, the conversion has been extremely successful.

Mowbray's Railway Inn   A letter from the husband of one of Joseph Mowbray's grand-daughters revealed that Joseph and his wife had two other children, both daughters, making it seven girls in all.

Home Park Call Office   In the recent (summer 1985) re-development of Outland Road both of these call offices were removed.

Tamar Hotel   A letter from James Pengelly's great great grand-daughter revealed that the two inns were not side by side and that the 'New Inn' was north of the crossroads, roughly where Thomas's garage now stands. Longest serving postwar licensee at the 'Tamar', incidentally, has been Herbert Stephens 1959–76.

Old Grammar School   Still at its Stone Barton location Plympton Grammar has recently changed its name again and once more honours its founder Elize Hele.

Bibliography

Abbreviations: *WEH—Western Evening Herald*; *WMN—Western Morning News*;
   Trans PI—Transactions of the Plymouth Institution; Trans DA—
   Transactions of the Devonshire Association; ALC—Aruthur L. Clamp,
   Publisher; PLHL—copy in Plymouth Local History Library.
Dates when known are those of editions referred to.

All About Argyle, W. S. Tonkin, PAFC (1962)
'Artillery Tower Plan for Oldest City Tower' David Hutchins, WEH (15.1.1981)
Barbican, The, and it's People Remembered, Arthur L. Clamp, ALC (1985)
Boniface of Devon, John Cyril Sladden, Jarrold (1975)
Borough of Plymouth, The Practice of His Majesty's Court of Record of the, Charles Bird, S. Rowe (1817)
Brunel's Royal Albert Bridge, Thomas Bowden & Bernard Mills, Peter Watts (1983)
Captain Robert Falcon Scott, RN, L. M. Forbes, Plymouth (1965)
'Central Park, From the Archives', David Hutchins, *WEH* (1982)
'Central Park, "Cancer in the Green Lung"', Pamela Leeds, *WEH* (1982)
'City of Plymouth, European Architectural Heritage Year', City Planning Officer (1975)
Crownhill Parish Church 1958–1979, John Barrett & Allen L. Freestone (1979)
Crownhill, Reflections, Arthur L. Clamp, ALC (198–)
Crownhill, Story of a Crossroads, Crispin Gill
Days in Devonport, Parts I–VI, Gerald W. Barker, ALC (1982–5)
Devon and Cornwall, Early Tours in, ed R. Pearse Chope 1918, David & Charles (1968)
Devonport Dockyard Story, K. V. Burns, Maritime (1984)
Devonport, Hail and Farewell to, F. S. Blight, Trans PI xii (1951)
Devonport, History of, R. N. Worth, W. Brendon (1870)
Devonport, Inns and Beer Houses of, 2 vols, Henry Horwill, Manuscript PLHL (1975)
Devonport Gaol, Prison Discipline with especial reference to, Frederick Row, Devonport (1870)
'Devonport, Official Guide to', Burrows (190–)
'Devonport, Plymouth's Snub', Geoffrey Hawks, *WEH* (29.11.1973)
Devonport, Stoke and Morice Town, Stonehouse & Plymouth, John Sanford (1830)
Devonshire & Dorset; the Beauties of England & Wales, Vol IV, John Britton, Edward Brayley, Vernor, Hood, Longman etc (1809)
'*Director* Class Naval Paddle Tugs', M. J. Gaston *Ship's Monthly* (Jan 1980)
Drake's Island, Mayflower Centre Trust (198–)
Drake's Island, a brief history of, P. J. Mowan, Old Plymouth Soc 1951)

Elburton, Ten Farms of, Arthur L. Clamp, ALC (1981)
Elburton, The Making of a Village, Arthur L. Clamp, ALC (198–)
Elizabethan House, 32 New Street, Crispin Gill, Plymouth (197–)
Emmanuel, The Parish of, Compton Gifford, Roy Harris, Church (1970)
'*Faithful* RMAS', Jon Bennett, *Ships Monthly* (Dec 1981)
First Across! US Navy Transatlantic Flight of 1919, Richard K. Smith, Naval Institute Press (1973)
Floating Bridge at Saltash, I. M. Rendel, Plan (1831)
From Pillar to Post, Henry Aaron, Heinemann (1982)
'George Hotel, Plympton' Henry Wheeler, *Plymouth Times* (1.11.1984)
George Rundle Prynne, A. Clifton Kelway, Longmans, Green & Co (1905)
'Hamoaze The Meaning of, Pheonicians in the West', Rev Worthington-Jukes, typescript, PLHL
Higher Stoke & Milehouse, a Short History of, David Ayers, Plymouth (1965)
HM Naval Base Devonport, Historic Architecture of, Jonathan Coad, National Maritime Museum 1983
'HMS *Drake*', Wardroom Mess (Dec 1973)
Honicknowle Remembered, Arthur L. Clamp, ALC (198–)
'Hooe, The Story of', R. H. C. Fice, *South Devon Times* (26.2.1960)
Hooe and Turnchapel Remembered, Arthur L. Clamp, ALC (1981)
Inn Signs, Introduction to, Eric R. Delderfield, Pan (1971)
It Came to Our Door, H. P. Twyford, Underhill (1946)
'*Kathleeen and May*', The History of, Richard J. Scott, Maritime Trust (1972)
Kelly's Devonshire, Directory also published by White & Billings (1856–1928)
Lord Morley's Flying Bridge, Keith S. Perkins, Rendel's News (1982)
Local Politics & Public Health in Mid Nineteenth Century Plymouth,
   Mark Brayshay, Vivien F. T. Pointon, Medical History (1983)
Making of a Cornish Town, Gladys & F. L. Harris, Torpoint Town Council (1976)
'*Mayflower* Supplement', *WMN* (1920)
Mannamead School, Story of, C. R. Serpell (1945)
Mount Batten, The Story of, Arthur L. Clamp ALC (198–)
Mount Edgcumbe, A Walk Around, W. Byers (1836)
Mount Edgcumbe, Duprez's Visitors Guide to, W. H. K. Wright, Duprez (1871)
Mount Edgcumbe Park, William Crossing, Hoyten & Cole (18—)
Mutley Bapist Church, Plymouth 1869–1969, Church Committee (1969)
Old Devon Bridges, Charles Henderson & E. Jervoise (1938)
Old Homes Around Plymouth, No 2, Pounds House, Patricia O'Neill, *WEH* (8.1.1937)
Old Plymouth, Sybyl Jerram, *WMN* Book (1913)

Old Plymouth, Ecclesiastical History of, J. Brooking Rowe (1876)

Old Plymouth, Nooks and Corners of, John McDonald (1883)

Old Plymouth, New Light on, James Barber, Plymouth Atheneum Vol IV 19

Old Plymouth Reservoir, Devon & Cornwall Notes & Queries, Vol XXVII

Old Plymouth, Streets of, C. Eldred & W. H. K. Wright (1901)

Old Plymouth, Views of, Sarah Foot, Bossiney Books (1983)

Oreston and It's People Remembered, Arthur L. Clamp, ALC (198–)

'Oreston, When Crusoe Came' Ivy Langdon, *Plymouth Times* (28.8.1979)

'Oreston, Tales of Old', Dorothy Warley-Pitt, *Plymouth Times* (31.12.1981)

Pennycross, Story of, Robert Groves (1964)

Pictorial Plymouth, Robert K. Dent, J. J. Allday (1900)

Pilgrim Fathers and the 'Mayflower' Ship 1620, Arthur L. Clamp, ALC (1985)

Pilgrim Fathers, Plymouth, Memorial to the C. W. Bracken, Devon & Cornwall Notes & Queries

Plan for Plymouth, A J. Paton-Watson Patrick Abercrombie, City Council (1943)

Playbill, A History of Theatre in the West Country, Harvey Crane, McDonald & Evans (1980)

Plymouth History of, Llewellyn Jewitt, W. H. Luke (1873)

'Plymouth', R. N. Worth, *The Graphic Magazine* (1878)

'Plymouth, History of', John Harris, Manuscript/typed PLHL (1808)

Plymouth, A History of, C. W. Bracken SR (reprint) (1931/70)

Plymouth, Ancient Heraldry of, some notes, R. N. Worth, Journal PI (1877)

Plymouth and Devonport Guide with Sketches H. E. Carrington, Byers & Son (1838)

Plymouth and Devonport in Times of War and Peace H. Whitfield, Plymouth (1900)

'Plymouth and its Potteries', Norman Stretton, *Antique Collecting,* Vol 17, No 5 (1982)

Plymouth and Plymothians Photographs & Memories Andrew Cluer, Lantern Books (1974)

Plymouth and Plymothians more Photographs & Memories Andrew Cluer, Lantern Books (1975)

'Plymouth and the West, Early Newspapers in', James L. Palmer, Trans PI Vol XIX (1944)

Plymouth and District Illustrated Commercial Guide W. H. K. Wright (1894)

Plymouth, The Ancient Buildings of G. W. Copeland & E. N. Masson Phillips, Old Plymouth Soc (1958)

Plymouth, A New History, Vol I Crispin Gill, David & Charles (1979)

Plymouth, A New History, Vol II Crispin Gill, David & Charles (1979)

'Plymouth, Arms of', Chris J. Smith, Standard Triumph Review (1961)

'Plymouth Blitz, The Story of the Raids', F. Crisp & H. P. Twyford, *WMN* (194–)

'Plymouth Blitz' S. M. Green & R. F. O. Cock, *Western Independent* (194–)

Plymouth Blitz, The Story of, Frank Wintle Bossiney (1981)

Plymouth, Book of Reference F. E. Sach F. E. Sach & Co (1916)

Plymouth Buildings of Architectural & Historical Interest, City of Plymouth/DOE

'Plymouth Churches, Laymans View of Same', 2 Vols, W. J. Power, type PLHL (1977)

Plymouth College, Ten Decades of Growth John Spear Plymouth College (1977)

'Plymouth Daily Newspapers and their Founders', James L. Palmer, Trans PI (1946)

'Plymouth Dartmoor &c, Place Names of', W. Best Harris, W. Best Harris (1983)

Plymouth, Devonport and Stonehouse, The Strangers Handbook to, (1842)

Plymouth, Devonport, Stonehouse etc, Handbook of, Henry Besley (186–)

Plymouth, Devonport & Stonehouse, (Post Office) Directories of (between 1812–1955)

Variously published by Longmann, Hurst, Rees, Orme & Brown (1812); S. Rowse (1814); Jenkin Thomas (1836);

G. Flintoff (1844); J. Williams (1847); F. Brendon (1852); M. Billings (1857); John Elvins (1862); W. J. Trythall

(1877); Eyre Brothers (1885); Swiss & Co (1905); Underhill (1932) and Kelly

Plymouth, Stonehouse, Devonport & South West Devon, various editions, Ward Lock (18—)

Plymouth, Devonport, Stonehouse, Wood's Handbook to, various editions, W. Wood (18—)

Plymouth Division, Royal Marines, Col R. D. Ormsby, Globe Laurel (1930)

Plymouth Dock Guide &c, The, Hoxland, Dock/Devonport (1792)

'Plymouth Friaries, New Light on the', Jennifer Barber, Trans DA, Vol 105 (1973)

Plymouth Gin, History of Jane Edward Plymouth (1979)

Plymouth Gin, notes Bill Burke (1975)

Plymouth's Golden Age of Trams, Arthur L. Clamp, ALC (1985)

'Plymouth, Heard its first telephone conversation', A. G. K. Leonard, *WEH* (1952)

Plymouth's Historic Barbican Arthur L. Clamp, ALC (1985)

Plymouth's Historic Hoe Arthur L. Clamp, ALC (1985)

Plymouth History of R. N. Worth, William Brendon & Son (1890)

Plymouth in old picture postcards Mary M. Davenport, European Library 1985)

Plymouth in Pictures Crispin Gill, David & Charles (1968)

Plymouth, Industrial Archaeology of ed Cynthia Gaskell Brown, Plymouth City Museum (1980)

Plymouth Memoirs Dr James Yonge (1647–1721), ec John J. Beckerlegge (1951)

Plymouth Muncipal Records ed R. N. Worth, Plymouth 1893

Plymouth Old and New Owen A. Baker, EP Publishing 1976

Plymouth—100 years of Street Travel R. C. Sambourne, Glasney Press 198–

Plymouth's Past Through Postcards Guy Fleming, ALC 1985

Plymouth A Portrait, J. C. Trewin, Robert Hale 1973

'Plymouth Public School', CWB, *WMN & Mercury* (10.9.1925)

Plymouth Public School C. W. Bracken, Underhill (1927)

Plymouth Royal Eye Infirmary notes by the Matron, Plymouth (19—)

Plymouth's Ships of War Lt-Com K. V. Burns, Greenwich (1972)

Plymouth Steam 1954–63 Ian H. Lane, Ian Allen (1984)

Plymouth Stonehouse & Devonport Illustrated handbook to W. H. K. Wright W. H. Luke (1879)

Plymouth, Stonehouse & Devonport, Nettleton's Guide to, George Wightwick, E. Nettleton (1838)

Plymouth, Story of R. A. J. Walling, Westaway (1950)

Plymouth, Story of, for young and old W. H. K. Wright, A. Wheaton & Co (18—)

Plymouth Theatres & Cinemas, P. F. Ghillyer & W.J. Power Type PLHL (1983)

Plymouth, The Book of John Gerrard Barracuda (1982)

Plympton Erle, A history of J. Brooking-Rowe James G. Commin (1906)

Plympton, History Beginnings of R. N. Worth Plymouth (1887)

Plympton St Mary J. Mercer-Cox Plympton (19—)

Plympton St Maurice Guide Audrey F. Mills Civic Association (1981)

Plymstock in Perspective Arthur L. Clamp ALC (1982)

Post School Education in the 'Three Towns 1825–1975, ed Alston Kennerley, Learning Resources Centre (1976)

'Pounds House History', Barbara Maslow *WEH* (20.4.1983)

Prysten House, Story of the, J. J. Judge (1955)

'Public School, A history of', Muriel Graham *WEH* (5.3.1983)

'Radford House, Vanished glories of', G. W. Copeland *WEH* (1954)

Royal Citadel Arthur L. Clamp ALC (198–)

Royal Naval Hospital Plymouth, History of, Surg Capt P. D. Gordon Pugh (1972)

'St Budeaux', H. Montagu Evans Trans PI (1913)

'St Budeaux, Growth of Through Peace & War', Rev T. A. Hancock *WEH* (23.1.1934)

St Budeaux, Historic Treasures', Rev T. A. Hancock *WEH* (16.2.1934)

St Budeaux, The Ancient Parish of, Marshall Ware ALC (1983)

St Edward, King & Martyr. Christopher Wood, G. Cumming (1959)

St John the Evangelist Sutton on Plym 1855–1971, Philip Mitchell (1971)

St Judes Church, A story of, Clifford Tretheway Parish Church (1976)

St Mary's and All Saints, Plymstock, Church history (19—)

St Mary the Blessed Virgin, Plympton, H. Wackett, Church Publishers (1969)

St Peters, Plymouth 1850–1950, B. M. Vere, Church (1950)

Salisbury Road Infants School 1903–1983, Muriel Graham, Pauline Membrey (1983)

Scouting in Plymouth 1908–82, Graham E. Brooks, Arthur L. Clamp, ALC (1982)

Seven Stars, The, Chris Wood Pages June (1980)

Sir Francis Drake and the 'Golden Hinde', Alex A. Cummin, Jarrold (1975)

Smeaton's Tower and the Breakwater, L. H. Merrett, Graphritre (19—)

Southway, One Hundred Years of ed Peter M. Bindschedler, Plymouth (1981)

'Stoke & Morice Town', F. S. Blight, Trans PI vol XXII (1951)

Stonehouse, Archaeological Survey Cynthia Gaskell Brown Plymouth (1975)

Stories from Plymouth's History W. Best Harris, W. Best Harris (1985)

Sutton Harbour Crispin Gill, Sutton Harbour Improvement Co (1976)

Sutton High School, A Short History Brian Moseley, B. S. Moseley (1970)

Sutton High, School at War Charles Jones, Plymouth (1948)

Tamerton Foliot Arthur L. Clamp, ALC (198–)

Tamerton Foliot Village, II, Portrait of, Betty Bryant & Arthur L. Clamp, ALC (198–)

Technical Colleges in the Three Towns, Terry J. Bickford, Digby Hole, Learning Resources (1976)

Theatre Royal, Plymouth, Building Study Peter Moro Partnership (1982)

The English Inn Thomas Burke, Herbert Jenkins (1948)

The Four Eddystone Lighthouses Robert Sanderson, Plymouth (198–)

The Inn, Explorers Guide Frank Bottomley, Kaye & Ward (1984)

The Letter Box J. Y. Farrugia, Centaur (1969)

'The Obsolete Plymouth Manors of Sutton Pyll', C. W. Bracken, Trans DA Vol 74 (1942)

Through England on a Side Saddle Celia Fiennes, Early Towns in Devon & Cornwall (1695)

'Torpoint Ferry, History of' Noel E. Purcell, *WMN* (Oct 1934)

'Torpoint Ferries', Nigel Howard, *Sunday Independent* (1982)

Transport Bygones in the Plymouth Area, Sydney V. C. Goodmann, ALC 1984

'Turnchapel', Gordon Hines, *South Devon Times* (21.1.1965)

Twelve Men of Plymouth, Gerald Hamilton Edwards, Plymouth (1951)

'Tything of Compton Gifford', R. N. Worth, Trans DA, Vol 28 (1896)

Universal British Directory of Trade Commerce & Manufacture, Champante & Whitrow (1798)

Vanishing Plymouth, Brian Moseley, B. S. Moseley (1982)

Vanishing Street Furniture, Geoffrey Warren, David & Charles (1978)

'Western Morning News, History of', supplement, *WMN* (4.1.1960)

White's 1850 Devon, William White, David & Charles (reprint) (1850/1968)

'Widey Court', G. W. Copeland, Trans DA (1955)

Window on the West (BBC Television), Tom Salmon (196–)

'Yogge's House or Prysten House', Jennifer Barber, Trans DA, Vol 105 (1973)

Unlisted but rich in information are: the many street and survey maps of Plymouth—Several of which are available as prints from Plymouth Local History Library or Museum; various editions of, *Doidges Almanac* which produced between 1868–1955 and the 'Christmas Cheer' booklets that followed it for some years; countless newspapers and magazine articles; souvenir programmes; advertising brochures; a variety of general reference volumes, books of facts and encyclopedias; census returns, old telephone directories and electoral registers. Copies of which can generally be found in the local history or reference rooms of Plymouth City Library.

Index